Ram Publications

Complete Book of Competition Treasure Hunting (The)
    Learn the INSIDE FACTS and you, too, can become a WINNER.

Complete VLF-TR Metal Detector Handbook (The)
    THE OPERATIONAL/TECHNICAL MANUAL ... thoroughly explains VLF/TR metal/mineral detectors and HOW TO USE them. Compares VLF/TR's with all other types.

Detector Owner's Field Manual
    The world's most complete field guide. Explains the total capabilities and HOW TO USE procedures of all types of metal detectors.

Electronic Prospecting
    Learn how to find gold and silver veins, pockets, and nuggets using easy electronic metal detector methods.

Gold Panning Is Easy
    This excellent field guide shows you how to FIND and PAN gold as quickly and easily as a professional.

"How to Test" Detector Field Guide
    Learn how to find QUALITY before you buy ... BFO, TR, VLF/TR, and discriminators.

Professional Treasure Hunter
    Discover how to succeed with PROFESSIONAL METHODS, PERSISTENCE, and HARD WORK.

Robert Marx: Quest for Treasure
    The exciting, almost unbelievable true account of the discovery and salvage of the Spanish treasure galleon, *Nuestra Señora de la Maravilla*, lost at sea, January 1656.

Successful Coin Hunting.
    The world's most authoritative guide to FINDING VALUABLE COINS with all types of metal detectors. The name speaks for itself!

Treasure Hunter's Manual #6
    Quickly guides the inexperienced beginner through the mysteries of FULL TIME TREASURE HUNTING.

Treasure Hunter's Manual #7
    The classic! THE book on professional methods of RESEARCH, RECOVERY, and DISPOSITION of treasures found.

Treasure Hunting Pays Off!
    An excellent introduction to all facets of treasure hunting.

Front Cover:

Karl von Mueller, the great-granddaddy of all TH-ers, searching for bits and pieces of metal which might help him locate the site of the treasure cave of the Valley of Secrets. This is an incredible story of a cave of gold that may be worth billions. The Valley of Secrets is located near the headwaters of the Purgatoire River in Southern Colorado.

THE TREASURE HUNTER'S MANUAL #6

by
Karl von Mueller

RAM BOOKS

ISBN 0-915920-29-8
Library of Congress Catalog Card No. 73-88545
© Copyright 1961, © Copyright rev. ed. 1973, © Copyright rev. ed. 1974,
© Copyright rev. ed. 1977, © Copyright 1979 by Gladyce M. Miller.

ALL RIGHTS RESERVED, including the right to reproduce this book or portions thereof in any form or by any means, electronic or mechanical, including photocopying, recording, or by any information storage and retrieval system, without written permission from the publisher. All inquiries should be addressed to Ram Publishing Company. P.O. Drawer 38649, Dallas, Texas 75238.

15022/482

Printed in U.S.A. by
Yaquinto Printing Co., Inc. • 4809 S. Westmoreland • Dallas, Texas 75237

For FREE listing of related treasure hunting books write
Ram Publishing Company • P.O. Drawer 38649 • Dallas, Texas 75238

Respectfully Dedicated

to

Bill "Hardrock" Hammond

of

Los Angeles

and

John E. Johnson

of

Weeping Water

Giants among men, both . . . They went through life, quiet and unobtrusively helping the little fellow, the down-and-outer, and those less fortunate than they. They built their monuments in the hearts of their fellowmen.
May God Bless Them.

Contents

Chapter		Page
I	What — Answers to	1
II	When — The	20
III	Why — Six Questions	26
IV	Who — About	32
V	Where — Buried Treasure	36
VI	How — Hunting	48
VII	Instruments and tools	65
VIII	Clothing	72
IX	Treasure hunting organizations	77
X	Publicity and secrecy	82
XI	Grubstakes and bankrolls	89
XII	Transportation	92
XIII	The law and treasure hunting	98
XIV	Taxes	105
XV	Research	109
XVI	Disposition of treasure	132
XVII	Use of instruments	139
XVIII	Gold Dredging	155
XIX	Maps	175
XX	Photography as a tool	184
XXI	History	195
XXII	Buried vs. sunken treasure	200
XXIII	First aid, lifesaving, and safety	202
XXIV	Legends and myths	216
XXV	Gold isn't everything	220

Appendix A—
State Historical Societies 230

Appendix B—
Slumbering Cities and Ghost Burgs 235
Treasure Literature 297

Introduction

This, the sixth edition of the Treasure Hunter's Manual, is my twenty-first published book. At the same time, it has been the most difficult to write and I believe it is my best book.

It has been written in twenty-eight different states and a part of it was written in old Mexico. Over 25,000 miles of automobile travel and an unknown amount of air travel has gone into the research and writing. Hurricane Donna and a Missouri river flood delayed the publishing of this edition, and several chapters were stolen from my car and then returned by the young chap who took them when he discovered what he had taken.

Publicity about this book has brought visitors from several foreign countries and hundreds of visitors from all over the United States. Armand Bouchard from France, Archibald Evans from England, Anthony Caccomo from Italy, and others came to visit me from overseas. Johnnie Pounds of Santa Monica, Joe Garcia of El Paso, Harold McBride and Ed Rich of Seattle, Tom (Cactus) Jones from Phoenix and no less than fifty others have come from across the country to visit and exchange help. Hundreds of Floridans have come to exchange views with me. And, all of this while the Treasure Hunter's Manual was being hatched.

Thank God, I have not been continually tied to a timeclock. Adventure has been my business and the area west of the Mississippi has been my beat. I have enjoyed driving, riding, and packing over the backroads and trails of western America. I have lived through some incredible experiences and still enjoy the desert, the mountains, and the backwoods. I have recorded so much of my experiences on film, and as time goes on I hope to write more and more books giving facts and instructions on how to enjoy adventure and make it profitable. Billions upon billions of dollars worth of wealth in the form of treasure, the natural resources, and precious metals remain undisturbed across the Nation. A pitifully small amount of this wealth has been recovered by a scant few hundred adventuresome men and women during the past few years. There is plenty of this wealth to go around and I want to help as many people as possible to locate and recover as much of this wealth as possible in a lawful and ethical manner.

Finally, this book tells all that is needed to know about treasure hunting to make it a profitable profession for you. For one reason or another, a good deal of vital information is concealed in this book in the form of hints, innuendo, and statements of double meaning. So, one reading will not make you an expert. You must read and study this book. It will not be difficult and if you have a genuine interest and flair for treasure hunting, every fact and facet of this business will be exposed to you. In any event, I hope you will find it interesting and enjoyable reading. I have tried to be prudent and tactful in presenting names, dates, and facts. No conflicts or discrepancies exist to my knowledge although some yarns may seem to conflict. For example, two Charlie Joyces are mentioned herein. This is two different people; not one man in two different, separated occasions.

I have not used the King's English herein. It is my common, everyday language with the 'pepper' removed. Neither have I used hundreds of yarns I'd preferred to have used. Laws, obligations, and other responsibilities have precluded my including some really unbelievable yarns and pictures. These may come in later books, when the 'coast is clear'.

This has been hard work, but now that it is done, I think it has been worth the effort. I hope you will agree with me.

KARL von MUELLER

Orlando, Florida

EDITOR'S NOTE:

TREASURE HUNTER'S MANUAL 6 was formerly printed by Eight States Associates, and in this current Ram edition we have, whenever possible, left the text intact — in the original lively, unique style so typical of Karl von Mueller. The style *is* the author, and his candid, often blunt, even apparently erratic manner of expression and violation of rules of grammar and syntax (he does know better!) are genuine reflections of von Mueller's knowledge of his subject and his basic attitude. To remove this individualistic style from his works would leave them still authoritative but — we think — much less fascinating to read.

Chapter I

What Is Treasure?

Most of the people who are interested in treasure and treasure hunting have a narrow, pre-conceived idea of what treasure really is. In fact, the word 'treasure' has only one meaning for most people and that is cash or money. In reality, insofar as I am concerned, treasure is a word which means anything of value which has been misplaced, lost, or concealed and which is no longer the known assets or property of a living person as such.

BEACHCOMBERS

There are many people who are actually successful treasure hunters in their own right who do not realize their categoric status. For example, the hundreds of people who quietly and inconspicuously scavenge the popular beaches around the world with rakes, sieves, metal detectors, and other types of paraphernalia in search of lost money, watches, and other valuables are treasure hunters, pure and simple. One of my acquaintances has worked the beaches of California for better than 20 years and he lives like a king. During this period of time, he has evolved a very efficient and almost foolproof system for searching the beaches and his success is such that short working hours during the late evenings and early mornings during the summer vacation season permits him to live plushly throughout the year He calls himself a beachcomber and, in some respects, he does infringe on the domain of the beachcomber, but, in the final analysis, he uses the tools and instruments of a professional treasure hunter and he finds and disposes of the valuables he is able to locate in the manner of the professional treasure hunter. Driftwood, the stock in trade of the beachcomber, is salvaged and sold by this man, but it is only a sideline and certainly not a 'bread-and-butter' item.

SCAVENGERS

The scavenger at the city dumps and disposal grounds of most towns and cities are treasure hunters in a sense and the products of their continual searches are varied and many. It is not a secret that many of these men (and women) become wealthy over a period of years and they accumulate this wealth by finding and selling property which has a value of some sort and by saving the money derived therefrom. You would be surprised at the amount of stuff that is deposited in trash cans on street corners, in the rear of homes, and behind business establishments which has a cash value. Old clocks, dishes, radios, appliances, and a multitude of other items, including furniture, all have a cash value. In fact, many of the treasure hunters I know, who are successful and have amassed respectable fortunes form treasure hunting, regularly shop the antique shops around the country to determine if there is anything 'new' which they might add to their list of merchantable items.

To digress a moment, I have contended for several years that many of the so-called 'antique stores' and 'antique dealers' in the United States are pure and simple opportunistic frauds or, at the very least, pitiful shops selling greatly overpriced merchandise which can often be bought in dime and variety stores at a fraction of the posted selling price. So-called 'milk glass' is something which must be almost irresistible to inexperienced and uninformed antique collectors and you will find it in so many antique shops, always bargain-priced at around $2 per dish and on up. However, there are hundreds of variety and department stores where this same identical dishware can be bought in a price range of from 10¢ per dish on up depending on the type of dish wanted. I do not mean to indict all antique dealers but I do want to point out that all is not kosher in the antique business.

ANTIQUERS

Antique dealers are often good buyers for items you may recover on treasure hunts, but you must be alert in most, but not all, cases as these dealers will usually buy what you have and they need at the lowest possible dollar. For example, my friend Bill Hammond and I salvaged a bunch of 'junk' from an Arizona cave which had been the living quarters for somebody years and years ago. One of the items we packed back to Los Angeles was an old wooden coffee-grinder. We had a car trunk full of this old 'junk' and stopped by an antique shop to see what we could sell all or most of it for. Bill pulled the coffee-grinder out and the dealer offered 25¢ for it, take it or leave

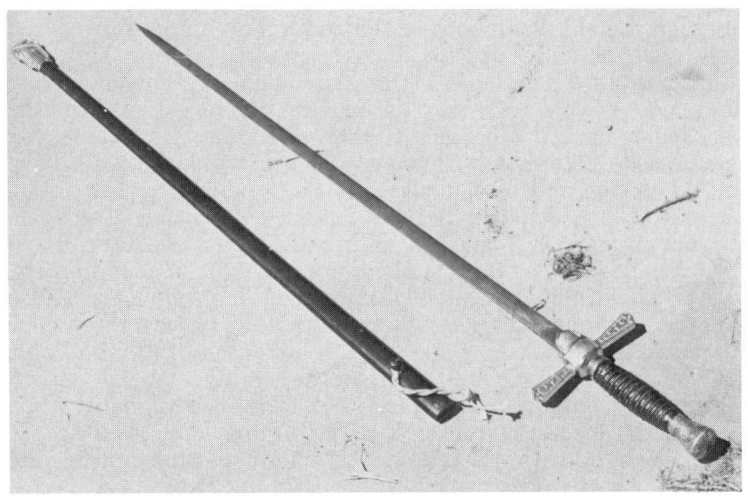

Ceremonial Sword. A peculiar weapon found in an Arizona cave, along with a rawhide saddle, guns, saddlebag. Handle is silver with a dye coating. Scabbard is polished leather with solid silver end-piece.

it. I spoke up and said I'd like to keep it as my wife would enjoy having it to add to her collection of old household wares. To make a long story short, I insisted on keeping it and the dealer continued to up his price until he finally bought it for $6.00. Since then, I have seen a number of the same or similar appliances in antique shops priced from $15.00 to $50.00. See what I mean?

As I said at the beginning of this chapter, treasure is anything of value that has been lost and so on. To list all of the items of treasure which come to mind would read like a merchandising catalog. Old guns, curios, documents, jewelry, money, bullion, tools, household implements and appliances, and even parts of old automobiles are a few of many which should set your imaginiation to whirling. Let's explore a few of these, topic by topic, so the uninitiated will have a better idea of what is potentially treasure and in the hopes that those treasure hunters who have had more or less reasonable success in the field can widen their vistas.

GUNS: I spent a day and evening with an old treasure-hound in St. Petersburg, Florida who had grown filthy rich prowling through the old plantations of the South recovering assorted and sundry items and shipping them to market in New York and Chicago. As we became better acquainted, he confided more and more to me. He was particularly interested in furniture and handguns in his productive days and it was from these that he grossed the bulk of his money. When I introduced the subject of old cannon and cannonballs, he was stunned. He had found an old boat which had become landlocked on one of the old bayous or bays in Louisiana or Mississippi (I don't remember which) and stripped it of its furnishings. On the boat and nearby were several old cannon which he called 'four-pounders' and a number of cannonballs and other sundry items of hardware which the climate had not dealt kindly with. Because of their condition, he had completely ignored them and it was my comments which aroused his remorse and realization that he had probably overlooked the most valuable accessories of the boat. During the Civil War, both the North and the South commandeered and pressed into service every possible land and water vehicle. It is my theory that this boat was one of the small trader boats which was fitted out with sundry armament and then used in clandestine commerce or as a military conveyance. I can imagine all sorts of adventuresome and exciting incidents this little mystery ship might have been involved in and which were not and never will be recorded in history. We may be sure that its final resting place does not reflect its active history.

WEAPONS

I have used the term guns, but the term 'weapons' would be so much more appropriate. Pistols, rifles, cannon, swords, knives, spears, brass-knuckles, and many other devices designed to injure, maim, disable, or kill other people lay hidden from view in thousands upon thousands of locations throughout the American continents (or the World, for that matter) and a few of them are uncovered from time to time. How many we do not know, but rumors which circulate would lead us to believe that many of these weapons are located each year and that many more remain for others to find.

Gun-buyers from the general public, people who buy old guns for the sake of having a historic or conversation piece around the house, will turn up their noses at anything that does not have the appearance of an unusual gun. On the other hand, gun dealers and gun collectors will often go to extremes to acquire an unusual knife or other weapon.

While on the subject of guns, I want to explode one myth or misbelief which has plagued many treasure-hunters from the year one. With very few exceptions, no particular item of treasure is confined to one locality, one area, or even to a single section of the country. As an example, let us use the Colt pistol. The mere mention of the word 'Colt' means only one thing to

Bottled Treasure. Old straw-sheathed bottle containing 773 dimes was found over doorway of tumbled down shack near Maitland, Florida 1960. Most recent date was 1917. Only 46 coins were 1916D but each is worth $100. Two 1895O and ten 1904S add to value. Metal detector used to find bottle.

many, many people; and this is the old West, with its cowboys, outlaws, and riotous living. Nothing could be further from the truth. Colt guns were sold and used everywhere and their sales certainly were not confined to the old West. In fact, at times, Colt had one whale of a time trying to sell his guns and anybody with the money in hand made a bargain buy at the factory. A similar statement could be made with respect to rifles. The fact remains that if you find a gun with a name and marks unknown to you, don't sell it for a song. You might have a valuable collector's item.

GUN APPRAISALS

It is not difficult to determine the approximate value of a gun or weapon. If you are located near a good library, the chances are that they will have a number of good gun catalogs and directories which will help you ascertain the approximate value of the weapon you own. If such a library is not available, write to the gun editor of any of the hunting and fishing magazines or the National Rifle Assn., Washington, D. C., and give him complete information about the gun, including the name and lettering inscribed on the barrel or breech and any marks which you might find on it. Quite often your local sporting goods dealer can help you along this line and almost as often he will try to buy the weapon for a song, so don't sell until you know what it is actually worth.

JUNKERS

All old guns have a cash value regardless of condition. Don't let anybody kid you! A rusted old weapon that can hardly be recognized may bring from $10 to $15 from a tavern or bar-owner or from some collectors. Later, you may be surprised at some of the strange tales which may become associated with such weapons when they finally go on display over a back-bar, in some motel or hotel lobby, or in some other public place. Americans like hokum and the hokum factories work night and day.

It is not at all uncommon to locate weapons in good condition in old buildings, in caves, or in carefully prepared caches. In the dry western and southwestern climates, nature seems to preserve things so don't be surprised to locate metal objects in good condition.

CANNON

Cannon are not as rare as we might believe but they bring good prices when sold properly. Remember: during the many military campaigns, which have literally blanketed the United States and Mexico, thousands of weapons of all types have been buried or concealed to prevent capture by enemy forces. An old cannon found in Arizona has been variously attributed to the Texas War of Independence, the Mexican War, the Civil War, and to various Indian campaigns. It could have been abandoned by any of the many military exploration parties. It was sold to a Los Angeles gun collector for $250. Was it sold for too little or too much? Who knows?

DERRINGERS

For some mysterious reason, derringers have always brought fancy prices from the casual collector and, in a sense, they are a drug on the market. While I do not have the facts and figures to prove it, I believe that almost twice as many derringers were manufactured between 1840 and 1900 than all of the other handguns combined. If you start snooping through history, you will find that not hundreds but thousands of manufacturers existed who made derringers, or as the name was corrupted 'deringers' (or vice versa). My curiosity about this little gun was whetted when I found three of them in a chamois bag in the walls of a barn in an old abandoned farmstead near Grand Island, Nebraska in 1942. After considerable correspondence, I learned that the three almost identical guns were manufactured by three different companies during the late 1800's. This started me to checking into the history of derringers and I learned some mighty interesting facts. I recall that one fellow got rich and then went broke duplicating better known guns. One fellow owned three competing gunshops in one city and all of these shops were making derringers. As I recall, the lowest retail price for a derringer was 65¢ and the most expensive over-the-counter model sold for $8.95.

Guns and weapons are a study in themselves and this is one of the reasons that treasure hunting is so interesting. The more you hunt and find, the more you must study and investigate, and before long you discover that you are literally a walking encyclopedia on some appropriate subject.

JEWELRY: Treasure consisting entirely or even partly of jewelry is often fascinating,, usually exciting, and always the source or basis of thousands of questions and doubts. Who owned it? Why was it buried or concealed? How did it happen to be concealed where it was? Where did it come from? These and hundreds of other questions arise merely from contemplating its history. Every treasure is different and, with the professional treasure hunter, much of the satisfaction and fun from treasure hunting is derived from attempting to fathom the history and background of a given treasure. Imagine unearthing an old Arbuckle coffee can containing two old watches, a spur, a beautiful agate-like pebble, a shoestring, and a letter obviously from a mother to her son admonishing him to come back home and, if he doesn't, to be decent and stay out of trouble. With a little imagination, we can conjure all kinds of ideas about the owner of this coffee can, his activities, and the reason for hiding these possessions in the floor of an old granary. Why did he hide two watches? Was there some sentimental value to the old spur? What was the significance of the pebble? Where was his home? Was he a shy youngster following the grublines, or was he a brash fellow who, because of a single mistake at home, had been thrust into the business of outlawry? Anyway you look at it, it is interesting; and the little pebble is all I have left of this small treasure. To the casual observer, it is only a pretty stone, but to me it is an exciting remnant of the life and activities of an unknown individual who certainly helped to settle and build the West. I never pick this little pebble up without literally tingling with excitement and curiosity. Why? I wish I knew!

GEMS

Despite all the stories we read in the newspapers and adventure magazines about the fabulous caches of precious stones, the instances are very rare indeed where a treasure cache is found to consist entirely of gems. It is not at all uncommon to find a cache which includes a few gem-studded pendents, rings, and brooches, but a cache of gems alone is rare. Even if you find one, the proof of the pudding is in the eating and I'll give you an example. In 1936, at the depth of the depression, Jack Richter and I slipped away from Ft. Crook on a 2 day pass and beat it down to the vicinity of Tarkio, Missouri to look for several treasures he had investigated through historical records of the Kansas State Historical Society. We located one of the treasures in a half-day's prowling and it turned out to be an old leather purse almost full of un-set gems. We thought we had found a bonanza. We took them back to an acquaintance in Omaha who operated a hock-shop and had them appraised. Believe me, not a single stone in the entire caboodle was worth a dime in the market then. They were imitations and why anybody saved them is beyond me, even today.

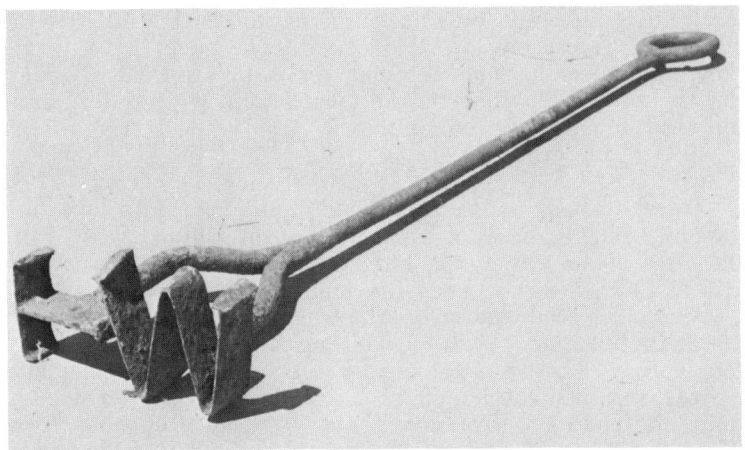

Mystery Iron. A branding iron which was uncovered in 700 block on East First South in the city limits of Salt Lake City. The W lazy T brand is a mystery to everybody. Can anybody identify it?

Naggatz and Dumphy recovered a bandanna-bag of gemstones in the El Cajon, California area a year or so ago. This was train robbery booty dating back to the turn of the century. When this lot of gems was appraised, only one diamond (worth $25) was in the collection. The rest were imitation stones. Obviously, the train bandits had sorted out the worthless stones and hid them while selling the good stones.

CURRENCY

Two harvest hands, turned treasure hunters, engaged in an interesting search near Last Chance, Colorado during the summer of 1957. They were working with an itinerant wheat combining crew and while harvesting in this particular wheat field, the big wheel of the combine dropped into a hole and stalled the rig. It was while digging the machine out that they literally fell into this treasure cache. After freeing the combine and pulling it from the hole, they enlarged the depression and removed a pouch of diamonds, a can of currency, some Mexican money, a saddle, and some odds and ends. The diamonds were found to be imitations, the saddle had long ago been ruined by rodents and rot, and the Mexican money was valuable only as curiosity items, but the currency which consisted of both

U.S. and Confederate bills made the cache worth while. Here again, the gems were worthless and their value lay only in presenting them to some museum for display purposes. Why this cache was deposited on the open prairie is a mystery and the answer will never be known.

DIAMONDS

To take a look at the other side of the coin, let's take the unpublicized discovery of a cache of gems within 100 feet of the ferry monument in the little town of Jensen, Utah where Hiway 40 crosses the Green River just southeast of Vernal. A grader for the road contractor who was building the new Hiway 40 through eastern Utah plowed up an old wood chewing tobacco box. These old-fashioned boxes were long, shallow, and narrow, so when he got off of his machine to investigate, he found the box to be unusually heavy. Instead of opening it on the spot, he placed it in his nearby car and went on about his business. That evening he pried the box open and discovered its contents to be hundreds of faceted gems. The man was endowed with more good judgement than the average person, and instead of going overboard and telling the world about his remarkable discovery, he proceeded with caution. He took one of the stones to a Vernal jeweler and learned it was a real diamond. Still uncertain about his stroke of good fortune, he sent several of the stones to his father in Illinois or Indiana for the purpose of getting them appraised. When a favorable report came back, he quit his job and proceeded to sell the gems in a systematic and profitable manner. Today, he owns a popular and profitable bar in New Mexico and is deeply involved in various mining and petroleum operations. Where all of these stones originally came from, or how they got to Jensen, Utah is a mystery. Some of the few people who know the story believe that possibly Butch Cassidy and his Wild Bunch hid them. This is unlikely. Others speculate that they are remnants of robberies in Montana in the early days. Still others believe that this cache may be in some way associated with the notorious 'Great Diamond Hoax' of Wyoming to the north, but since the stones were all genuine, this is unlikely. Anyway, they were found.

WATCHES

Old watches and pendents are often found in treasure and these items are always valuable. Solid gold watch cases were the rule in the early days and it is this fact that often dates a treasure cache when it is found. A treasure cache containing modern gold-plated or gold-filled watch cases places it in a recent category. The old solid gold cases, often beautifully engraved, are valuable items and bring fancy prices on the open market. Needless, to say, many train robbers made it a practice to rob the passengers as well as the express cars and the jewelry taken in these robberies was often ditched or buried with the idea of recovering and selling it later when the excitement of the robbery had died down. In so many cases, the robbers were caught or killed before they could recover their buried or hidden booty.

Any device made of gold which is found in a treasure cache is valuable, not so much due to the gold content but more from the antique value. Curiously enough, it is not at all uncommon for a professional treasure hunter, or an amateur for that matter, to find some item of jewelry in a treasure cache which is gold and which he cannot identify. Unfortunately, in the past, many of these items have been sold for their gold value alone and often melted and sold through the regular channels as gold.

SNOB HARDWARE

Hundreds of personal items were manufactured from gold and it often takes a person with some knowledge of history and antiques to recognize items for what they are. The nature of an item can multiply its actual cash value on the market. Here are a few items which were manufactured of gold and which are valuable: women's hair combs and hair clips, money clips, watch fobs and charms of peculiar design, belt and shoe ornaments, tie and lapel pins, door ornaments, table jewelry, cigar clippers, tinsel-thin stationery ornaments, snuff boxes, and hundreds of other items which would be scarcely identified by the uninformed.

Too, many valuable items of gold have been found and sold for extremely low prices simply because the finder did not believe they were gold or because the buyer convinced the finder that they were not gold. For the information and guidance of the beginning treasure hunter, I want to list a number of items which have been found and which were solid gold. Among them are: button hooks, horseshoe nails, vanity sets, door knobs, paper weights, cigar holders, coat buttons, manicure outfits, and even writing pens. Because of the soft and heavy characteristics of gold, these items demonstrate how vain people can be, especially when their judgement is warped by wealth and prosperity. Imagine, if you will, the torture of smoking a cigar through a heavy cigar holder, or trying to trim your fingernails with solid gold nail clippers, or trying to write a letter with a pen weighing 3 or 4 ounces. Button hooks of solid gold are about as functional and sensible as a screwdriver made of lead; either or both would bend before they got the job done.

Brooches, pendents, lapel pins, and chains were common pieces of jewelry in the early days and they often turn up as treasure. Usually they are solid gold. Earrings were common and are certainly not rare in today's treasure finds. These are usually of the type designed for pierced ears and not the clamp-type which are so common today.

ANTIQUES: This is a category which is absolutely fraught with confusion. Not knowing what the legal or accepted interpretation of the word was, I asked several different antique dealers and got just as many different answers. I asked historians and got still different answers. To this day, I have received only a few similar interpretations of the term.

AGED IN THE HEAD

One dealer told me he used the 'antique car' yardstick; that is, anything over 25 years old could be considered an antique. A college professor (historian) told me that he considered anything prior to 1900 as 'possibly' an antique. Another historian told me that he considered anything over 100 years old as antique.

In the final analysis, antique dealers, in essence, felt that it took a shorter period of time for anything to become antique than did anybody else. And, understandably so, because antiques are their business, so the quicker they can 'make' antiques, the more profitable their business.

Historians, on the other hand, were more inclined to let objects become steeped in age before they would grudgingly convey antique nomenclature to them. This is the more logical and sensible application of the term.

Anyway, for the treasure hunter, it is safe to consider anything old and unusual to be an antique until proven otherwise. This rule can be applied to anything which is found in the pursuit of treasure hunting: hardware, clothing, jewelry, money, furniture, dishes, silverware, art objects, or anything else that can be used to decorate homes, rooms, business premises, or for display in museums or other public and private places. Just for example, let's take the case of gold or silver doorknobs which adorned the entrances to some of our mining tycoons homes in the latter part of the 19th century. Whether they are gold or silver, they unquestionably have a considerably greater value as 'antiques' or 'collector's items' than they do for their actual cash value as bullion. A few items such as these have been found in treasure caches and there are, unquestionably, many more still unfound. Another good example is old, hand-carved picture frames. Their value as simple picture frames is questionable, but as antiques you will find that they are often worth many times their original purchase price. Yet, many of these old, valuable frames are thrown into trash cans every year by the younger generation in their attempt to 'go modern' and, in consequence, many of them are lost forever while, in other cases, these discarded frames will be picked up by scavengers in the city dumps and sold into the antique market at high prices.

If you are going to devote much time and effort to treasure hunting, you can do worse than spending a little time studying the antique field so that you can recognize many valuable items on sight. There are a number of low-cost books in print on the subject, including several good paper-backed books (so-called pocketbooks) at 50¢ each.

DOCUMENTS: This is a category that covers a multitude of sins: checks, family records, mortgages, promissory notes, stock certificates, bonds, indentures, certificates of indebtedness, bills of lading, mail and letters, business records, letters of credit, and the multitude of other paper work that goes with the horrible affairs of living in a civilized world.

TRASH

When you get firmly entrenched in treasure hunting and go on a treasure trek with the same informality as a hunter embarks on a duck-hunting trip toward the end of duck season, you will begin to amass a room, shed, or barn full of odds-and-ends of various and questionable value. Among all of this 'trash' (as some people prefer to call it) you will have various and sundry documents. These documents will have various values, but none will be worthless. If and when the time ever comes that you believe they are worthless; don't throw them away or burn them . . . ship them off to your state historical society for inspection or give them to your local historical society, if there is one.

The value of any document is not vested entirely in its age or the name thereon. More often than not, the historic significance of a document controls to a great extent its value. For example, when the television show which dramatized and whitewashed the life of Wyatt Earp appeared, any documents bearing his signature or name skyrocketed in price. Then, as the real, documented facts pertaining to this character out of the West became known, the value of these documents was deflated.

The same applies to Davy Crockett. Although Crockett was reputedly illiterate, thousands of spurious documents appeared bearing his signature and they brought fancy prices until the matter of his capabilities of signing his own name became generally known.

GILT-EDGED WALLPAPER

Some old mining stocks are valuable merely because they were sold in conjunction with a famous mine or 'floated' by a famous mining tycoon. Some of these old stocks are valuable, too, because they still represent an equity in a valuable mining property. On the other side of the ledger are the boxes-ful of mining stocks that can be found in various mining camps throughout the West and which are as worthless as the paper they are printed on. In fact, I can cite some valuable uses for these old documents; the chipmunks use them to make cozy nests and some of the old denizens of the abandoned mining camps have used them to paper and weatherproof their cabins. Nevertheless, they are worth from a dime, to a quarter, to a dollar apiece as curiosity items and some of them have been sold on souvenir counters in resort towns as such.

Old bills of lading, checks, vouchers, and other documents of famous outfits like Russell, Waddell, & Majors, Wells Fargo, the Mormon Church, Union Pacific, the Burlington & Missouri, and various famous people are usually extremely valuable.

Many old documents are a drug on the market but others are priceless. It takes time and research, more often than not, to ascertain the value of old documents, but it is worth it.

Deeds and any convenances of land are usually valuable but don't over-estimate the value of old mining and railroad stocks.

CURIOS: This is a term which has been corrupted to mean anything unusual, and we will use this interpretation here. So, under the corrupted heading of curios we will include such items as trinkets, toys, items of adornment, artifacts, and most of the other items which we have not placed in other categories. Into this category, I have placed all of the hardware items which do not properly fit into the antique classification.

CURIOS

Although most certainly not treasure, items such as buffalo skulls, longhorn cattle horns, and the Indian armament of bows, arrows, lances, shields, and other similar items have a tangible value that varies with condition and the individual characteristics of each item.

There are hundreds of items which fall into the *curio* category and the sincere treasure hunting enthusiast should train himself to observe for them when in the field and carry them home for preservation and profit.

BULLION: This is a word that strikes terror in the heart of any successful, professional treasure hunter. *Bullion* . . . a word incorporating disappointment, grief, regret, sorrow, and troubled wealth.

Many a time I have sat by a campfire in southwestern United States or in Mexico and heard true tales spun about fabulous caches of bullion laying yet where they were found. To the uninitiated, this sounds like fiction; to the professional, it is unquestioned fact.

In Liberty, WA, Roy Lagal looks on as Charles Garrett demonstrates dry panning with the "Gravity Trap" gold pan to miners Jack Kirsch and Frank Duval. The gold pan has become an important tool in practically every aspect of prospecting, even electronic prospecting. Electronic prospecting has rapidly come to the forefront as one of the best ways for the treasure hunter to recover Mother Earth's gold. The new VLF/TR type metal detectors with their ability to cancel iron earth minerals and search deeply for gold nuggets have made it all possible.

MONEY: This is something that you never have enough of until you have too much and then everyone tries to get it away from you. You don't really have to wait that long, because when you begin to show signs of prosperity the sharpers will begin to show up in the form of salesmen, charity workers, beggars, solicitors, and the Lord only knows how many other forms.

Contrary to some mighty well-known rumors, there is no such thing in treasure hunting as worthless money, be it coin, bullion, or currency. Even the counterfeit or facsimile Confederate currency which was printed in the North at the start of the Civil War is valuable, and don't let anybody tell you otherwise. The same applies to all money.

$1

A good example is the experience of a young fellow by the name of Don Seyler who found a whole gob of new one-dollar bills hidden in the attic of an old, abandoned house in Maryland. He noticed that they were all dated in the early thirties, and he had presence of mind enough to consult a coin dealer about them. The coin dealer was either crookeder than a snake or else didn't know his money (take your pick) because he pointed out to Seyler that they were the old so-called Republican dollar-bills and therefore were worth at the most only 10% over the face value. Seyler sold them to him for face value plus 10%, but could have done much better by checking with another dealer before selling.

For the benefit of the uninformed, the term 'Republican Dollar' is commonly used to designate the first of the new size dollar-bills which were printed during the Hoover Administration. They were taken out of circulation as soon as possible due to a legal and technical error on the face of each bill. If you will look at the face of a dollar bill, you will notice that it says at the top 'This certifies that there is on deposit in the Treasury of _____. The so-called Republican bill states 'This certifies that there has been deposited in the Treasury of _____.' One is present tense and the other is past tense. Merely a legal technicality that may or may not have rendered the currency worthless. Back in those days it bought a whole dollars worth of groceries and nobody cared.

COINS

If you do stumble onto some coins or currency, don't sell them to the first buyer! Take your time! Get a copy of some good money guide books and check your treasure out by them. The Whitman Publishing Company, Racine, Wisconsin prints a number of good guides. One book, for example, "A Guide Book Of United States Coins" costs $3.95 and lists all coins back to the year 1616 and illustrates most of them in addition to giving appraisals of current values for them. You can get the same books on U.S. currency and Confederate money.

In the case of Confederate money, don't let anybody kid you into believing that it is worthless! It is NOT. Some of it is worth several times face value to collectors. Check the market before selling any Confederate money you find at bargain prices.

And, finally, the matter of gold coins and bullion must be considered as a good deal of this is found every year. Gold coins in very good to fine condition are worth from 10 to 100 times their face value. Generally speaking, any U.S. gold coin that can be identified is worth at least 5 times its face value. A hundred years ago, a number of banks were coining their own gold money, and it is usually this money that brings the premium prices on the market. For example, an 1849 $5 (Five D) gold coin minted by the Massachusetts and California Company at San Francisco in worth $4,000.00 in fine condition and the sky is the limit on one in uncirculated condition.

A few gold coins turn up quite often in various treasures and in the most unlikely and unexpected places, so if you should find any gold coins, check the coin Guide Book mentioned above or some other equally reliable reference book.

GENERAL: An entire book could be written on WHAT is treasure without exhausting the subject. A good deal of time and space has been consumed here to familiarize you with what treasure is generally and it has been handled as it has so that you will be able to exercise some good judgement when you do find that unexpected treasure which you might not have recognized as such otherwise.

Generally speaking, anything of metal that dates back prior to 1900 is valuable, even though it is just part of an implement, gun, or some other device. Almost anything that is old is valuable. Keep these few facts in mind and you will be less likely to pass up something good.

Harry and Lucile Bowen, owners of Bowen's Hideout, Spokane, Washington, made a thorough search of the ghost town of Quesnel Forks, British Columbia, Canada. This is one of the oldest ghost towns in that area. These finds are among the more unusual relics they located. The gold and silver ingot in the upper righthand corner was evidently highgraded by a worker and hidden behind a brick in an old kiln where it was found by Lucile Bowen with a Garrett Master Hunter transmitter receiver detector. Note the 1894 presidential election medallion, the old Chinese cleaver, the zinc jar lid with its porcelain picture inset, and the old Union Pacific lock. The Bowens are well known for their contributions to the hobby of treasure hunting in the Pacific Northwest.

CHAPTER II

When

One of the most amazing examples of when to hunt treasure was related to me some years ago by a fellow known as Charlie Forbes. Forbes was not his real name and I have never been able to determine much more of his background than he related to me. Here is Charlie's yarn:

OHIO

Back in the early 1930's, Charlie was committed to prison in Pennsylvania for burglary. His crime, said he, was for burglarizing a store to feed his family. He was a personable fellow and apparently managed to get along with everybody in prison. While assigned to the prison laundry, he became acquainted with another prisoner who was serving a 101 year sentence for murder. Prior to Forbes release they became close friends.

As Forbes days in prison became numbered, the murderer confided to Forbes that he had a fortune in currency buried in Ohio and that if Forbes would deliver one-half of it to his mother, he would tell him where it was. One of the ironic twists to the story is that Forbes was to tell the mother that her son was a merchant seaman and that the money was an accumulation of several years at sea. It was required that Forbes would get the mother to write a letter to her son 'in Spain' and that Forbes would mail the letter as a receipt to the prisoner without ever telling her any different. Forbes agreed and received his instructions by committing them to memory.

The money was inside a copper wash boiler which had been sealed with solder and then buried in the bed of a lake in northern Ohio. It was buried and recovered in a most unusual and peculiar manner. On the shore and about 60 feet from the waters edge was a large tree with a hitching ring partly embedded in it. Between the tree and the shore was a Government survey benchmark. By affixing the end of a 100-foot length of rope to the ring and then aligning the rope directly over the benchmark, the end of the rope would be precisely over the buried money. But, the cache was located about 3 feet below the lake bed, almost 40 feet from the water's edge, and in two feet of water. It would be an almost impossible job for one man to recover the old boiler with its contents under these circumstances without arousing a lot of curiosity.

This is the way the cache was concealed originally and here is the way Forbes recovered it. At the time the money was concealed, it was just as 'hot' (using the parlance of the underworld) as was the party who hid it. So, to get it out of sight and circulation for a while, he conceived the idea of burying it in the bottom of the lake after the ice cutters had passed over the area. Anybody who can recall the late 1920's and early 1930's will remember that the mechanical refrigerator was a relatively new device and the old icebox was still in common use. Consequently, in many areas ice was still being harvested from lakes and streams, and stored in icehouses for use in the summer. Consequently, the boiler with its valuable contents was buried in the bottom of the lake and old scraps of ice were probably strewn over the cache. When the first thaw came, water naturally seeped into the area which had been harvested of ice, and there would be almost no possibility of anybody ever finding the cache accidentally. Eventually, the person who concealed the treasure became involved in other crimes and was eventually captured and given a maximum sentence. Thus, he had no hopes of release and the treasure he had so carefully and successfully concealed was lost to mankind. That is, until an unusual trust and faith in Forbes resulted in its disclosure.

When Forbes was released from prison he managed to get a job as a farmhand in Ohio. He spent his first summer following the wheat harvest from Texas up into North Dakota and carefully saved every possible cent. After the wheat harvest, he picked corn and increased his savings. Finally, with a respectable bankroll, he returned to Ohio and settled in a community near the lake and got a job with a small newspaper. In his activity as a newsman, he managed to investigate the site of the buried-sunken treasure and found the hitching ring and benchmark. However, a drouth had depleted the water level of the lake and instead of being submerged in two feet of water, the exact spot was at the water's edge.

When the lake was solidly frozen over, Forbes began his excavation through the frozen silt and recovered the treasure. According to his story, he extracted slightly more than $44,000 in old Republican currency and delivered $22,000 to the convict's mother in Illinois. He complied with the requirement of getting a receipted letter and mailing it to the convict.

Forbes did not squander his money. He bought a farm, and sold it. Became a popular hardware dealer in Minnesota and sold it in 1942 to enter the armed services. Because of his prison record, he was rejected. He entered defense production work and was a machinist at a Naval ammunition depot when I got acquainted with him. My interest and activity in treasure hunting aroused his interest, and he finally confided this remarkable story to me. I have presented the yarn here because it so logically demonstrates that 'when' is not always 'now.'

Treasure hunting is not necessarily a seasonal avocation, occupation, or profession. Yet, the seasons, climate, and weather have always, to a great extent, controlled the hiding and the recovery of treasure. Except under certain circumstances, extremely hot or cold weather precludes treasure hunting in many areas and localities. Likewise, crowds, traffic, vacationers, and sportsmen often makes treasure hunting untimely or undesirable at certain times of the year.

On the other hand, 'when' is the difference between success or failure in locating or recovering buried treasure. Here is an illustration of a case showing that 'when' can and is often 'now.'

COLORADO

A few years back, the Denver Post ran a feature article on a pack-train tragedy high in the Rockies near the turn of the century. This article related the fact that a sizable amount of cash had been lost as well as considerable tools, equipment, and other items. An employee of the Denver and Rio Grand Railroad in the Steamboat Springs (Colorado) area immediately associated this tragedy with local stories he had heard while assigned to jobs at various towns in the area of the tragedy. It being early on a Sunday morning when he read the story and he being certain that this story was closely associated with the other yarns he had heard, he drove over to the vicinity of the tragedy. Picking up a fishing friend of his, he went over the close relationship between the printed story and the local yarns and in a matter of minutes they were in the treasure hunting business. By eliminating the unlikely and impossible from the data at hand, they quickly estimated the probable location of the treasure and started searching.

The ravages of nature helped them, and in a matter of

minutes they found the exposed back of a mummified burro, but no pack. They reasoned that due to their weight, the packs would have come to rest higher on the slope or else tumbled to the bottom of the canyon if they became unhitched from the pack animals. Operating on this premise, they started a systematic search at a ledge some thousand feet below the trail level and worked upward. The first productive discovery was another burro with pack still in hitch, and still covered with debris and float. A little farther up the slope they found another mummified burro with broken pack askew and a few ruined rifles strewn around. Inside the pack a couple semi-serviceable rifles were found. Finally, at the top of the slope and just below the trail they found another pack. With two unbroken packs and a third broken pack located, they decided to call it quits for the day. The heavier pack near the top of the ledge was carried up to the trail and opened. It contained the cash carefully packaged and packed between items of hardware.

The second pack was broken open where it was found and it contained an assortment of 'new' old handguns, ammunition, and an assortment of tobacco. The guns and ammunition were carried up to the car, and a few of the rifles from the broken pack were also recovered.

The week following revealed the area was literally swarming with persons following the newspaper lead. By the next weekend, most of the pack animals had been found, the packs recovered. Nobody ever reported finding the pack with the money, and the search for it went on for several years.

This yarn refutes the old saying 'Better late than never' and substantiates another 'There's no time like the present.' Above all, it demonstrates that timing is often extremely important in treasure hunting and that each buried treasure must be dealt with in its own peculiar way. While these two Coloradoans were probably at least slightly interested in buried treasure by virtue of many local yarns and legends, it is interesting to note that within minutes after an interesting article in the Denver Post 'lit their fuse' they were serious treasure hunters, and within hours of the 'fuse-lighting' they had attained success.

This yarn was related to me by the brother of one of the participants and I wish it were possible for me to identify the individuals. However, due to circumstances and events which occurred later, it is better that these two men go down in treasure hunting history anonymous so that their descendants may be spared any embarrassment or notoriety.

TIMING

Professional treasure hunters usually research several different treasure caches simultaneously, and it is not at all unusual for a professional to have more than one cache pretty accurately located at one time. Some amateurs have even adopted this practice.

Actually, the practice serves several good purposes. It often saves a lot of backtracking thru the same museums, libraries, newspapers, and other sources of information and, in effect, it lets the cook have two or more skillets on the same stove. It so often happens that a treasure cache is accurately and definitely pin-pointed but cannot be recovered at the moment due to a number of reasons, so another project, or idleness, is imperative for the treasure hunter. If he has another project or two in the works, he can devote his time and efforts to upgrading the information and data on his other projects while he waits for the opportunity to recover the cache he has previously located.

The element of timing permits him to make his recovery unobtrusively, quietly, and usually unnoticed.

The timing, or the 'when,' of treasure hunting is an elastic or flexible value that must and can usually be adjusted to the values or requirements at hand. It can be required by, or established by, such widely assorted variables as climate, the immediate weather, the seasons, the attitudes and edicts of people, disease, and many other conditions. Here is a typical example:

Along about 1955, Jack Davis (an amateur from Los Angeles) became involved in a program in recovering some of the famous Joaquin Murieta treasure. During the course of his research, he became interested in the antics and affairs of a long-deceased character by the name of Hyler. Eventually, he made a full-time project out of the Hyler mystery. After numerous investigatory trips to San Bernardino, Bakersfield, Oatman, and other places, he decided he was ready to strike for paydirt. The most likely site for the Hyler fortune to be buried was in the area around the old man's cabin in the Angeles National Forest high in the mountains behind Los Angeles. To his dismay, he found the area closed during the fire season and he had to postpone his final search until the area was opened.

On the first weekend after the newspapers published news about reopening the area, Davis entered the area and located the old Hyler cabin-site and numerous landmarks. Further progress was stymied by the presence of numerous visitors who were enjoying a day's trip to the mountains for the first time since the area was closed. When the season came around to where there were few visitors, the snow came. It was one frustrating obstacle after another. Finally, during a mid-winter thaw, Davis managed to get into the area, get his work done, and get out. I do not have the slightest idea about what he recovered, but he would neither admit nor deny a successful project.

Members of Search International use every available means to recover silver from this river located near Creel, Mexico. VLF/TR and BFO detectors were used to locate black sand deposits which were then worked with "Gravity Trap" gold pans and dredges. When rich pockets were found, it was not uncommon for one ounce of silver to be recovered from a single panning. If you wish to learn more about electronic prospecting with VLF/TR and BFO metal detectors, read two Ram books, THE COMPLETE VLF-TR METAL DETECTOR HANDBOOK and DETECTOR OWNER'S FIELD MANUAL.

CHAPTER III

Why

By far, the most difficult, confusing, and perplexing question to answer regarding treasure hunting is: WHY? The question has many facets, but the most important is: why was the treasure hidden, or lost, and then why look for it? In so many cases, the question is extremely difficult to answer, even when the facts are known, because of the human factor. The human factor is merely the knowledge that human beings do the goofiest things for the goofiest reasons at the most outlandish times.

FOR EXAMPLE

Just for example, let us take a mysterious event that occurred during the late 1930's. Harry Hopkins, advisor to President Roosevelt,, drove into Lincoln, Nebraska one day and visited the State WPA headquarters there. Next morning, Hopkins and D. F. Felton (who was State Director of the Nebraska WPA) drove westward to Kearney, Nebraska where they visited a couple WPA projects and then on to North Platte, Nebraska where they spent the night. Next morning, they drove on up to the Mirage Flats Irrigation project, which was under WPA supervision, and spent a part of the day looking around the area. Late in the afternoon or early evening, they stopped at a point designated by Mr. Felton and concealed three copper containers which were about half the size of a 5-gallon oil can, and then departed. This series of events has picked at my curiosity for years and years. Not only have I wondered and wondered what was in the cans, but WHY were they concealed at this particular area.

This yarn was related to me in the strictest confidence by Bill Lanham of Lexington, Nebraska along about 1940 and his was first-hand information. He had been called by Mr. Felton from somewhere along the line to meet him in North Platte for the purpose of visiting some WPA projects. When Lanham arrived in North Platte, he was sworn to secrecy and then proceeded to act as chauffeur for Felton and Hopkins for the trip north into the Mirage Flats area. Who else Lanham had told, I do not know; and I have never mentioned this matter to anybody except in the most general manner while 'fishing' for other information. Nevertheless, in late 1957, while visiting in Seattle, I chanced to meet a man by the name of Fred Bacon who has been known to me for years through the professional treasure hunter's grapevine. Bacon has been no slouch of a successful treasure hunter and when it comes to trading and bartering recovered treasure he has become relatively well known throughout the field. Through mutual use of jargon and lingo common only to the treasure hunting fraternity, Bacon and I established each other as 'in' and we began talking treasure and exchanging gossip.

Surprisingly, he introduced the subject of the Hopkins trip to Mirage Flats and when I expressed some knowledge of the event, we began comparing notes. Bacon had picked up the story from a man who had been an attorney with the Federal Works Agency and the story he passed on to me was identical in detail to that related to me years before by Lanham. Only difference was that Lanham had related the details to me just a few months after it had occurred, while Bacon's theory was that these three containers held more than a million dollars worth of brand new currency and that there were probably many more such caches around the United States if there was just a magic means of locating them. So it might be. I mention this yarn to demonstrate one important fact: that treasure is often concealed for unknown, unusual, or unreasonable reasons. Who is there who will hunt over 10,000 square miles of land without the slightest idea of what they are looking for or where it might be in the area? I'd like to try, but time is fleeting and I've got more certain things to find.

Or, take the case of the crane operator in Florida who was excavating a drainage canal and unearthed a container which belched out over $30,000 in cash, plus some old jewelry, a curling iron, a pair of woman's shoes, and some other trivia. Who hid this cache? Why?

Bankers, as a general breed, have never been famous for charity, honesty, or for impartiality. Yet, for some reason which escapes rationality, many bankers have concealed various amounts of money in caches far removed from their banks. One professional treasure hunter has claimed that in one out of three cases when he has heard of a banker dying, he has found concealed cash when he searched the premises of the banker's professional hobby. This means that if the banker had farm which was a showplace, or a resort, or a ranch, for example, this treasure hunter was reasonably sure of making a strike on the premises. Why? Why do the bankers and money-lenders so often conceal their assets, or a part of their assets, in places which, in essence, seem ridiculously unsafe?

$10,000 INSURANCE

Another good example is the usually unknown reasoning behind so many wealthy people secreting and concealing their money in the most insecure locations around their homes and premises while all of the local banks belong to the FDIC which guarantees all depositors to the extent of $10,000. Of course, a lot of this is justified or imagined distrust and mistrust of the banks and bankers. When the occasion arises where questions can be asked, you get a variety of answers. One old miser will say it is none of the bank's business how much money he has. Another will tell you that the bankers tell the lawyers and then the lawyers will use every means at their command, both legal and unlawful, to wrest the money from you. Still another will recall the early 1930's when he lost every cent he had to the banks and then had them foreclose on his property. Many of these fellows can pretty well justify hiding their wealth, but most of them cannot or will not. Why?

LAWYER'S $$$

Although it is treasure in the most remote and broadest sense, I think the following yarn is thought-provoking and it most certainly arouses a lot of curiosity. Just a few short years back, a young outlaw in a small midwestern city was informed, somehow, that a young, local lawyer was carrying a toolbox full of cash in the trunk of his car. By various and devious means, this youngster 'cased' the lawyer's car and definitely established the fact that a toolbox was in the trunk of the car, that it was padlocked, and WELDED shut with spotwelds and that the trunk was always locked. Consequently, he actually believed the 'toolbox full of money' tale and proceeded to make plans to get possession of it. He did! By studying locksmithing from a book on the subject and getting possession of a device for opening locks, he managed to get into the trunk of the car one night while it was parked at the side of a local social and fraternal club. Nothing ever appeared in the newspapers regarding this 'robbery.' Yet, a year or so later, when this young outlaw was convicted and sentenced for a robbery, he confided in his cellmates that he had pulled the 'trunk' job and found 500 $100 bills in the box. He further assured his cellmates that he had most of it left and that it was so well concealed that it would be there when he got out. OK, why was the shyster carrying this amount of money ($50,000) around in the trunk of his car? Why had it been there for over two years? Why did he not report its loss to the police? And, finally, where did the young outlaw hide it? It's yarns like this that arouse your curiosity and, yet, make almost any kind of treasure story interesting and acceptable.

NO ANSWER

These few examples, and there are many more, go a long ways toward demonstrating that the answers to so many treasure problems are not obtainable by deduction. There are so often odd, unreasonable, and crude reasons for the secreting of wealth. Another good example is the discovery in the basement of a house at Chadron, Nebraska (I believe) of over $26,000 after an elderly woman passed on. This happened in the last year or so, and nobody suspected she was so well bankrolled. Still another example is another lady in Biloxi, Mississippi who passed on and left a fortune on the premises and only a few dollars in the bank. I always wonder WHY when I read of these affairs or when I hear of them.

WHY LOOK

On the other side of the ledger is the question that always arises and this is: Why waste my time looking for these will-o-the-wispy Eldorados?

I have never tried to 'sell' anybody on treasure hunting. When help has been asked, I have tried to lend a hand. Despite this reluctance to try to 'sell' this activity, I have been challenged from time to time for one good, justifiable reason for going treasure hunting. This, I can usually answer, and here are a few of the 'answers.'

Treasure hunting can be a very profitable avocation, hobby, or activity. I know many fellows who would still be going to work at 8 AM, punching a beastly timeclock, and leaving work at 4:30 PM if they had not got interested in searching for 'ghost gold,' treasure, loot, and other tangibles which would otherwise be lost forever. Some people enjoy the society of the timeclock, office gossip and politics, and the reasonable certainty of a weekly paycheck. For people with families, or those of faint heart and lack of guts, or those who cannot endure mental gymnastics, treasure hunting can be a chore, bore, and a psychological calamity.

Treasure hunting is an adventuresome activity, and many of us love adventure. Most of us who love adventure prefer to actively engage in it rather than read about it. We can save the reading for the rainy, stormy, or snowy days; but we can make hay when the sun shines. So, rather than hang around the beer joints, the poolhalls, or loaf in the public parks, we spend our time in the most enjoyable pursuit of outwitting fate, history, and economics.

HEALTH

Treasure hunting is a healthful activity, and it provides us with good, solid, all-around exercise, both of mind and body. Did you ever notice this new breed of prosperous pauper who lays out in the yard in his shorts soaking up the sun and actually believing he is really living? He's generally mortgaged to the hilt and will probably never see the day he is out of debt. To me this is a form of psychological dereliction: the poor boob thinks he is really living and actually he is just 'relaxing' his body into a coronary condition or that inevitable heart attack. On the other hand, we have all noticed the robust, healthy appearance of the fellows (and their families) who break away from the city on weekends and get out and do a little gadding around the country. You can spot these fellows in the office, or in the shop, or anywhere else. They have an entirely different appearance, a fresh outlook, and they are invariably more alert.

EDUCATION

Treasure hunting is educational and you just simply cannot engage in it without learning a lot. The wise, alert beginning treasure hunter will give due heed to everything pertinent to this activity. As he progresses, he will find his knowledge of geology, botany, biology, economics, psychology, law, and all other matters will have increased slowly, steadily, but vastly. And these are only a few of the subjects in which he will make great strides. Subjects which were formerly dry and uninteresting will suddenly become so absorbing. History and mathematics are notoriously the driest subjects in our schools, but these become interesting when there is a need to know in treasure hunting. A railroad depot agent in Wyoming once told me that he doubled his knowledge of the arts and sciences after he was 50 years of age simply because he developed new capability for learning when he became interested in treasure hunting. This is significant. One thing about all of this learning is that you take it as you like it; it's not forced on you and you just naturally get a consuming curiosity and eventually become amazed at how much you did not know beforehand.

I could go on and list a number of other good reasons to justify activity in treasure hunting, but those above vindicate any arguments to the contrary. You can take it or leave it, as you wish, but the benefits are there for all to enjoy, if they will.

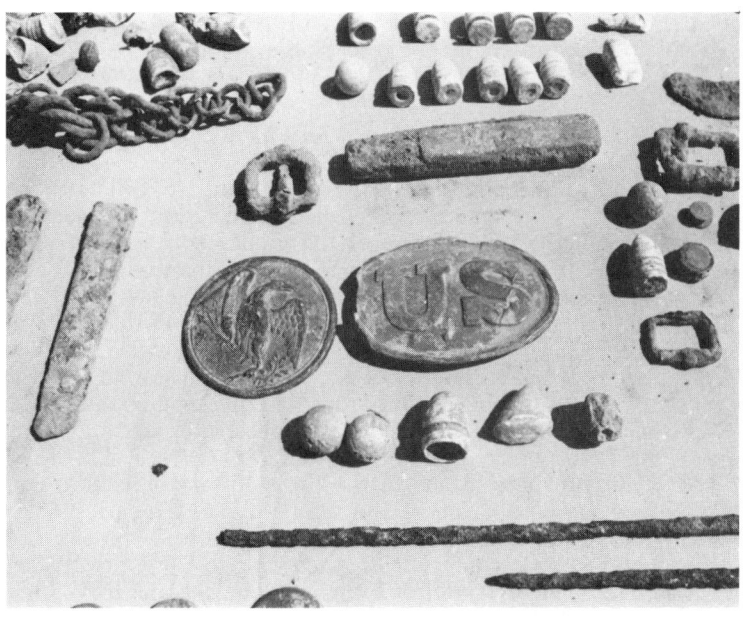

The number of active relic hunters is growing rapidly. New, deep seeking detectors and new hunting methods are causing battlefields and ghost towns to yield countless quantities of rare and valuable artifacts. The value of most relics continues to increase even though larger quantities are coming out of the ground than ever before.

CHAPTER IV

Who

The matter of WHO works two ways and we must consider who hid, lost, or abandoned the treasure and who may or can find it.

This, in itself, is an all-inclusive subject and entire libraries of books could be written about the dull, exciting, tragic, happy, deranged, or normal lives of the people who conceal treasure and those who seek and find it. The annals of history contain frequent items that directly or indirectly allude to treasure in some form or other. On the other hand, many thousands of incidents are not even hinted at in history and some of these pertain to treasure caches of respectable amounts.

CODY

As a good example, millions of words have been written about Buffalo Bill Cody and his trek across the stage of American history. Of course, a great deal of the "Buffalo Bill" history, as we get it, is pure, unadulterated fiction and must be accepted as such to get the true picture of the great Cody. When all is said and done, Cody was a mediocre frontiersman whose attractive appearance and unusual neatness caught the eye of a publicist and writer who elevated him to a pedestal that he was never able to forget or ignore. Don't get me wrong! Cody was a man, through and through, but any informed historian will tell you that thousands, not just hundreds, of frontiersmen outranked Cody in the realm of downright, perilous, valorous activity in the West, both before and after his time.

Anyway, nowhere in any of the Cody history or fiction have I ever found any mention of the time William Frederick Cody returned to his ranch from downtown North Platte, Nebraska with $17,000 on his person, *and lost it*. According to Cody's own story to John and Ellen Rylander of Farnam, Nebraska and to William Stebbins of Gothenburg, Nebraska, he received a payoff in North Platte for services rendered and thereupon proceeded to get roaring drunk. As far as he could remember, he got home alright and hid the money, but he never realized nor could he remember where he had concealed it. He could faintly remember something about the well, the granary, one of the stock tanks, and the cellar; but search as he might, he never did find the lost money. His wallet was gone and he was sure that his pockets had not been ransacked. He had a faint recollection of handling the wallet in the granary and at the stock tank, and that was the extent of his memory about the incident.

Insofar as is known, he never recovered the money and it is entirely probable that it lays today hidden somewhere on his ranch or concealed somewhere between downtown North Platte and his ranch.

EARP

Another equally ridiculous myth surrounds the great Wyatt Earp, now of TV fame. Not until the appearance of Frank Waters fine book 'The Earp Brothers of Tombstone' has any widely circulated literature appeared which exposed the darker side of the Earp legend. Here again a writer singled out a frontier character and totally ignored the bad; bloated, emphasized, and fictionized the good; and made a hero out of a bully. To my knowledge, nothing in print has pointed the finger toward any of the buried Earp loot, payoff, and other financial accumulations, but there have been treasure hunters in the Southwest who have pursued the Earp histories in Arizona and Kansas and accumulated fortunes from recovering caches that were directly connected with the Earp faction. Of the several Wyatt Earp biographies which have been both publicly and privately printed, the serious or veteran treasure hunter will find that they are all loaded with fiction, myth, inconsistancies, and downright misstatement of fact and are therefore worthless as historical references. Frank Waters book, to me, appears to be the closest approach to genuine fact that I have yet found in print. All of this literature adds up to a pretty solid assumption that the Earps did operate as thugs, racketeers, and not-so-honest lawmen and that they concealed a pretty substantial sum of loot in Arizona and probably in Kansas.

Why mention the great Earps and the famous Cody here? It is merely to point out that 'who' can include anybody. A person's apparent station in life has nothing whatever to do with his, or her, capabilities to acquire or conceal fortunes of various sizes. It makes no difference whether they are in business, in government, or some other activity; this matter of temptation and the human intrigue of secrecy make them vulnerable and they often stoop or bow to the whims of avarice.

There are those who believe that treasure is the same as loot, and this is untrue. Neither is it the caches of misers. Nor is it solely included in any other categories. There are those who believe that it was only outlaws, embezzlers, and other dishonest persons who concealed treasure. This is not entirely true.

EVERYBODY

The people who concealed treasure were in all walks of life. Yes, there were outlaws, thieves, embezzlers, forgers, burglars, and others. But, there were also the honest businessmen, farmers, settlers, peddlers, and thousands of others who hid their money in various places because they had no other place to protect it or they did not trust the banks and bankers. We still have these people with us today and maybe their reasons are entirely valid and justified.

So, the people in the past, as is true today, who buried or hid treasure, came from all walks of life and they hid their 'wealth' in various amounts. Even law officers have been known to confiscate loot and hide it for their own future use. So, the 'who' with respect to the actual concealing of treasure can be all-inclusive; it can take in just about everybody.

The 'who,' with respect to seeking and recovering treasure, can likewise just about take in anybody and everybody except the bedridden and the prisoner. The ranks of the professional treasure hunter, the man who devotes the bulk of his busy hours to treasure hunting or who derives most of his income from treasure hunting, have been filled with men and women from all walks of life. Carpenters, cobblers, blacksmiths, clerks, mechanics, cowboys, sheepherders, artists, writers, housewives, brakemen, aviators, druggists, and retired people, to name a few, are among those who have lived solely from the proceeds of their treasure hunting activities. None of them began as treasure hunters but merely drifted into the activity. One success led to another, and another, and another; so they finally devoted fulltime to it.

PROS

There are, of course, some very successful treasure hunters who have amassed fortunes from treasure hunting, but who still pursue their normal professions or businesses. For example, one professional treasure hunter is first, last, and always a very successful oil man who successfully hunts treasure as a hobby. A Wyoming rancher is a fulltime, wealthy ranch owner-operator; but at the same time he is a very successful professional treasure hunter. A California seed-merchant owns and operates a thriving wholesale-retail seed store; but at the same time he has graduated into the ranks of successful professionalism in the treasure hunter world.

Not so surprising is the fact that some youngsters still in school have done some mighty successful treasure hunting in various sections of the country. They have pursued local gossip, rumors, and legends and hit the jackpot.

LAWMEN

County and city officials have been known to be unusually successful in treasure hunting efforts. Whenever a group of professional treasure hunters get together to gab, the subject invariably comes up for discussion about the BILLIONS of dollars that have been secretly recovered by various sheriffs and police officers throughout the country. In the course of their work, they naturally come upon many facts that are never made public and it is natural for a treasure hunter to speculate on how many of these facts relate to funds which have been buried by various individuals, or otherwise hidden.

In the final anlysis, anybody can engage in treasure hunting and their success can usually be controlled by their own resourcefulness, doggedness, and their ability to rationalize and THINK.

FINALLY

A final comment to those strong of wind and leg who have not received the final nudge to 'git out and git rich'! A gentleman by the name of Julius Deverne was confined to a wheelchair for years and was often entirely bedridden by arthritis.. This man made himself, his family, and his helpers wealthy during the depression by reading, writing, and researching buried treasure. His family and his friends would do the legwork. He'd read articles and books, makes notes, order maps, and pinpoint a treasure location without ever going near the site, and he was often successful. In very few cases was he ever able to be on the site and see the results of **his work come to a climax.**

If there is a will, there is a way. Don't ever forget it!

Chapter V

Where

A few years back, I did considerable visiting (some people call it lecturing) with treasure hunting clubs and other interested groups around the United States. I always tried to get the various groups to enter into discussions and to ask questions as I showed a series of color slides of various projects I had been on in times gone by. Invariably, somebody would ask from the audience just where to look for all of this treasure that was yet undiscovered; my stock answer was 'Right under your nose!' Sometimes I got some mighty humorous rebuttals, but I meant just what I said. Believe me, there is treasure in various amounts laying in secret places in every city, town, village, and hamlet and I would almost be willing to bet that every old farmstead in the United States has its own little treasure cache.

REMEMBER?

To begin with, almost anybody who is in his late forties, or older, can remember back when wages were paid in cash and mother kept the family funds in a sugar bowl, pitcher, or some other receptacle. I remember when I was a kid that $15 per week wasn't bad pickings for a lot of hard work and I can remember when my closest friend, in those days, would go to the sugar bowl in the cupboard to get grocery money when we had to go to town for a few groceries. I mention him particularly because his father and mother kept their folding money in a Prince Albert can in the icebox right beside the ice. Nobody would think of looking there for money. In our own family, my mother kept her currency in a pan which was kept in the warming oven of our kitchen range. So it goes: everybody kept their money somewhere in the house, but never carried any large sums on their person if they could avoid it.

Remember now, we have been speaking of spending money, or money that was needed to keep the house going, groceries in the pantry, coal in the coalshed, and to pay for the other ordinary expenses. When it came to larger, more important amounts of money, it was an entirely different story.

CELLARS & TICKS

If the amount to be kept around the house wasn't too large, it might be folded into little bunches of two or three bills and hidden under the pickle jars or canned goods in the cellar, or it might be enclosed in a small envelope and hidden behind the coffeegrinder on the kitchen wall, or it might be hidden in one of the little niches of the old grafonola (phonograph to you youngsters), or it might be secreted in some manner in one of the big pictures on the living room wall. Quite often, pretty good sized chunks of money would be hidden between the mattress and springs of the master's bed. We still had featherticks which were the forerunners of mattresses in those days and these old feather- or straw-ticks hid their share of money. In fact, I've often wondered how much money has gone up in the smoke when these old ticks were burned after somebody had died in the bed it was on.

In the above, we have been thinking of relatively piddling amounts of money, but sometimes it is these piddling amounts that add up to a big score. It was a rare case indeed that over a few hundred dollars was concealed around the house in pots, pans, pitchers, baskets, and other similar receptacles. There are exceptions to this general rule and these exceptions ran into the hundreds of thousands of dollars in some instances, but this is something that is almost always beyond the legal or physical reach of the average treasure hunter and it is mentioned only to record the fact that money is oftentimes hidden in the most unusual places and sometimes in astonishing amounts.

Actually, treasure has been found in so many different and surprising locations that the number of actually used and possible places for caches is infinite. Experience has proved that money has been concealed and then lost, forgotten, or abandoned in the most ridiculous places as well as in the most common and expected places. Here are a few examples which are given to demonstrate the lengths to which people will go or have gone to hide their wealth and resources.

WINDMILL

A wealthy Jacksonville, Illinois farmer patiently sealed a fortune in flat sardine cans and submerged them in the grease in the gearbox of his windmill. Years after he had passed on, the two windmills on his place were dismantled and sold at auction. Still later, one of the gearboxes was bought from a junk yard by a young farmer near Lafayette, Indiana. While overhauling and cleaning the gearbox, this young fellow found $10,000 which had been sealed in the cans as mentioned. Sometime after this, the farmer was surprised to learn that still another windmill had existed on the same farm, but he was never able to trace it to its final owner. Does this other gearbox still harbor a fortune in cash, possibly even more than $10,000? Is it still in use? Who knows?

PIPE

In another case, an amateur treasure hunter from Atlanta, Georgia took his newly acquired metal detector to a Union campground on the outskirts of Decatur, Georgia to try it out. Along a fence, he located a piece of pipe which had been driven into the ground at an angle. For some unknown reason, he pulled the pipe and found that it was capped at both ends, unusually heavy, and about eight feet long. The pipe was so heavy that he assumed it was a rod of some sort, but the presence of caps at both ends perplexed him. They were so badly corroded that he could not screw them off, so he rammed it back down into the hole part way and attempted to bend it. It broke and inside he found over $550 in half dollars. This is another peculiar situation because this certainly was not Civil War treasure as newest coin inside was dated 1920. Who hid it? Are there any more pipes in the area? Could be!

There are so many of these treasure stories that would make some mighty exciting reading if only the facts behind the treasure were known. Many is the time that I found an old gun, saddle, bridle, a few wallets, or some other property in a most unusual place and sat and wondered about the fellow who left it there. Many of these items could have been left by some young fuzzy-faced kid who was being pushed onto the owl-hoot trail because of some minor trouble at home, or it could have been some hardened, bloodthirsty old scoundrel. It's just my nature to wonder, when I find things like this, where the guy started and where he wound up.

Where to hunt for treasure? This is an extremely difficult and confusing question to answer; yet, logically, the only sensible answer is ANYWHERE. However, such an answer will not do for most practical purposes and so, categorically, we will list known locations for caches which have actually been discovered.

I am not going to try to list them in any logical order, as this would merely make them logical in one way and illogical in several other ways. They are listed according to trade or profession and it is obvious that any of the trades or professions not mentioned will fall into one of those listed.

EMIGRANTS

EMIGRANTS: In and around old campgrounds along the old trails. Around the sutlers store at the old forts. Around fordes and ferrysites on all rivers which were crossed by the emigrants. Around campgrounds and corrals at the old trading posts and land offices. In the vicinity of boat-landings at the starting point of various trails. At burial points along the trails where plagues and scourges took a great number of lives. At campgrounds at junctions and terminal points of the old trails. Around the sites of squatters' and traders' cabins along any of the trails. In and around any and all early day settlements particularly where the

This group of treasure hunters gathers on the Borrego Desert. All across the country treasure hunting groups like this one assemble regularly for field trials and group hunts. These gatherings are excellent opportunities to share experiences, detector knowledge, and just to have a good, relaxing time.   Photo by Russell Gish.

town built away from the original townsite as it grew. In and around all popular rendezvous for parties along the trails. At points where the relatively easy-going ends and the rough-going starts.

OUTLAWS

OUTLAWS: In and around their campsites and hideouts. In and around townsites where they hung out or dominated. Around the line camps where they worked while employed. Around the ranches, stores, dwellings, and posts which were owned and operated by friends or sympathizers. In and around natural hideouts such as caves, tops of buttes, wooded canyons, and waterholes which they used in travelling back and forth across the country.

GAMBLERS: On the outskirts of towns where they operated. In the walls and floors of dwellings used by them. Along the foundations of dwellings owned or rented by them. In the linings and under trays of old trunks and valises used by them. In various property which was owned by them.

THE GIRLS

PROSTITUTES: This category covers a number of categories including dancehall girls, barflies, roominghouse operators, and other occupations followed by females who capitalized on the lonely male. Their most usual hideouts were in the walls of their domiciles or places of business, and any money will usually be found to be neatly stacked or folded and carefully sealed or sewn in cans or packets of oilcloth or some other water-resistant material of the day; or sewn into folds of their finest or best dresses; or concealed on the bottoms of drawers or on the bottoms of furniture.

MERCHANTS

MERCHANTS: Actually, this category includes all businessmen in the old frontier towns and settlements, and it must be pointed out that banks, banking, and bankers were extremely suspect in the old days. Consequently, while banking was part and parcel of doing business in the early days, many merchants and businessmen kept a certain amount of money on deposit at different banks and concealed the rest of their funds in secret places. Known caches of this money has been found in the dwellings and business places of the merchants, in their cellars and basements, packets nailed to the underside of stair-treads in closets, fastened to the underside of counters, concealed behind removeable bricks in fireplaces, chimneys, and basement walls, in old vases and urns, and between the leaves of old ledgers and books. Remember this, this is a partial listing of places and objects around and in which treasure has been found. Some of the oldtimers were very imaginative and sometimes even perplexed themselves with their clandestine deposits.

HORSE TRADERS

HORSE TRADERS: There were a number of horse traders who travelled through the country with their covered wagons followed by herds of horses in various numbers. Some readers who were around as early as the late '20s and early '30s will remember the last of them. These fellows tried to not carry large sums of money and most of them followed one 'modus Operandi' when ditching their money. That was permanent railroad installations such as whistleposts, switchblocks, and yard-limit signs. Why they predominately favored railroad property is not known. However, during World War II, when so many old railroad tracks were removed for the iron and steel, it was not at all uncommon to read in local newspapers or hear yarns about the railroad crews finding various sums of money hidden in and around various installations. Along some of the old abandoned, or little used, railroad lines in the middlewest, it is quite likely that a person with a good metal detector could do quite well along this line. The customary manner of concealment was to wrap currency or gold coin in leadfoil or oilcloth and stick it in a can. The can would be buried with the open end down so that water would not drain into it.

FREIGHTERS

FREIGHTERS: There are several known large caches of cash which was hidden by freighters that has never been found; and anybody's guess might be right on the number of caches of which nothing is now known. Freighters, emigrants, and others often hid their cash when they expected to be held up by bands of robbers, or to be attacked by Indians, or when otherwise in danger. These caches will usually be found along the trails, especially at campsites, which were used for commerce. There were many trails which were not popularly used by emigrants and information and history on these can usually be easily obtained from local or state historical societies. These caches quite often run into amounts of $50,000 or over.

FARMERS

FARMERS: The ethics and honesty of bankers has never been held in particularly high esteem by the working man and this was particularly so of the farmer. Consequently, the famous 'posthole bank' became popular prior to the landrush and homesteading days. For the benefit of the uninformed, the posthole bank was nothing else than a cache of money or valuables at the side of or base of a fencepost or other similar landmark. To many people, the posthole bank could only be associated with fenceposts. To the contrary, others have always considered any clandestine cache outside of a building constituted a posthole bank. Anyway, for convenience, we will list a few proved posthole bank depositories as typical examples: fenceposts, windmill anchor posts, trees, guy-stakes, and mailbox posts.

RANCHERS

RANCHERS: Experience has more or less indicated that the early day ranchers were more inclined to conceal their cash in and around the house. It is no secret in the professional circles that thousands upon thousands of hours have been wasted in searching through outbuildings and yards of old ranches without success.

FERRYMEN

FERRYMEN: Often overlooked in history, the fellows who built and operated ferries were often the most prosperous men in a community or area. If a true book is ever written solely on the business of ferrying on the old Oregon and Mormon Trails it will be a book packed with greed, lust, murder, robbery, pathos, and exciting human activity. In the vicinity of Casper, Wyoming, alone, several ferries were operated across the North Platte River and several fortunes were made there and some of the vilest intrigue in the west was engaged in here by individuals, cliques, and organized groups. The sites mentioned at Casper or at adjacent Fort Caspar (note the difference in spelling) are merely a few. Many nice-size caches have been located within a half-mile radius of either end of ferry sites and there are unquestionably as many more caches which have not been found. Exact location of either approach to ferry points can usually be easily determined through state historical records and local inquiry.

FELONS

MODERN BURGLARS & ROBBERS: The small bands or gangs operating today as burglars or robbers are generally confined to youngsters in their late 'teens and early twenties. For some unknown reason, their caches or hideouts for loot are usually located in old buildings (houses, sheds, or barns) on the premises of one of their band or some other confederate. Not so often, the loot will be concealed in several different locations and when an arrest is made in the case only one of the hideouts is usually exposed. When cash is involved, a good portion of it is usually hidden along with the rest of the loot which may be appliances, car parts, furniture, or other valuable items.

EMBEZZLERS

MODERN EMBEZZLERS: Most, but certainly not all, embezzlers today engage in the activity to meet current expenses and, quite often, to meet gambling debts and therefore do not actually come into the scope of the treasure hunter. However, no small number of embezzlers by any stretch of the imagination become involved by taking only a small amount of money to meet some current pressing obligation. After becoming so far involved, many of them make a calculated crime out of it by embezzling large sums over as long a period of time as possible and hiding the money at various places. This, on the assumption that they will be confined for so many years and retrieve the funds when they are released. By carefully investigating these cases and analyzing the activities of the embezzler, it is often possible to locate some of the absconded funds. According to the statutes of most states, these funds should be surrendered to a proper public official or turned over to the firm from which they were embezzled. This involved considerable hardship and trouble in some cases, so the state statutes should be consulted in this respect before making an extended or detailed search for such funds.

MISERS

MODERN MISERS & MIDAS'S: As our mode of living changes, so changes our personal characteristics. In most instances, the habits of the modern misers, midas's, and hermits have changed accordingly; not to such a great extent but they have changed. Let it be realized first that the homes and abodes of all people is their legal domicile and to enter such domiciles without authority or permission constitutes burglary, breaking and entering, or other felonies depending on the state or local statutes, or both. After such premises have been abandoned and if the treasure hunter has the right or permission to enter, then these following hints and tips may be followed. The more common hiding places for funds for these people are in bed clothing, old books and papers, behind or in picture frames, in old stacked dishes and utensils, and practically any possible container or receptacle. Not so frequently do these people hide their funds outside of their domicile, but when they do it is with learned discretion. For example, an old recluse in Iowa was a farmer on the outskirts of town. He had an orchard close to the house in his farmyard. The orchard was fenced and over the top of each fencepost he had nailed a tin can upsidedown and most local people believed this was to keep the birds away. Several years after he died, and a new tenant had moved on the place, it was discovered that some of the cans were spotted with tar over the head of the retaining nail. When one of the cans was removed, it was found that a number of $50-bills had been neatly folded and placed beside the retaining nail inside the can. Every one of the cans which had the water-repelling blob of tar contained a substantial sum of money. In another instance in Louisiana, money was found concealed inside the small hub caps of an ancient car which had been driven into a hog lot and parked at the end of its useful days.

These are some of the things which make treasure hunting so interesting to those who pursue it professionally, and it is also one of the reasons that beginners and amateurs lose interest before they ever manage to make a discovery.

WHO

Another example which should probably be placed in the WHO Chapter are the fellows (and there are a number of them) who make fantastic profits over a period of a few years, conceal the money and make accurate income tax returns but don't pay, and then dispose of or conceal all of their assets so that the Government cannot place a lien on their property. No longer are safety deposit boxes an absolutely safe clandestine depository for funds, particularly, insofar as the courts and law is concerned.

Consequently, many of these fellows revert back to the old methods of concealing their funds. Their hiding places may be in their automobiles, but this is unusual, in or around homes they owned and conveyed to relatives to prevent liens and confiscation, and in similar ordinary places. Some of these fellows have been known to convert their cash into gold nuggets and use the nuggets as aggregate in concrete for porch steps, patios, and even mortar for laying bricks.

RATIONALIZE

WHERE is a complicated and confusing question but it can often be solved by rational consideration of the person who hid the object and the area. A partial list of known hiding places for money, gems, jewelry, and other objects of great value is as follows: mattresses, pillows, car seats, under the car dash, in car radios, in the car trunk fastened to the bottom of the package tray, fastened to the bottoms of shelves in closets and pantries, in the water tank of bathroom stools, under tables and chairs, in tractor tool boxes, on sills in old garages and barns, in holes in old gun stocks, in tobacco cans in outbuildings and sheds, in hollowed-out books and even in hollow doorweights, and in such places as stovepipe holes in chimneys.

FLUES

This last item certainly deserves some discussion. All of us remember when the wood and coal stoves exhausted the fumes and smoke through a stovepipe into the chimney. Any student of physics knows that heat goes up. Consequently, anybody smart enough to acquire and save any amount of money also was capable of realizing the wonderful possibilities of a chimney as a hideout, *and many did.* In every instance that I am aware of, money was stowed into old tobacco or other cans and stuck in the soot at the bottom of the chimney. Thus, regardless of how hot a fire was built in the stoves, the fire, fumes, and heat would pass over the can and race up thru the chimney. It was entiretly unlikely that anybody would withdraw the stove pipe and fumble around in all of the soot, so it made a good hiding place. Not only this, but if somebody did happen to find the money, in all likelihood they'd leave a trail of soot and make it easy to catch them. It was just that simple and there is still plenty of money still lying hidden and lost in the chimneys of many of these old time homes.

HIDEOUTS

At the risk of being repetitive and possibly presumptious, I want to list a few locations for treasure which are by no means all-inclusive, but they will give your think-tank exercise and possibly help you if you ever get on the trail of a known treasure and can not fathom where 'it' is actually concealed.

Remember! Treasure has actually been found in these places and locations, so they are not speculative locations, but they have been proved by experience.

Old iceboxes and refrigerators, ash compartments of old coal stoves, under door and window sills, tacked to floor joists, in nests in chicken coops, in rain troughs and spouts, tacked to the underside of eaves, stuffed down into the roof eaves from the attic, tacked to the bottom of lower cupboard and pantry shelves, behind the reflectors in old auto headlights, in household goods storage rooms, nailed to the bottom of weighing scale platforms, submerged in glass jars in stock tanks, hidden at the bottom of kegs of nails or staples, sealed in old inner tubes and tires, concealed in old farm machinery, sealed in heavy containers in cisterns, attached to well pipes, behind automobile dashes, in old cream cans, hidden in unopened mail (sealed in an envelope and then mailed to himself), in old dishes, in and around the cold air ducts of furnaces, in ash pits of old furnaces, and in many other stranger places around the premises. Old trunks, fruit barrels, and other containers are relatively common.

Many fortunes have been placed in cans and covered with melted grease or lard. Over $300 was scraped out of an old black axle-grease can, by accident, when the grease was finally used by a person who salvaged it from a city dump. That's the way the cookie crumbles, and you never know what comes next.

CURIOSITY

Curiosity is one of the 'tools' of a good treasure hunter and in closing this chapter I want to relate a little yarn about this characteristic. For years and years, the old livery stable in the ghost town of Atlantic City, Wyoming has been decaying and falling in ruins. In a lean-to, two old Dodge cars have been gathering rust and age. An old, bullet-punctured gasoline tank hung from the roof of the lean-to for as long as anybody can remember. In 1958, part of the roof fell and with it the old gas tank. Sometime later, a forest ranger and an old prospector were rummaging and prowling through the old stable. The prospector rolled the tank over with his foot and noticed the sound of gravel or rocks inside. Days later, the prospector's curiosity was aroused about the sound and he went back to Atlantic City and opened the tank. Inside he found several hundred dollars worth of silver and gold coins. Many of them were dented and damaged by the bullets which had been fired through the tank by pinheaded sharpshooters. Perhaps a thousand, and maybe thousands, of people have walked under this tank while it was suspended from the lean-to roof and probably another few thousand people walked across or around the tank while it lay on the floor of the lean-to. Whose bank was this old gasoline tank? Nobody knows.

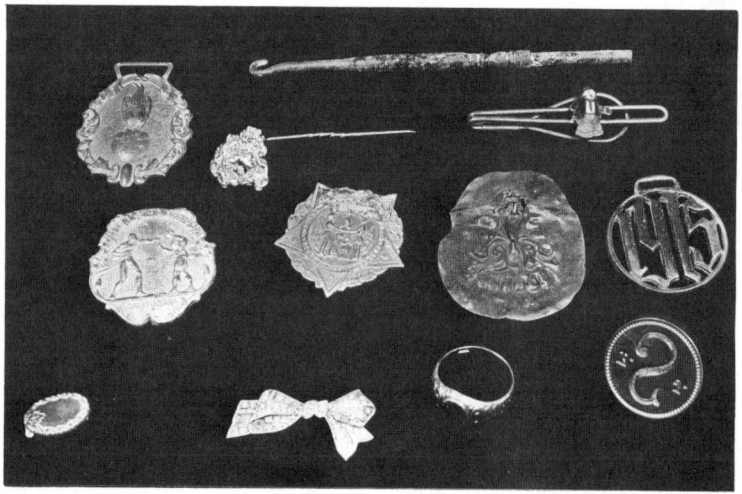

Roy Gene Rolls, Forest Ranch, California, is an extremely active coin and relic hunter. These medallions and old, unique jewelry items were found by Gene during his Old West ghost town searches.

CHAPTER VI

How

Back in 1956 I wrote an article 'Treasure Hunting Made Easy' and I packed just about all the information I could into 4,000 words. This article was written in response to hundreds of inquiries and to just as many questions from the floor at various places around the United States where I had lectured on treasure hunting. After this article was published in the National PROSPECTOR'S Gazette, more questions came in. These enabled me to pick out the weak and the uninformative parts of my article and, consequently, I have included all of this information in this book.

The section dealing with research was unquestionably weak, but I did the best I could with the available space. I know a lot of fellows made some pretty productive strikes by virtue of the information and guidance contained in the article and I imagine a lot of fellows never let me know of the help it gave them.

TEDIOUS

In the procedures and processes of treasure hunting, you can scratch it down in your little memory book that the toughest, roughest, most tedious part of MOST treasure projects is the research. To begin with, most big treasures are first located in libraries, county clerks' offices, or in newspaper files and then they are actually recovered from the site where they have usually lain for years. A guy with a million dollars worth of instrumentation doesn't stand a chance against a good research man in most cases. Instruments are often extremely important, but common sense tell us that you should know the most likely places to use them AND HOW TO USE THEM.

RESEARCH

I have always maintained that 90% of the work for successful treasure hunts is done in the form of research. In fact, let me give you a little example. An acquaintance once telephoned me in Santa Monica, California and asked me to meet him at the Venice Library an hour or so later. This I did. He was reading through some California records and less than an hour later we were on our way up Sepulveda Boulevard for the San Fernando Valley. We passed through the city of Pacoima and into the mountains past a sanatorium and at a lookout point, he stopped and searched around for some time looking for a marker. He found it and we drove on for a few miles and he got out again and found another marker. Back to the car he came and took out a measuring tape and metal detector and started measuring away from this last Government marker. In a matter of about 20 minutes, he kicked a hole in the ground to mark the spot and went back to the car to get a shovel. In another half-hour he had recovered a treasure of guns, old coins, and some jewelry. I would venture to say that in less than 2 hours after leaving the Venice Library he had this treasure cache located, unearthed, and in the trunk of his car. On the way back to town, he mentioned that every bit of the work on this project was done in the Culver City Library, the Venice Library, and in the historical files of the historical museum on the USC campus. He had never been to, past, or near the site before.

ARIZONA

I would venture to say that a man could spend a full lifetime in Arizona (or any other state, for that matter) researching through old newspaper accounts and locate two treasures a year, at least, and still not scratch the surface of the state's actual buried treasure.

Not only a single book, but an entire shelf of books, could be written about the exact and precise procedures to be used in locating different treasures and this is simply because every treasure cache poses different and distinct problems.

McDERMOTT

For the sake of actual, constructive example, let us take a typical fairly recent successful treasure jaunt and see how it works out. In 1917, a rancher by the name of Tom McDermott, residing on his ranch south of Gothenburg, Nebraska sold a few more than 1,000 head of horses to a horse-buyer for the Government for over $27 per head. This adds up to a little more than $27,000. He was paid in cash at Gothenburg in the presence of a banker and businessman, Will Stebbins, and left the bank. Outside of the bank he was met by his brother-in-law, Jud

Burrows, and together they drove back to the McDermott ranch in a buggy. McDermott was a bachelor so while Burrows prepared supper for the two, McDermott went to a sod barn and was gone for some time and then returned. He did not say a word to Burrows about how much he had received for his horses or if he had banked the money. It was well-known throughout the community that McDermott had absolutely no faith or respect for bankers or lawyers, and it would naturally be assumed that he brought his cash home with him.

Along about 1927, a veteran of World War I rented a farm a mile or so south of the McDermott ranch and eventually he became a very good and close friend of Tom McDermott. He bought a new 1927 Ford roadster and people in the community assumed that Tom McDermott had paid for it since the Madsen farm was considered a rather poor place and Madsen, a casualty of World War I, was not able to farm as he would have liked. Madsen also became a good friend of the Burrows, too.

One Sunday in 1927, Madsen drove McDermott over to the Burrows place which adjoined the McDermott ranch on the west, and during the customary visiting, Tom McDermott mentioned that he had received a $27,000 pay-off for this one particular lot of horses and had hidden it in the barn and completely forgotten it. Sometime later, either in 1927 or 1928, Madsen became completely disabled and went to the veterans hospital and home in Grand Island, Nebraska. While there, he related to several other patients the fact that Tom McDermott was careful of who he let handle his money and how they handled it but, at the same time, he was careless in how he kept it at home. In the discussion, he mentioned the facts as related above.

The facts of this yarn as mentioned to the point where Madsen went to the hospital are a matter of record in the North Platte, Gothenburg, and Farnam newspapers. Not the hiding of the money in the barn, but the selling price, number of horses, McDermott being accompanied by Burrows, Madsen buying a new Ford Roadster, and Madsen and McDermott (both bachelors) being frequent Sunday guests of the Burrows and vice versa. These and many other important facts are spread out in the newspapers and the Farnam Echo, particularly, gives a number of clues to the social affairs of the community.

Finally, Madsen died and then McDermott died. The McDermott estate went to the various members of the family (after the lawyers got their share) and after a lot of the neighbors and others got through snooping over the McDermott ranch things got pretty quiet around there.

About this time, Byron Jones (now dead) recalled the facts and figures that Madsen had related in the soldiers' home and hospital in Grand Island and upon learning that McDermott had passed on inaugurated an investigation into the old man's financial dealings. He was astounded by the wide property holdings of Tom McDermott and the size of his dealings. When he was positive that he was on the right track, he quit his job as a mechanic and devoted his full time to checking the McDermott history through local and area newspapers, county records, and by visiting with neighbors and acquaintances of the McDermott-Madsen-Burrows trio. He checked into the railroad and stockyard records at Farnam, Ingham, Gothenburg, and other Nebraska towns in the area and compared his findings against the known expenditures of McDermott. Even the probate and court records were checked and Jones finally came to the conclusion that McDermott must have been a mighty wealthy man in cash alone, not considering his extensive land holdings and other interests.

Thereafter, he concentrated on gathering information on McDermott's personal activities. Information was scant as neighbors could offer very little information and local officials in nearby towns knew only that he was extremely wealthy, tended to his own business, and steered completely away from any kind of trouble.

Finally, according to Jones own diary, he concluded that he would have to search the premises if he was to be successful. His research had disclosed that a line camp existed several miles north of the ranchhouse and corrals, and he made his first search there without results.

He then began a systematic search of the ranchhouse and most of the outlying buildings which were soddies, that is, made from sod. After searching through every nook and cranny and locating only token sums of money, Jones evolved the idea of using an ultra violet light to discover any disturbances which had been made in the walls of any of the buildings.

UV LIGHT

By use of the UV light, he located the World War I horse money in the barn, plus some other caches and then went over the inside walls of the house and found a few more. His total take from the premises in a week's time was over $40,000. $40,000, that is, if we are to believe his diary which is in the possession of Ted Garvin of Los Angeles, California.

Thus, Jones research established the fact that a treasure existed and gave clues to possible locations. Through ingenious use of an instrument, in this case an ultra violet lamp, he was able to ascertain the definite locations of the caches and recover them. This is not an exceptional example of where research has led the treasure hunter right to the treasure, but it does demonstrate that 'facts make figures.'

LEADS

So many people ask 'How do you get a lead on a treasure cache?' There are actually many ways. Through an article in a magazine, an item in a newspaper, or a piece of gossip related by some unknowing local resident or former resident of a community. Sometimes these combined clues cause a chain reaction that leads you a long ways away from your original goal. For example, along about 1957, my good friend Bill Hammond and I went to the old Vallecito Stage Station state park in San Diego County, California to check on a ridiculous treasure story about the area. At that point, we picked up another tale that lead us to Winterhaven (near Yuma) and then up to the old Picacho mine and Picacho Peak with all of its superstitions and tales. A day and evening there shooting the bull with George, the caretaker, sent us on up to a spring and tank in the Piute Mountains between the city of Needles and the town of Essex. We looked the scene over carefully and returned to Victorville and Los Angeles to do considerable research on the area and certain characters who had passed across the stage of the area. After exhaustive research and making as much headway as we could through records in Los Angeles and San Bernardino, we visited with (interviewed) a few oldtimers in Barstow and returned to the Piutes to make our final search. We found a small treasure which hardly compensated us for our time and trouble and, because of the heat, we left to make another try at it during the cooler winter months. Later, we became involved in prospecting in the area and never did get back to our treasure hunting around there. Someday, we may go back.

This is not a perfect example of treasure hunting because all this hopping around is not especially conducive to success. The ideal and proper way is to pursue each project to a conclusion.

In case you are interested, the trip to Vallecito was in response to curiosity aroused by a notarized article in one of our big circulation adventure magazines. The article and everything about this treasure was pure hokum. The article was merely a rehash of another ridiculous story printed years prior in another magazine by a writer who had never been out of Michigan and was at the time of the writing laying flat on his back in a hospital. Hammond and I were not alone in investigating the story as hundreds more from all over the United States went to San Diego in pursuit of the fictional El Dorado.

GOSSIP

Quite often residents of towns and communities will relate a yarn that is a direct lead to a treasure. It might be about a banker or businessman who absconded with funds and died before they could be located, or an old tightwad (whata name) or recluse that reputedly hid all his money in the area, or a robber who 'pulled' a job and was killed shortly afterward without the money being recovered, and so on. Many of these yarns bear investigating and when you hear the same stories related over and over again by different people in different areas, it gives some credence to the stories. As often as not, these yarns are amplified, magnified, twisted, distorted, and generally confused with each telling. Only good research can determine the facts and even then it is sometimes difficult to tell.

Research, as I have said time and again, is hard, tedious work and it is sometimes difficult, if not impossible, for a man who loves the outdoors to sit in a library, newspaper office, or one of the county offices and go through mountains of documents and books. This is pure misery for many men who really are exalted in the open spaces and I know many of them. Some are doctors, some dentists, some lawyers, some farmers, some mechanics, and men who formerly followed other trades and professions. Now, they prefer to let the sky be their blanket and the good earth their mattress; all happy, honest, sensible men who are doing what they like best and know it. Nevertheless, intensive research is usually a most necessary part of treasure hunting and often absolutely mandatory to the success of a project.

THE BEGINNING

There must be a beginning to a treasure hunting project,

and this is usually the rumor, gossip, yarn, statement, or even a magazine article mentioned previously. Starting with this we have to first prove that any treasure actually did or does exist. From here on, it is merely a matter of developing a web of facts that unquestionably supports or refutes any possibility of treasure existing as suspected, implied, or believed. Naturally, when all facts point toward the non-existance of an alleged treasure, the search is abandoned. On the other hand, when facts indicate or prove that a specific treasure exists, it is only prudent to pursue the research to a successful conclusion or, at least, until we are certain that sufficient facts cannot be obtained to assure finding the treasure. Considerable data and facts can be found in the public records and it is through these records that we can often verify the actual existance of a person, place, or thing and it is often in these public records that we can often find detailed and factual reports on events that took place up to a hundred years or so ago.

Many people are confused regarding what is and what is not a public record, and there are also many people who are totally unaware of the existance of such documents. Essentially, public records are the official records and documents of a government be it precinct, township, city, county, state, or Federal. Many organizations which are not precisely governmental activities may also come under this category, depending on the statutes, such as historical societies, cemeteries, power and irrigation districts, and agricultural societies and districts.

To provide a list for easy reference purposes, the following most-likely public depositories and custodians of public records are given here.

    Federal Government:
        National Archives, Washington, D. C.
        Historical Section, Department of Defense
        Department of Agriculture
        Historical Sections of the various bureaus in
          the Department of Interior
        Department of Justice
        Smithsonian Institution

    State Government:
        State Historical Society
        Attorney General
        State Sheriff or State Patrol

Secretary of State
State Treasurer
State Land Office or Realty Board

County Government:
County Historical Society
Sheriff
County Attorney, or his equivalent
Clerk of County or District Court
County Surveyor
County Assessor
County Commission

City Government:
Mayor
City Clerk
City Engineer
City Library
City Museum
Police Department
Street Commission
Utilities Commission

Depending on what state you live in, you will find that some of the departments and bureaus listed are either non-existent or operate under another name. For example, your county surveyor might be known as the county engineer, or your assessor as the tax collector, or your county commission may be known as the board of supervisors. The names may be different but their functions will be quite similar to those in other communities and states.

In the realm of semi-private and private records which may quite often be available to you, you will find the files of the following businesses and people helpful so often:

Attorneys
Bankers
Businessmen
Newspaper Files
Auctioneers
Private and public libraries
Private and public museums
Doctors
Authors, writers, and artists

Another source of information and records which has not

been listed above is your local justice of peace and the constable. Those who have held their offices, which are public, for a considerable time are unusually well versed in what has gone on in the community. If these constables and justices of peace will cooperate and help, they can usually provide a lot of assistance in establishing facts for a project. However, take it from me, so many of them are so obstinate, suspicious, and, in some instances, actually stupid that it is a hit-or-miss proposition to approach them. I say this not because I have any bone to pick with these offices, because I do not, but I have so often found that they greatly over-estimate their importance and are completely reluctant to do business with anybody unless they are brought before them on some misdemeanor or unless you can help them serve a summons. Nevertheless, I mention them here because they can often be of great help through their knowledge of a community or through their records.

CLUES

We have already established the fact that you must have a lead or clue to start a treasure project. This may be rumors about a miser in your community who reputedly hid a fortune somewhere, or it may be a local legend about a robber who hid some loot in the area, or any of an almost unlimited number of leads. Quite often somebody accidently locates a treasure cache in the community and this stirs up rumors and speculation about other treasure still unfound. The way to start is to first determine that a treasure actually does exist, or to at least determine that there is a good probability that a treasure does exist.

The next step is to determine what it is, if possible, and where it is. In many instances, the nature of the treasure is obvious or well-known, and the job remains to determine where it is.

The matter of determining where it is is the part of treasure hunting that often requires exhaustive research. Of one thing you may be certain, if a treasure does actually exist, there is most certainly enough information in the form of the written or spoken word to enable a diligent treasure hunter to find it. This statement has often been the cause of arguments and discussions, but the fact remains that there are too many known cases where law officers have searched for years for hordes, loot, or other treasure in order to close a case and have done so without success. Later, a professional (and sometimes even an amateur) treasure hunter has come along and recovered it in a few days or a few weeks. It is merely a matter of gathering together the right facts and then piecing them into the whole cloth and then picking up the winnings.

ZANE GREY

I think that one of the most phenomenal true treasure stories I have ever heard is one that pertains to a lead which was found in one of Zane Grey's books. Some years ago, Charles Forbes, son of a paving foreman, read a copy of Grey's book dealing with the Overland or Oregon Trail and one of the yarns in the book related to the hiding of a fortune some distance from the covered wagon camp by an elderly gentleman. This story, maybe through hunch or intuition, stuck in young Forbes mind and when he was old enough to go out on his own he made plans to follow up the story. Several years of intermittent research led him to a point along the trail in Wyoming and he concentrated on diaries and documents pertaining to that particular area. To make a long story short, he garnered enough information to actually make the search and he found this treasure. I have heard of several other similar stories of fellows finding treasure which was mentioned in books of fiction, but these I know nothing about. Young Forbes, now middle-aged, lives in Mexico and I discussed this story with him in 1957 in Ensenada and he confirmed the entire story.

BOOKS

Many tips and directions on research are covered in Chapter XV of this book and you will find that I have duplicated some pieces of information in various sections of the book. This is because they are especially important or because they require rementioning. Millions of hours have been spent by writers, historians, and others in researching and investigating events, places, and people for books and articles. The wise treasure hunter seeks out these books and facts and uses them in his own research. For example, it is not necessary to go to a particular site or community to look over the ground while researching a treasure there. In all probability, there are several good books, complete with maps, that already cover the area more completely than you are likely to, and more often than not, these references will reflect the actual conditions at the time the event took place which you are researching.

MAPS

There are thousands of detailed maps of the Oregon Trail and its vicinities, but the maps which were made a hundred or so years ago do not necessarily reflect the exact geography we see today. So, if a person follows a lead from a diary dated 1857 and attempts to correlate it with the geography of the Trail or the Platte River, for example, today, he is either lost or misled. However, all one needs do is to leaf through a good old-fashioned Atlas such as the Crown Series and he will find the geography compares with the diary. Thus, by reconstructing the old geography from the actual geography of today, he can come pretty doggone close to orienting himself to within a few feet of the point he seeks. The original maps of the Crown Series are in the Denver Library, but reprints of them can be found in the libraries of many state historical societies. There are many others and the librarians at most historical society libraries and museums can help you locate the best possible or the only applicable maps for almost any year you name.

Because of the several good reproduction processes available today, it is possible to get a copy of almost anything in a matter of a few minutes and at very small cost. I have a number of the old Crown Series maps of the Oregon Trail covering the stretch from Independence, Missouri to Independence Rock, Wyoming and it seems to me that they cost me 20¢ per page. This makes a lot of them expensive, but if they save you considerable mileage and time, they are more than worth the price.

In fact, I would like to know how many treasure caches along the old Oregon Trail have been found by treasure hunters who used the Crown Series maps to orient and locate the treasure.

When you really get into treasure hunting, you find that it can become a mighty difficult and complex activity. A Chicago newspaper once referred to me as a 'specialist' and when a friend sent me the article I could tell that the writer or his consultant knew what they were talking about because the article mentioned things which are not at once obvious to the uninformed person. I guess I am what would be termed a 'specialist': my forte is old frontier treasure and it is almost a mania to me to locate old guns, equipment, money, and other treasure of the century past. I'd pass up an opportunity to locate $25,000 worth of treasure which was concealed last year to prowl around in the West or Southwest looking for a few old guns and money.

In fact, I have already done just about the same ridiculous thing several times and I don't regret it a bit. So, when I often refer to some of the old Trails or frontier towns, you know I am merely expressing a restrained love for the West and the outdoors. Even today, I get worked up over an approaching treasure hunt like I did when I was a kid the night before our big football game, or the day before the opening of hunting season. I can't explain it; I just get completely unsettled and excited. Then, when I finally shove off and get engaged in the research or the 'hunt,' I find that I am completely in command of my wits and all of the exhuberance is gone. I guess it is gambling in its worst form, but I enjoy it and I haven't missed a meal . . . yet.

HOW IN BRIEF

Roughly, here is a brief outline of the procedures for seeking a treasure of almost any kind. You can apply these procedures to practically any treasure cache you have in mind or might become interested in, later. Just remember one important point and that is: Every treasure project is different and you must use your own ingenuity.

    A. The Lead or Clue
    B. Research
    C. Search
    D. The Recovery or Abandonment
    E. Converting the Tangibles

On the surface, that is all there is to treasure hunting, except paying taxes and spending the money. The various procedures are explained as follows:

LEAD

A. The Lead. Professional treasure hunters follow many leads which are picked up in a great variety of places; a magazine or newspaper, comments overheard in the barbershop, a bit of news over the radio, a paragraph from a book, neighborhood gossip, or even a portion of a personel letter received from somebody. Leads and clues to a treasure can actually come from anywhere and at the most unexpected times. It is important that you become capable of recognizing a good treasure lead, that is, if you want to enter the ranks of the professional repeater. Of course, the leads mentioned above are only a few of an almost infinite number of sources. Believe it or not, occasions will occur when different persons will relate a local treasure legend and almost lead you to the cache. The most usual actual reasons they did not pick it up is that they lacked the initiative or else they did not believe the story themselves. You can take it as a general rule that there is no treasure rumor, yarn, or story that is not potential and it pays to give at least a cursory investigation to any stories that sound potential.

WELL

Take the case of an old scavenger and hog-raiser on the outskirts of a town near Camden, New Jersey. Apparently he made a pretty good living picking up bottles along the roads and highways and, at the same time, he raised a few hogs and did other things to augment his income. His acquaintances kidded him about his 'high' income and when they asked him what he did with all of his money he'd say "Throw it in the well." Several years after he had passed on, several cronies were sitting and sipping in a beer joint one night when someone mentioned the old scavenger. His remarks relative to throwing his money in his well were mentioned, and in their alcoholic exhuberance they decided to check and find out. Thereupon, they went to his vacant and abandoned old place and lowered one of the men into the well. Lo and behold, he found a number of packages floating around on the water, so he stuffed several of them into the waist of his trousers and called for them to hoist him out. When they broke the first one open they found a sheaf of currency. He went back and recovered the rest of the packets and the old man's story had come true.

His ingenius method of waterproofing the packages and still keeping them afloat was very simple. He had cut corrugated cardboard from boxes to a size just a bit larger than the currency. Then, he'd sandwich the currency between the boards, wrap the 'sandich' in a breadwrapper, and coat it with paraffin. Then, he wrapped it again, and again, until it was thoroughly waterproofed. Then, as he said, he'd throw it into the well.

Consequently, it is often profitable to accept the fact that in so many instances fact is stranger than fiction. It has been proved so many times.

RESEARCH

B. Research. The very first thing to do in handling a treasure lead is to determine insofar as possible if the treasure actually exists, if it ever did exist, and if there is a possibility that somebody else has already found it. If it appears that the treasure did not exist, the project can be layed aside in favor of a more certain project, and then worked on further at your leisure.

When it is reasonably established that the treasure does, or did, actually exist, then is the time to begin an orderly and logical investigation to determine where it is. Since it is granted that every project will be different than any other, we must sensibly eliminate all false facts and information and concentrate on the known, proved facts. This is easier than it first appears since more often than not old newspapers, city and county records, and often local citizens will verify the presence of a person or persons at particular time or period and probably a lot of the other facts which are uncovered in the investigation.

It is possible to ascertain deposits and withdrawals from the accounts of deceased persons at many banks, for example, or to determine the amounts of money involved in real estate and other transactions by checking the county or state records. I cite these examples to show that if there is a will there is a way to ascertain almost anything you need to know.

In instances where the treasure is probably located on private land, you will need to know who owns the land, where he is, and if his permission is required to recover the treasure. It is no secret that over 90% of the treasure which is recovered on private property is never reported to the property owner, nor, for that matter, to anybody. One of the principle reasons for this is discussed at length in Chapter X (Publicity and Secrecy).

When the treasure is possibly located on your own property, or on public domain, you can usually follow the rule of walking away with the prize and telling no one.

I think all treasure research should answer the following questions to the greatest possible extent:

1. Does the treasure actually exist?
2. Can it be legally recovered?
3. Has it already been investigated and possibly recovered?
4. What were the circumstances around its concealment? Who did it? A fugitive? An embezzler? A miser? A deranged person? Somebody else?
5. Where is the most likely location that it is hidden
6. Precisely and exactly where is it hidden? This is the fine research.

These questions are not nearly so hard to find answers for than it would appear, and a good treasure hunter finds that everything after work on question 6 is the anti-climax, or the dull point, of treasure hunting until he actually locates the cache and opens it to see what he has recovered.

SEARCH

C. The Search. This can be the most interesting or the dullest part of treasure hunting and it all depends on your own temperament. This is the part where you can use your tools and instruments and ever so often get out into the open spaces and enjoy yourself. The search can have only one of two outcomes: you either find the treasure or you abandon the project. There is no in-between at this stage of the game.

It is difficult to categorically distinguish types of searches. They can be, for example, in buildings, around buildings, in farm lots, in canyons, on the prairies, in cellars and basements, under and around large boulders, in caves, or in a zillion other places. It is extremely difficult to correlate a search of a business building with a house or barn, or a big baseball field with a farm lot, or a monument of the city fathers with a giant boulder, or a telephone booth with an outhouse. And, don't think for a minute that treasure has not been concealed in telephone booths.

While not exactly a 'must,' a metal detector is a mighty handy gadget to have when you close in for the kill. When I first started treasure hunting back in the late '20s and early '30s, I had to use the tailbolt from a lumber wagon and I'd run it into the soil on an old Oregon Trail campground near Ft. Kearney, Nebraska, and when I hit something hard, I'd dig. It's no secret that I found quite a bit of treasure, but I sure did my share of digging, too. Today, with either of my metal detectors in use, I could probably find as much treasure in a week as I found in several years, then.

The use of instruments is covered thoroughly in Chapter XVII and need not be covered at this point.

However, I do want to point out some things. First of all, when searching buildings or anything else that can burn, be careful of fires. Take no chances on fire. This pertains to fires in buildings, on the prairies, or in the forests. Another thing is don't damage property!!! If you can not get in and get your treasure and get out without leaving any signs that you have been there, you most certainly haven't brains enough to keep out of a jam if you are fortunate enough to find a cache. Damage to buildings, property, or anything else is the mark of a rank amateur or a very ignorant person.

I know probably one hundred, or more, professional treasure hunters around this old world and I know from talking with them, working with them, and going on treasure projects with them that they all carefully avoid leaving any evidence that they have been around . . . whether they found their treasure or not. These fellows are so careful that they'll even paste wall paper back into place without ever tearing it, or they'll cement bricks back into walls or chimneys and then smudge the cement so it looks like the old, or they'll remove the sod before digging a hole and then carefully replace it after they fill the hole.

Some professionals go prepared for anything and carry a little lime and cement with them, and kits of bolts, nuts, and screws, and little bottles of paint, and a multitude of other items which are neatly and conveniently packed in their warbags. These are the expendable tools of the professional and he leaves no sign behind him.

Searches can be unusual and strange. A metal detector might be the thing for one search, while an ultra-violet lamp might be just the thing for another. In still other instances, just your hands and eyes might be all that is needed. You've got to apply the proper operation to the task at hand. Sometimes only your hands will do as when searching old log and frame buildings where you must reach over a sill into a niche or crevice for the cache. Even then, you must often wear gloves to avoid insect and snake bites.

Almost every search is different and the use of a little common sense is actually all that is needed.

RECOVERY

D. The Recovery. In itself, the recovery of treasure does not seem important, but it is something that cannot be overlooked, ignored, or even passively handled. Here is why: For every dollar that you'll ever recover, or find, there are a hundred people who would haul you into court if there was the slightest chance that they could nick you for a part of it. Thus, if you openly and publicly unearth a treasure cache, you are setting yourself up for a long and expensive law suit, or maybe several.

FINDER'S KEEPERS

While the courts have pretty well established that the old saying 'Finder's keepers . . . .' is true, there are many people who will persist in testing it in court and since these are good bread-and-butter cases for lawyers and shysters, you'll find these characters ready and willing to take such cases in the absence of anything better. So, publicizing your treasure discoveries is a mighty poor way to convince the public that you are a mental giant, a superman, or anything else but a damned fool. They'll admire you as you pull your million dollars out of that hole in the ground, but they'll laugh at you and pity you as you march into court time after time after time. That's just the way the cookie crumbles.

So, arrange to make your treasure discoveries and recoveries with as much privacy as possible. Do this even if they are on your own property!!!

When you have completed the recovery, cover your tracks! Fill all holes, nail back all boards with the original rusty nails, putty up the nicks and crevices you made, stick the porch steps back into position, fill up the stake holes if you used stakes to zero in on the cache, and leave everything just as it was to begin with.

When all of the hokus-pokus is boiled out of treasure hunting, you find that it is mostly common sense. More often than not, there is so much treasure that is literally 'right under your nose' and all you have to do is think and use just plain, old, ordinary horsesense to find it.

CHAPTER VII

Instruments and Tools

One of the most discouraging things that can happen to you as a treasure hunter is to need a certain tool and not have it handy. This doesn't sound like much of a world-moving statement, but let me give you an example. A few years back (when I had more horsepower than I do today) I located a treasure cache in a cistern some 12 miles from the nearest town. I had a full complement of tools and equipment in the car, except what I needed . . . rope. I did have 15 feet of rope but nothing to anchor it to, so I drove my car as near as I dared to the cistern, hooked my tire chains to the bumper, and then attached the rope to the chains and dropped it down into the cistern. And, down I went. I located an old iron chest I was seeking, and then came the problem on how to get it up to daylight. The rope lacked about 5 feet of touching the floor of the cistern and I didn't dare try to attach the chest to the rope and then go up and pull it up after I was safe and sound because I was not sure the rope would stand the combined weight of the chest and me.

Here's how I worked it out. I jacked up the car and took off the wheel nearest the cistern, layed it under the brake drum, and let the car down. Then, I took the spare tire and lashed it to the other wheel by using the long battery cable from the car. Then, to this rig I attached the tire chains, and then the rope, and down into the cistern I went. This allowed the rope to lack just a foot of hitting the floor of the cistern. I pulled the chest over under the rope, made a sling of two barrel-hoops which were there, and then attached the rope to the barrel-hoops and the hasp of the chest. I shinneyed back up the rope and out of the cistern and pulled the chest up by heaving and then snubbing the rope around a post layed across the opening. I got it out OK.

I could give a dozen more examples, but this one demonstrating what a mere 3 or 4 feet of rope might have prevented is a doggone good one. If the rope would have broke, I could have been stranded in that cistern for hours or days depending on how long it would have taken somebody to notice my car standing there. There are other possibilities, too, that might have happened.

The assortment or complexity of equipment needed and used by the treasure hunter is limited only by how extensive his operation will be. It is only logical that the man who is going to search around old townsites which are devoid of any buildings is not going to need the same equipment that the fellow who is going to search through a ghosttown. By the same token, the fellow whose research leads him to a cave is not going to need the same equipment as the fellow whose project requires the location of an old 'posthole bank.'

I had pretty good luck at treasure hunting back in the late '20s and early '30s and I never owned an honest-to-goodness metal detector until after World War II. I did a lot of clandestine prowling in old buildings and abandoned houses and I never owned an ultra-violet light until about the mid-1950's. This proves one thing, if nothing else, and that is that you can get along with almost nothing if you have to. However, the more we discover, the more we are inclined to invest in good equipment, and this makes sense. I can truthfully say that treasure hunting paid its way for me; I didn't subsidize it.

I like fine tools, equipment, and instruments. Generally, when I buy, I buy the best that is available. Despite this respect for fine equipment, it seems that I have given, loaned, or had stolen most of my expensive tools. Yet, my car is loaded with junk when I'm on the trail.

INVENTORY

Here is my entire complement of tools. It changes constantly due to losses and additions, but this is essentially what makes up the toolhouse in the trunk of my car.

Prospector's rock pick	4# sledge with short handle
Chisel assortment	8# sledge with long handle
5 to 7' pry-bar	D-handle square point shovel
LHSP shovel	Bricklayer's trowel
35 LF of light strong chain	50 LF of ¼" rope
Assortment of pulleys for rope	50 LF of ½" rope
Trench spade	6' probe rod
Carpenter hammer	Carpenter saw
600 LF builder's cord	Nail and screw assortment

Screwdrivers Small box-opener
Socket wrench set Misc. small tools

Equipment is an all-inclusive term and for equipment I include the following:

Snakebit kit Cooking gear
Sleeping bag Portable radio
Small camp stove Spotlight
Flashlights Hand-level
Cameras Note book
Water bags & containers Pencil
First aid kit Ball point pen

My instrumentation includes the following.

Garrett Master Hunter Spartan 175
Geiger counter Ultra-violet light
Inductance loop Portable intercom

At first glance, it will look like it is impossible to get all of this gear into a car, but it can; and much more. I haven't mentioned many items which you will learn to use by experience such as a harness awl, a hoe, a rake, a scythe, paint brushes, a pistol, and oodles of other items which will be peculiar to your own 'warbag.'

HEAVY GEAR

As you enter the professional ranks and begin to let treasure hunting pay its own way, you probably find that a lot of more expensive items are needed such as a housetrailer, an air compressor, a jackhammer, a light plant, and even a dry washer for gold dust recovery. However, when you get to this stage, if you follow the usual pattern, you will have a number of associates and acqaintances in the same fix as you and you'll wind up owning an item or two of this equipment and loaning or borrowing as you need to for your projects. Save your money! Learn to get by with the minimum amount of equipment possible.

One item I have not mentioned above is maps. You can not get too many of them or too great a variety. They can be a nuisance around the house so learn to keep them in an orderly manner and stored away. This is a subject which is covered in Chapter XIX and enough has been said here about them.

There are a few treasure hunters who will need to accumulate all of the items I have listed here. Every piece listed is handy to have around, but your experience will teach you what you need and what you can do without. In fact, quite often you will pick up some item on one of your hunts and it will become a most important part of your equipment. One of my most valuable pieces of gear is an old hoof-trimmer which was used by blacksmiths years ago. For me, it is a tool of a thousand uses. I have used it as a bottle opener, can opener, pruning knife in the New Mexico and Texas brush, a glass-cutter, nailpuller, rope-splicing tool, and in Mexico I even pulled teeth with it.

I want to visit as briefly as possible about certain items I have listed for the benefit of those who need to know. These little pointers are passed along in good faith and I'll try to give them out in short slugs.

FIRST AID

Snakebit kits and first aid kits are not sissy stuff. Either or both may save your life, or that of somebody else. So, get one of each, at least, and don't forget them. With respect to the snakebite kit, learn how to use it and if you ever need to use it, don't get excited, don't rush. Make your incisions and start the suction going. To hell with the snake, let him get away, if necessary.

A sleeping bag is almost a must. I've slept in my car and flopped on the ground a lot of times, but I prefer a good sleeping bag. It's cozier, more comfortable, and you won't have a lot of bugs or snakes crawling up to your back or belly to keep themselves warm. If you've ever woke up to feel a cold snake snuggling up against your legs or back, you'll not forget it for a while. I've had snakes lay on my sleeping bag at night but never try to get inside.

For cooking gear, I like the good old GI mess kits. I also like one of these cast iron skillets and I have finally gotten down to a 6- or 8-inch one as being the size for me. Most of my cooking is done over an open fire and I like to broil anything that can be put on a spit. Some things can't be broiled, so the skillet is almost indestructible and you can cook anything in it. By the way, aluminum foil is handy to cook everything in. Almost anything to be cooked can be wrapped up in it and cooked that way.

I have a small camp stove and rarely use it, but when I do use it, I really need it. Open fires are useless and dangerous in the wind, and a camp stove can be set up in the trunk of the car or some building to permit cooking.

RADIO

A portable radio is convenient to use to get news and weather reports when you are out of reach of civilization. The car radio can be used for this, but sometimes you have to pack some distance and the car radio is out for the period you are gone. Also, most portables can be used as direction finders by zeroing in on nearby or local stations. Remember this!

FLASHLIGHT

Flashlights are almost indispensible and, yet, are so often forgotten or overlooked by camper, outdoormen, and others. Don't forget to use fresh batteries and take along spares if there is a chance they might be needed. I have mentioned a spotlight but I do not mean the ordinary kind. The kind I have plugs into the cigar lighter of my car and a long cord permits me to take the light to the front or back of the car. Thus, it is valuable for making repairs after dark, or searching around the car after dark, or for sending out distress signals, if necessary. It fits under the driver's seat, out of the way, and is always handy when needed.

In the matter of instruments, there are those who say an ultra-violet light is absolutely worthless to a treasure hunter, but I have proved to myself otherwise. You can quite often determine if any bricks have been removed from a basement wall and which ones with a UV light. In the walls of sod and adobe buildings, you can often ascertain if the walls have been tampered with. Even floors that have been excavated in spots can be seen under the UV light. Not only does this device enhance your chances of finding certain types of treasure, but you can use the instrument in your prospecting.

My lists of equipment will probably discourage a lot of fellows. However, I have already stressed the fact that you do not need all of this stuff. My first treasure hunting equipment consisted of the tailgate bolt from a lumber wagon and I did pretty well with it. So, you can start out only with the few tools you need and then add to them as necessary. In fact, most men who like to get out of doors probably have all the equipment they need right now. I like to get by with the least possible equipment and I'm slowly learning to use one tool to do several things. It makes less of a load whether driving or packing in.

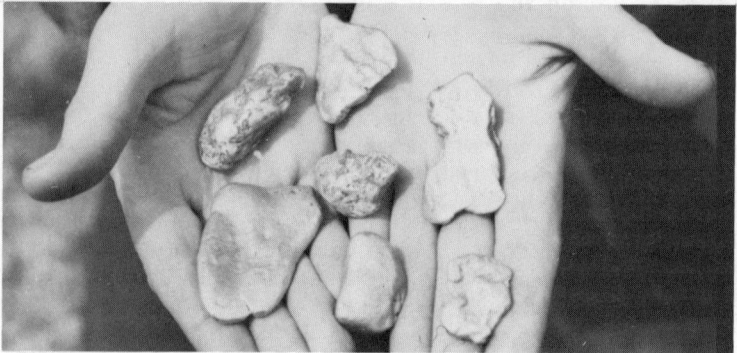

Don't be misled into thinking that there is no more gold left to be found! Actually, there is more gold in the ground than was taken out by the early-day miners. Of course, the gold that is left is not easy to find and recover, but it can be done by investigating the gold producing areas of the 19th-century and selecting the most promising sites, especially those where veins and large nuggets were found. In those areas, your chances of finding gold are greatly increased with the use of the new universal VLF/TR ground canceling metal detectors. These instruments have the capability to ignore the disturbing effects of mineralized ground while detecting gold. ELECTRONIC PROSPECTING, a book published by Ram Publishing Company, provides the reader with the complete information needed to select and use these new detectors in successful electronic gold recovery. See page 303 for complete details on this electronic prospecting guidebook.

George Mroczkowski (with hat and vest), president of the Gem and Treasure Hunting Society, stands next to a Mexican Army soldier who happily shows off his rifle that George found for him. During a recent Army maneuver, the soldier and one other lost their rifles in a swollen river. George and his recovery team were called in by the Mexican Army, and after several days of searching this river bed they found the two rifles. Needless to say, George was well honored for his success.

"Hardrock" Hendricks, Roy Lagal, Jim Mitchell, and Charles Garrett conduct an investigation in West Texas of a well-documented silver cache. Often, several treasure hunters will get together to combine their various experiences, know-how, and equipment expertise in order to increase their chances of successful recovery.

Chapter VIII

Clothing

I have several perpetual critics around the country who continually find fault with many of the things I write and say. I write the following without malice, but to prove a very interesting point, and that is that not a single one of these self-appointed critics has either the 'proverbial pot nor the window.' You all know what I mean.

Anyway, After one of my advertisements for this Treasure Hunter's Manual had appeared in a magazine, one of these critics wrote me to ask just what in the hell difference clothing made in the art of treasure hunting. I wrote back a single sentence to test his thinking and in this sentence I asked him what kind of chairs were in his automobile. He wrote no more.

The choice of clothing is important primarily for health and comfort only. I know a very successful treasure hunter who is a nudist. You know, one of these always-healthy people who are part human and part bare. I asked him once if he practiced nudism while on his treasure jaunts and he said he did only when he was in camp. So, even he wore clothes, sometimes.

I know that I am extremely selective in clothing for treasure hunting, prospecting, and just tramping out in the desert and mountains. You'd never know it to see me decked out in my brush-clothes, but I have selected all of them for a purpose. I'll go over my outfit for you and explain why I have selected them.

BOOTS

For footwear, I prefer 8 or 10" boots. I particularly like these because they are easy to put on and take off, they are lighter than knee-boots, and they make doggone good pillows to go with my sleeping bag. When necessary, I can tuck the bottoms of my pants into them and let the pant legs droop over and keep out seeds, burrs, sand, and dirt.

SHIRTS

For shirts, I like good wool shirts and heavy synthetic cloth shirts. If you have two of each, you are equipped for pretty warm or pretty cold weather. During the summer, the synthetic shirts are nice for the daytime and then at sundown you can slip on one of the wool shirts and wear it like a jacket for the additional warmth. One wool shirt is usually sufficient for daytime wear during the winter, except when the wind is blowing, and when it cools off all you need to do is slip in the other wool shirt, or a jacket.

COATS

I've had a multitude of jackets but my favorite is a cheap $8 one I picked up on the spur of the moment in the Sears store in Seattle several years ago. I have worn it from coast to coast and from Canada to Mexico and it still has a lot of mileage left and it keeps me warm in the coldest weather. It is a plaid mixture of wool and orlon, and bulky but light.

PANTS

In the matter of trousers, I always like to wear a pair of nylon or orlon trousers underneath and a pair of tweed or denum trousers outside. During cold weather or in snow, I wear the nylon pants underneath and a pair of water-resistant hunting pants on the outside. I have the hunting pants with the knit bottoms and tuck the knit part into the top of my boots to keep the snow, dirt, and weed seeds out. The reason I like the synthetic fabric pants underneath is that they are cool and, above all, I think they offer some protection from snakebite. I was struck by a rattler in Wyoming several years ago but I was saved by a pair of nylon pants I had on under my tweeds. When I sad down to administer first aid to myself I would find no punctures and when I looked at the trouser leg, there were two telltale wet spots. His fangs just didn't make it through the fabric.

Hunting pants have certain limitations. Most of them are water-repellant and on a cool, sunshiney day are extremely hot. Even if you waddle around in the deep snow, they just don't give enough ventilation and you are soon soaked with sweat. On the other hand, they are tough and do not rip or tear easy in the brush and if you have much crawling over and through rocks to do, they'll wear like iron. Too, they are pretty good protection against snakebite, insects, and thorns.

SOX

Socks are far more important than would appear. If you are a city dude and go into the hills, mountains, or desert for an extended stay, you'll probably learn to live with blisters from one end of your feet to the other at first. I'll never forget my first go-round with George Lanning. He was an old desert rat who had managed to amass a nice bank account honestly and he was in a party I went prospecting with once. At our first camp, he noticed by footwear and said, 'Dod gam, look at this fellow and his foot pillows!' It was funny to him, but not to me. He hadn't worn sox for 50 years and he thought I should get in line. However, I was a tenderfoot compared to him.

I like to wear a light pair of silk or nylon sox, and then pull a heavy pair of wool sox on over them, then my boots. This is the easiest way I know of to prevent a lot of blisters and callouses. In the hills, your feet and shoes really get a workout; not only are your feet sliding back and forth, and then up and down in your boots, but when you walk along hillsides, your feet have a tendnecy to roll in your boots, too. Alum, hypo, iodine, salt, or any of the other toughening treatments do not work near as well for me as do heavy socks, so I stick with the heavy socks and leave the drugs at home.

RED

I also have a red vest and red cap that I wear whenever I am out during hunting season, but I don't do this much. Somehow, some of these mighty hunters shoot at anything that moves during hunting season, and I've had several close shaves, so like a smart old bear, I stick as close to my den as possible when there are so many lead-slinging idiots in the field. Believe me, we had a mental giant from Chicago once shoot a plain old hereford cow within 100 feet of our campfire and he actually believed it was a deer. Yep, he came down and cut its throat to bleed it and thought he had bagged a prize. This is the type of characters you can run into during hunting season, so I stay home as much as possible then.

WATER

If you go into the desert or wilderness areas, play safe and take along one item of clothing that you can carry water in, if necessary. A hat, water-resistant jacket or trousers, or some other item will do. Don't forget in a pinch, you can use one or both of your boots to contain or carry water.

SUNGLASSES

Not necessarily an item of clothing, but sometimes almost as important is a pair of sunglasses. At high altitudes in the mountains, on the desert, along the beach, or in snow they are almost a must. A lot of fellows do not use sunglasses because they think it is manly to go without or that it makes them a sissy to use them. These are the guys who invariably wind up with poor eyesight.

Clothing is much more important than many of us like to admit. Our city cousins are hesitant to dispense with many of the items that are shown, advertised, or listed in the sports magazines, and they will suffer untold discomforts just to make themselves believe that they are right. Fortunately, for their own sake, if they spend much time in the field, they invariably relegate themselves to the fashions of the old-timers. It not only costs less, but it is so much more practical and comfortable. We like to think of ourselves as being 'modern' (whatever that means) and most of us are unaware that we are constantly sold a bill of goods by the advertisements which appear in the magazines. Just for example, the color telephones. Everytime I move to a new location and have a telephone installed, the girl always tries to sell me a colored phone. Yep, seven and one-half bucks worth. I don't argue with her, I just tell her if a colored one works better, I'll take it; and if it doesn't, they yank the damned thing out and put in a black one like I've always had and cancel the charges. Pure idiocy! But, people have to keep up with the guy next door or down the street, so we have color telephones and pay $7.50 for them. Telephones are just one example of what advertising does. Look at the junk they hang on automobiles that is absolutely worthless, yet the public wants it.

The same goes for your field clothing. Don't for Heaven's sake, go out with an oldtimer and wear a necktie. Maybe he won't, but he should, take the dripping end of the necktie and hitch it to a tree limb. By the same token, don't go into the field wearing a pair of oxfords and expect to get very far without suffering for it. In the field, a cap is usually about as practical as a BB-gun; it will shade your face while your neck and shoulders roast. You'll be aware of this that night and the next day. Short-sleeved shirts are out; wear long sleeves to protect you against the cold and sun, alike. Tight pants are NG; wear the baggiest things you can find. In fact, if you are going to buy clothes especially for your first trip into the 'sticks,' make it a policy to get everything (except hat and boots) one or two sizes larger than you usually wear.

Just use that noggin the good Lord put on your shoulders and don't try to be a fashion-plate because you will impress absolutely nobody, and the chances are that if you go out dressed fit to kill you'll be the laughing stock of the area. Nuff said!

Somewhere near the Apache Trail, east of the Superstition Mountains, Charles Garrett searches with the new BLOODHOUND two-box deepseeking attachment. This attachment connects to any Garrett VLF/TR instrument to give true two-box operation. Much needless digging is eliminated because the BLOODHOUND does not detect small trash. Also, the very low frequency operation does away with many of the faults of earlier model, high frequency two-box detectors, such as detection of water, minerals, and tree roots. This new type instrument is sure to become popular with those who search for large money caches.

Chapter IX

Treasure Hunting Organizations

Unity is strength. That's what I read in some books, and, while not always true, this statement pretty well summarizes an established fact.

There are well over one thousand treasure hunting clubs in the United States. Some of them are probably inactive and may exist in name only. There are others which are always active and have weekend events 52 times a year.

Many of these organizations parade under obvious treasure hunting titles while others use titles which would be misleading to the casual observer. Some of them are incorporated under the laws of their home states as non-profit corporations or as profitable entities; whichever the membership desires.

In addition to the many local clubs, there are several national organizations or clubs. I want to point out here that it is impossible or imprudent for me to list many of these organizations in this chapter because the groups do not desire publicity in any form. In fact, the publicity angle is one reason for many of the treasure organizations using the misleading names. There is no fraud nor dishonesty involved; some of these groups are private groups organized for the mutual benefit of the membership only and their activities are nobody's business but their own as long as they observe the law.

Clubs and associations have much to offer but you as a member have to also give as well as receive. Don't ever expect to pay for your membership and then just sit back and reap the harvest. It just doesn't work that way. To begin with, your dues go to pay expenses of the club and it is rare indeed that anybody makes a salary from your dues. Thus, the officers serve without pay and are thereby entitled to the support and assistance of the entire membership. You will find that you gain the most by getting in and doing more than your share and it is fun once you get started.

Jim Alexander of Alexander Enterprises, Pasadena, Texas, President of the Treasure Hunters Association of Pasadena, oversees a THAP competition hunt, held in Houston, Texas. Jim has been active in TH-ing for many years and is well-known in treasure hunting circles for his finds, club participation, and willingness to share his leads for "good searching" areas with all TH-ers.

"Rocky" LeGaye of Houston, Texas, is shown as he photographed a THAP competition hunt. "Rocky" was a well-known writer and authored the book, THE ELECTRONIC METAL DETECTOR HANDBOOK.

Bob Ulman awards a detector prize to a lucky winner of the Junior Open Contest sponsored by the Prospectors Club of Southern California during an October club meeting. Estee Conatser, program chairman, assists in the award presentations. Estee is co-author, with Karl von Mueller, of THE JOURNALS OF EL DORADO (A Descriptive Bibliography on Treasure).

Charles Garrett and Dick Waters assist Mrs. Lake Erie Schaefer (now deceased). Mrs. Schaefer was the well-known author and book publisher responsible for publishing Frank Fish's book, BURIED TREASURE AND LOST MINES. From Frank's diary she compiled and published the book, DEAD MEN DO TELL TALES. The photos were taken by Herb Polson.

Roy Lagal tests a BFO over the extremely highly mineralized magnetic sand of the Mojave Desert. Both the VLF/TR and BFO instruments are all-purpose instruments. While the VLF/TR has ground canceling and greater depth, both instruments are equally at home whether cache or coin hunting or prospecting. In spite of the greater popularity of the VLF/TR, the BFO continues to be used by cache hunters and prospectors, especially in building searching, cache hunting, ore sample identification, and black sand deposit locating. Roy, author of several of the most popular treasure hunting and prospecting books, is designer and inventor of the "Gravity Trap" gold pan. Photo courtesy of Bob "Doc" Barr.

CHAPTER X

Publicity and Secrecy

There is something about treasure hunting that is like a disease: the bug may bite and bring about a violent, temporary reaction; or it may result in brief, intermittent spasms of treasuritis; or a severe chronic infliction may occur whereby the victim (?) pursues a treasure hunting avocation with consistent diligence to the end of his time.

The very nature of treasure hunting with all of its implications requires that every bona fide search must be conducted with the utmost care and secrecy. This is especially true for buried treasure which might be located on private property or treasure which might be located on public property but which may have legal strings attached through existence of legal heirs or estate of the party or parties who originally deposited the treasure.

PARASITES

It must be remembered that in the relatively few instances where actual discoveries of bona fide buried treasure have been publicizd, one or more parties have gone into court to claim legal ownership of the treasure through heirship or they have induced lawyers to seek out-of-court settlement by virtue of heirship claims. There are a couple of cases where the plaintiff asserted that he had personally concealed the treasure and attempted legal recovery. However, in each of these cases, the court found in favor of the defendant. In most instances, the finder may be sure of retaining the treasure he has found, but he can also be absolutely certain of 'wasting' a minimum of 40% of the value in court and legal fees, and these and other fees might take more than the actual value of the treasure so that he winds up poorer but wiser.

Consequently, secrecy is the rule! It is a good policy to suppress any desire or inclination to confide in casual friends. In fact, most of the really successful treasure hunters confide in absolutely nobody until they have the treasure safely out of reach of any or all parties who might possibly covet it. And, then they confide only in trusted members of long acquaintance in their own fraternity. It is an undeviating rule that you never see a successful treasure hunter's name in the newspapers or magazines as a treasure hunter.

The professionals use some mighty clever ruses while on or near a treasure site to conceal their purpose or identity. Because many of these ruses are almost stories in themselves, I am going to list a few of them so you can see how they work and why. The names have been changed to protect the identity of the actual individuals, but the facts are essentially correct as they were related to me.

BOTANIST

Tom Thompson had researched a treasure project in Kansas and determined that the treasure must be hidden on a farm site along the Big Blue River near Marysville. Knowing that his presence would be quickly noticed and excite considerable curiosity, he approached the farmer and advised him that he was an amateur botanist and would like permission to trespass on his land in order to study the flora and fauna in that area. Permission was granted and Tom spent several days going over the area with a magnifying glass and other botanical paraphernalia with all of the zeal of a student. At the same time, he was closely studying the terrain for a potential treasure site. When the area's curiosity had settled, he hauled out his metal detector and spikes and began a minute search of the area. He found it!

WATCH

Dave Moore followed a lead on a treasure deposit along the Mormon Trail near Bayard, Nebraska. The landmark was the famed Chimney Rock. When he was certain that he'd found the right location, he asked for and received permission from the landowner to look for a pocket watch of considerable sentimental value which he had allegedly lost during the hunting season. With permission to make the search, he assembled his metal detector and found what he was looking for.

Henry Signa is another who used the lost watch ruse to obtain permission to make a search. Through research he believed that a treasure deposit was located at the upper end of the right-away near the 'Parting of the Ways' of the Oregon and Mormon Trails above Farson, Wyoming. He searched and found the location and then secured permission from an employee of the Wyoming Highway Department to search the area for a watch he had lost. Permission was received, and unmolested, he recovered the treasure.

ROCKHOUND

Charlie Harper took a slightly different tack. He heard the rumor that highgraders at the old Baldwin Mine near Lake Baldwin and Big Bear Lake, in southern California, had poured small portions of molten gold thru cracks in the crude refinery and that a confederate would pass by and push loose dirt over the discs of metal so that they could be picked up at night. A fight between the highgraders resulted in at least one of the hiding places being forgotten or lost. Charlie decked himself out as a typical rockhound and with his rock pick scoured the area until he was familiar with all possible locations. Then, in midweek when traffic was at low ebb, he started digging. Fortunately, he carefully refilled each unproductive hole. A ranger discovered him and informed him that it was unlawful to dig. Charlie told him that he was merely getting a few mineral specimens for a school, and the ranger allowed him to continue since he was refilling each hole. Yes, Charlie found what he was looking for and not a trace of this treasure hunt remains in the San Bernardino Mountains.

ANGLER

Emil Blotky followed a lead which took him to the banks of the Wabash River near Berne, Indiana. Since the location was on private property, Emil equipped himself with license, tackle, and other gear and spent considerable time fishing near an old covered bridge between Berne and Geneva. When the fish were not biting, he was searching. He found his treasure and nobody knew any difference.

BIRDWATCHER

Herb Nelson turned bird-watcher to gain his end. Near Jacksonville, Florida, an old retired gentleman had evidently concealed a fortune on his property since he had absolutely nothing to do with banks. When the old gent passed on, Herb took it upon himself to investigate and he found that the deceased had been involved in numerous real estate transactions but had never maintained anything but a small bank account. With these and other facts as the incentive, he began a careful survey of the properties around the deceased's home. He posed as a bird-watcher to prevent any undue curiosity from neighbors, and so with field glasses and camera he was free to roam and wander as he wished. The liberties associated with his harmless hobby of bird-watching enabled him to make his activities fruitful.

"Hardrock" Hendricks, well known full-time treasure hunter, locates a tiny gold coin apparently dropped by the storekeeper many years ago. "Hardrock" pinpointed this deeply buried tiny metallic object by using his VLF/TR instrument.

VERMIN

Tom Dort used an interest in naturalism to help him search for treasure without restriction near Carthage, Missouri. He had several leads on buried treasure resulting from the Mormon War and the Civil War, so he started digging for ground squirrels with the property owner's permission, of course. His big problem was children hanging around to see what he was doing and offering to help. Because of the necessity of putting on a convincing show, he did actually dig out a number of ground squirrels and this solves the problem of why a number of colleges and universities received unsolicited crates containing pairs of these little vermin from time to time. He shipped the little critters to schools at random to make his activities more convincing. Anyway, he did quite well for himself as a result of a summer's digging.

There are many, many more examples which could be listed. Some of them are extremely interesting and others could be considered drole. The fact to be pointed out is that these fellows maintained complete secrecy and thereby managed to keep all of the values they found. Not a word ever appeared in the local papers pertaining to any treasure hunting activities, although some back issues of local papers do mention the men in relation to their obvious activities. Nor have any of their names ever appeared in print anywhere because of treasure hunting activities. The successful treasure hunting fraternity shun publicity like a plague, and that is why they are able to continue their successful projects.

There have been hundreds of articles appear in magazines and newspapers under the bylines of alleged successful treasure hunters. There has also been published a number of books on the subject. My own investigation has never disclosed a single instance of a successful professional treasure hunter ever authoring any such articles or books. In a few instances, a successful professional has given help and information to a writer.

BUM STEER

On the other hand, a mighty lot of useless, even harmful, information has been allegedly disclosed in some of these articles and books. A doggone good example is the article which appeared in Tiger Magazine a few years ago pertaining to the 'fictional' Vallecitos Stage treasure, or as the magazine named it 'The Mine with the Iron Stove.' This article was backed up with a notorized affidavit which was published at the head of the article. This was a treasure I had heard some uninformed rumors about, but one which was a mystery to me. So, when the article appeared, I beat it down to Vallecitos, on the edge of the Anza-Borrego Desert State Park in California. The warden informed me that my car was the 249th car that had driven in looking for the treasure and that it positively did not exist. He should know as he was intimately and thoroughly familiar with the local history, its legends, myths, and actual events. He informed me that the original yarn had appeared in another magazine years before and that it had been rewritten and 'jazzed' up by a man who had no outdoor experience whatever. Thus, over 200 automobiles had converged on the point from as far away as Connecticut and Georgia. Several of these people became lost or stranded on the desert and had to be rescued by the wardens and rangers.

I could go on with more examples, but the point I am trying to make is nobody is going to pinpoint a treasure for you or anybody else, and I think it is almost criminal for alleged writers to foster such yarns that send greenhorns into dangerous areas or cause people to spend more than they can afford to spend on wild-goose chases.

In the final analysis, don't ever believe any of these 'bona fide' tips which are published in the adventure, or other magazines because in 9-out-of-10 instances, the writer was merely writing to make an 'honest' dollar and has had probably less experience than you in the field of treasure hunting.

THE PROS

Now, don't think for a minute that there aren't professional treasure hunters who have not researched so many treasures that they will never be able to go after them all. These guys have merely had the know-how to work on several projects at the same time, and it is not unusual that they'll pass tips along to friendly acquaintances to help them out. But to plaster a prepared article in some big magazine is absolutely ridiculous. It never has been done and it is unlikely that it ever will be.

I have absolutely no argument with an author who compiles a lot of lost mine, buried or sunken treasure, lost loot caches, and other yarns and publishes them for entertainment purposes. But, I do vehemently resent any of the 'authoritative' articles which are poor fiction at best and result in unnecessary risks and expenditures of money by men who do not know how to establish the actual existence or non-existence of a treasure. I call it downright fraud, and it is nothing else.

So, don't publicize your treasure hunting activities unless you are merely toying around with the activity for the purposes of becoming a local hero. Operate entirely on the QT. Use good judgement and common sense and don't take unnecessary chances. Don't accept every treasure yarn you hear as a bona fide fact. Remember one thing, first, last, and always; these well-known treasures have been sought by professionals if there is anything to them, and if they found them, they're gone, and if they didn't find them, you will find them only with luck. It's just that simple.

Chapter XI

Grubstakes and Bankrolls

It doesn't take big money to hunt buried treasure! The authority for this statement is Jack Plummer who I believe has been one of the most successful treasure hunters on the American continents. Who he is and where he is, I do not know; but this fellow is an unbelievable story in himself.

I first became acquainted with him in California and I learned to respect him for his straightforward honesty, his squareshooting with his fellowman, and for his charity toward the underdog. He was constantly on the go and I was amazed at the number of aliases. For example, I drove him to the International Airport in Los Angeles once and he confirmed a plane reservation under one outlandish name. A minute later, he was on the telephone under another name advising some acquaintance that he would be in Chicago that night. He was truly an unbelievable character that even fiction writers would find trouble writing into their stories.

I have often pondered whether Plummer was actually engaged in some illicit activities, but this I doubt. He knew the established techniques of treasure hunting inside-out. He knew every principle depository of literature in the country and he could reel off the actual names of curators at museums, the librarians for historical societies, and other important sources of information for treasure hunters almost by the hour. He had the anticipation of a prospector and the memory of a camera. He knew the professionals by the score and he could spell off the phoneys like counting the days off on a calendar. He was a remarkable man.

BROKE

I mention him particularly because he recited to me on different occasions the number of times that he had been flat broke, with nobody to turn to, and how he had made it back up the ladder. I remember when they were organizing the Long Beach Treasure Society (now defunct) about 1955, Plummer was present and gave the club a $100-bill and a pep talk. In his talk he mentioned that they could set him down in any city in North America, flat broke but with a belly-full of food, and he could be a millionaire in a year; without breaking any laws, without being dishonest or unethical, but just by finding treasure. I believe him.

I know, personally, of several instances where fellows did pretty well for themselves by devoting their evenings and weekends to treasure hunting without depriving their families or themselves of the necessaries for comfortable living. On the other hand, not a month goes by but what I am not approached by somebody with a 'surefire' lead but who needs a walloping amount of money to get the necessary amount of equipment to finish the job. Imagine, if you will, a total stranger telling you with a straight face (and probably actually believing his own story) that he needs a new 4-wheel drive pickup, a big air compressor, a light plant, and a lot of other equipment to go into an area and locate a lost mine which he has definitely (?) located. I have before me a letter from a fellow I met once with this information in it. First of all, I don't believe in lost mines. In the second place, he doesn't need a pickup with hoist, compressor, and a lot of other cumbersome equipment; he needs a couple of horses. And finally, just how in the hell does he know the 'lost mine' is where he 'knows' it is. This fellow actually wants from $20,000 to $50,000 of my money to take this vacation. Fact of the matter is I wouldn't give him over $10 for all of the information he has on this 'lost mine' and if I paid him this much it would be just for the story for possible inclusion in some future book. You never know whether these guys actually believe these stories they tell or whether they are trying to con you out of some of your dough. All you can do is back off and run like blazes. Sometimes the temptation is great; sometimes it isn't.

GRUBSTAKERS

I know and know of a lot of fellows who have grubstaked treasure hunters and prospectors. In a few cases, the payoff has been big, but in most cases the money goes down the drain. It is a calculated risk at best, but often for very high stakes. I have done my share of grubstaking, too, but I have finally settled on a firm policy of grubstaking only the older hands who are thoroughly familier with the area and terrain and who have enough common sense and experience to keep out of danger and trouble.

Regardless of whether you seek a grubstake or are approached for a grubstake, it is usually difficult to make an equitable agreement at the onset. There are too many variables, so it is up to the individuals to be completely honest with each other. Then, in the event of a successful discovery, they must be most scrupulous in making a fair and honest settlement. Sometimes the grubstaker or investor wants to go whole hog on the results and in very few instances he does not want enough to cover his risk. It is a pretty thin veil we have to hide behind and I say it is not only wise, but mandatory, that the grubstaker and the treasure hunter or prospector treat each other as they want to be treated. In other words, let greed not enter into their affairs.

Let's face it! You and I as individuals are pretty small potatoes, justice-wise, in this world. A doctor can treat us for years for the wrong ailment and we still have to pay him. A lawyer can intentionally lose a court case for us and he can still demand and get his fee. A bank can charge us a standard fee for overdrawn checks, but if it makes a mistake that entails hours of our time in correcting it, they don't pay us a penalty or a fee. A car dealer can sell us a worthless automobile and there is little we can do about it. Our telephone company can give us lousy service for months on end, and still demand and get payment for it. In fact, if all of us actually knew how often we come out on the short end of things, we'd be a pretty sad and dejected lot. The world is changing: people are no longer ostracized for committing a crime, but they are for getting caught.

Being familier with these facts and philosophy, it is better to observe the law of the jungle. This means to go about your treasure hunting quietly and without fanfare, ask assistance from nobody, and keep all of the winnings for yourself. Greed invariably enters into 90% of all grubstaking entered into by all but the oldtimers, so avoid trouble by being a 'lone wolf' until you have the capitalization necessary to stand on your own feet. By that time you will have learned for yourself whether you are a man or a mouse. If you are the latter, your money and you will soon be parted, one way or another. It's your life, and you just got to navigate for yourself.

What this all means is that if it is at all possible ask and receive financial aid from no one and you'll be better off in the end.

CHAPTER XII

Transportation

One evening, a few years ago, when I was lecturing in an Illinois city on treasure hunting, gem polishing, prospecting, and mining, I was scheduled to visit with an adventure group. A few moments before this earth-rocking event was to take place I was standing in the lobby shooting the bull with a few of the members when a fellow asked me what I was going to talk about. I told him I was broadminded and asked what he'd like to hear about. Without blinking an eyelash, he came back at me with the statement that he'd like to know where a lot of treasure was that he could dig up without a lot of work. He didn't want me to tell everybody, just him.

BIG-TOWN HILLBILLY

I told him that I had kinda planned to talk a little on maps, transportation, and a few other items and then we'd all have a discussion and I'd answer questions to the best of my ability. I'll never forget the retort I got from this mental giant who had the desire but not the know-how to get rich quick without working: "Who the hell needs to know about transportation? There's cars, buses, cabs, bicycles, trains, and, let's see, the elevated." There you have it! If you have had any real outdoor experience, you know I had a genuine city dude on my hands; and if you have not yet experienced fighting the elements, day and night, without the benefits of flush toilets, electric lights, telephone, and almost nekkid women, I'm telling you now that ever so often you run into this type of educated soul who has more guts than brains and that you can't trust anywhere, any time, or anyhow.

So, according to this acquaintance, we have cars, buses, cabs, bicycles, trains, and elevated railroad. Just how these conveyances are going to help me in the vicinity of Rhyolite, Nevada or Christmas, Florida or Last Chance, Colorado beats me, but I'll take his word for it.

LEGS TO BOATS

A lot of treasure hunting requires nothing more than minor leg work. A walk to edge of your own town, for example. On the other hand, a good deal of the professional treasure hunter's galavanting around is done in a more difficult manner: jeeps, cars, pickups, buggys, wagons, or horseback or muleback, or afoot. Yes, even some pretty tortuous boat trips have been involved in getting to or from treasure caches and some rough and dangerous airplane trips have resulted from the pursuit of treasure.

Iceboats, snowboats, skis, snowshoes, and even dunebugs have been used. To the uninitiated, a dunebug is literally an engine and frame mounted on large oversized tires which is used in various parts of the country to traverse sand, loose soil, and swampy areas. It is not at all uncommon for owners of these rigs to have Sunday rallies and see them literally floating over the sand dunes, creek and river beds, and other unusual places, side by side, or in a line, at speeds up to 60 to 75 miles per hour.

Actually, what we are interested in here is transportation for YOU! And your transportation requirements are probably considerably different than those of many others. So, we will attempt to establish some standards, but not list them as such, and give the requirements as demanded by experience.

A standard automobile or pickup will fill most of the treasure hunting requirements in the United States. In some areas, though, a more positive type of transportation is required to get to certain areas and, in this event, we usually turn to the most popular local type of transportation for getting into the sticks. This may be the jeep, the horse, or it may require hoofing it. You must use the most applicable form of transportation. And, at this point, I want to admonish the uninitiated to not try to revolutionize transportation in an area with which they are not familiar. In other words, don't try to show up the natives by attempting to use a motorcycle where they are using horses, or a car where they use a 4-wheel-drive vehicle. All you are apt to do is become the laughing stock of the community to start with and end up being a guest at your own funeral. It is that serious.

SMART

I have always maintained that our country cousins are every doggoned bit as smart as our city dudes. I've lived both places and I know. The country boy might not punctuate his sentences right, or wear the right colored tie, or polish his shoes every evening: but you'll rarely find him sitting along the roadside helpless with a flat tire, or lost within a half-mile of a highway, or freezing in the center of a forest. So, if you have any astounding new ideas, better discuss them with somebody who can give you good advice before you risk your life with them.

Make your transportation fill the bill and worry less about comfort. If a pickup will do the trick, use a pickup. But, if there is any doubt, you'd better step down to a critter; a horse, mule, or burro. This is particularly true in the rocky desert areas and in the mountains. Look at your problem from both sides, and don't forget that it is a long walk back. It is better to ride a horse on a 40-mile round trip, than to walk back 20 miles.

The new automobiles are built for pavement and nothing else, regardless of what the salesman tells you. They simply will not take many of the fair to good mountain and desert roads without getting hung up on some of the gulches and dips. On some of these humped railroad crossings in the eastern U.S., the new cars will scrape right under the doors. So, you can take it for granted that when you get onto the rural roads anywhere in an automobile, you are possibly heading for trouble. Not always, I agree, but trouble is always lurking near.

FWD

In Wyoming, Utah, Arizona, New Mexico, Washington, California, and old Mexico, I have ridden hundreds of miles in 4-wheel ambulances which had been converted for prospecting and I have also ridden a few miles in half-tracks and jeeps. I can tell you honestly I have cussed the vehicles almost every mile of the way, BUT we got there and we got back, and we never would have in an automobile. In fact, we helped a good many automobilists get out of 'squeezes' and get started back.

I have also travelled a few miles in an old two-wheel trailer (without tires) behind an old Fordson tractor. It was rough, it is true, but I got there and back.

RENTALS

Lots of these items you will have to rent, if you need them, because very few prospectors or treasure hunters keep a complete array of transportation equipment around. There are generally three price ranges for all gear: the native price, the civilized price, and a price in-between.

The native price is an entirely reasonable figure, or it might even be low. The civilized price is completely out of reason; and the in-between price is a reasonable price.

For example, I have rented burros for $1 per week in old Mexico and some parts of Arizona. I have also paid $5 per day for burros in California. I have rented old pickups for $1.50 per day in California and Arizona, and I have also paid as high as $7.50 per day for a pickup in equal condition. In Montana, a fellow took me out for a whole day with his snowmobile without charge just for the lark of a treasure hunt; while in Utah it cost me $25 to rent a power snowsled for a day.

Much 19th century treasure awaits today's treasure hunters, proof of which lies in the fact that just recently a large cache of Spanish silver was found near the tree which was directly in the center of this early-day mission.

ABUSE

You are often charged outrageous fees. Yet, sometimes when you consider everything, these fees are not so out of reason. A good half of the renters do not give the slightest thought to taking care of other people's property. In fact, some renters figure they have been pretty smart if they can do $50 worth of damage to some rented item while only paying $25 rental. I have seen horses come in from trips with their hooves split and bleeding, saddle and pack sores all over their backs, and with a coat of salt all over them. The idiots who abuse animals like this should be institutionalized and given shock therapy for as long as it takes the critter to get back into condition. I have also seen rented equipment being driven and ramrodded in the desert and in the mountains while it was boiling. This just doesn't make sense to me, but it apparently does to some of my more educated brethren as it happens every day.

When equipment and critters are abused like this, it makes it tough on all of us because we have to pay higher rentals the next time we need equipment, or else it takes the rentals completely off the market.

A short time back, my good friend, Bill Hammond, and I were a little flush with money and we gave a lot of thought to setting up an equipment rental business out near Victorville or Barstow, California. Profit was the last thing we had in mind; we figured we could help the other fellow out and have a kind of center where any and all prospectors, treasure hunters, and rockhounds could meet, rest, and rent any equipment they needed. The entire idea was good except the rental. We found we would have to charge exhoritant rents in order to break even because of the way people take care of things today. We abandoned the idea, even though I still think it would be a wonderful help to the majority.

PLANES

The airplane is a form of transportation we have not mentioned yet. It is not nearly so important as we would like to believe. Its principal value lies in not only providing a fast means of getting there, but in the unusual reconnaissance potentialities. While you can see things from the ground that you can't from the air; you can see things from the air that you can't from the ground, too. This is especially true when looking for the exact route of old trails, or for old ghost towns or townsites, or old farmsteads and abandoned farmyards, for example.

First, you need to have some idea of the approximate location of what you are looking for. Then, you can cruise in at around 2,000 feet, and often spot your location without trouble. I like to take pictures of everything and you can do the same. Shoot your pictures from 2,000 feet, and then drop down to around 500 feet and look the immediate location over and set up your landmarks on the area so when you get back on the ground you'll have no trouble in locating your search area. If you do this wisely, you'll have little trouble getting around the area on the ground.

When using aerial reconnaisance like this, don't forget to make notes on the easiest way into the area on the ground. You can often pick up signs of old wagon roads and trails that you might never spot on the ground. Save yourself a lot of trouble by learning to orient the location with landmarks. Use towering landmarks such as mountain peaks, hills, trees, windmills, and watertowers instead of depressions in the earth. You can't usually spot the depressions from the ground, while you can see the higher places.

Airplane rentals will usually average out at $20 per hour, although I have managed to make a few rentals at $8 and $10 per hour. This rental price includes a pilot to fly you. At established airports where there are operators who offer charter service, the price will often go up to $35 to $50 per hour. These operators will usually be flying more expensive airplanes and I think they are usually safer to fly with, but others say this is not always correct.

However, for over 90% of your treasure hunting you will have no problems at all. I will venture the estimate that over 95% of the hidden and buried treasure in the United States is easily within reaching or walking distance of somebody, and this is saying, essentially, that it is within easy reach. I like to get out into the lesser settled areas and, consequently, I have an inclination toward treasures which are not right in town. Thus, this discourse on transportation and what you might be faced with along this line if you do hit for the open spaces at some later date.

Chapter XIII

The Law and Treasure Hunting

I have before me twelve books pertaining to laws of the States and the United States with respect to treasure, treasure hunting, and the ownership thereof. If anybody can read and digest these twelve books and not come out thoroughly confused, I'd like to meet the man. Seven of these books were written by laymen, and the other five by alleged lawyers; two of the laymen's books make a lot more sense than the lawyers' books. In fact, one lawyer writer has managed to contradict himself in three places that I have already found so, for my money, here is one shyster who not only wasted his time but also the customer's money. Thank God, I have one of the very few editions of his treasure law book that I have ever seen or heard of, so it is quite likely that few others became confused as I have.

FINDER'S KEEPERS

When American treasure law is boiled down to its final essence, it comes to the old saying: **Finder's Keepers, Loser's Weepers!** Remember that, because it is correct.

To begin with, it is better to do your treasure hunting so that you do not become involved with the laws. If you do become involved, the chances are that you will win your case, but still come out on the short end of the horn. It is no secret that lawyers have a peculiar, but legal, way of getting the lion's share and leaving the drippings for the client. Sometimes, lawyers do not use entirely legal means to get more than their share, and who is there to prove otherwise. I prefer to have absolutely nothing to do with lawyers or anybody who threatens to sue at the drop of a hat. I have cast off several alleged friends when they started talking about taking somebody into court to get something that wasn't theirs to begin with. In plain, simple English, I have damned little respect for 9 out of 10 lawyers and even less respect for anybody who is constantly consulting a lawyer.

My philosophy is this: If these characters live such a perilous and reckless life that they must be in almost constant touch with their shyster, they are not the caliber of people I want to associate with at any time. To me it proves that they so often doubt their own honesty and integrity and must rely on our confused laws and statutes for guidance and protection.

IT'S YOURS

Generally speaking, if you dig up or find buried or hidden treasure anywhere of which no one else was aware, it is yours. For example, if you go out to Tom Jones' ranch and dig up $100,000 in gold coin, and if he was not aware that it was there, and if nobody can prove that they lost it there, it is legally yours. But, let a word of your remarkable discovery appear in the newspapers and you will find that Brother Jones will lay claim to the entire amount and legally impound it until the case is settled. With an amount of this size, you can be pretty certain that at least 6 other persons will file suits claiming they hid it. So, when the entire matter is over, 10 or 15 years from now, you will find that your original $100,000 has dwindled to maybe $6,000 or $8,000. Lawyers, court costs, and other expenses will have eaten up the rest of the money. Mind you, $100,000 at 6% simple interest for 10 years should have grown to at least $160,000, but you will come out with less than $10,000, if you are lucky. Note well, if you have not already spotted the fact, that nothing has been said about income taxes. Actually, they come right off of the top, so you can very well finish the last day in court with a hundred-dollar bill in your pocket, and lucky to get even that.

Every state, if it has any statutes directly pertaining to treasure, has laws which are usually slightly or greatly different from the others. Court rulings and judgments are not always the same, although they usually follow the same philosophy. Thus, if there is ever a book written pertaining to the American laws of treasure trove, it will be a monster in size and it will incorporate thousands of citations and judgments, and it will be so confusingly cross-referenced that it will be literally worthless. The book I speak of here is the one that has not been written and which will incorporate every possible facet of treasure trove and its recovery. It will never be written; we are sure of that.

GOOFY LAWS

We, as treasure hunters, are faced with a number of confusing, conflicting, and even antiquated laws and this applies to every state in the union. If we are to comply with the letter of the law, and all its manifestations, we are literally chairbound; we can not move without infringing upon some law that applies directly to us; or one or more that can quickly be tailor-made in the prosecuting attorney's mind to apply to our activities. I do not say that all attorneys and all prosecutors are over-diligent or dishonest, but I do say that too many innocent men have been sent to death-row or convicted of other crimes to give the legal professional a completely clean bill of health. In my own little hometown of slightly more than 1,000 souls, I remember an INNOCENT bank robber being railroaded by an over-diligent county attorney as a warning to others. A few years later, the actual bank robber was arrested in another state and confessed to the crime. I attended the first trial and went along with the majority that the man the court convicted was innocent. Too bad the witnesses, the prosecuting attorney, and the almighty judge can't be legally tortured for miscarriages such as this, but they can't. They go right on mis-seeing things, building up phoney and slanted evidence and testimony, and a few gutless judges go right on presenting courtroom shows that prove that justice has a dollar sign on it.

This chapter up to here has been prepared to show that you can not be a successful, or even a plain unsuccessful, treasure hunter without running the risk of laws, courts, and possible imprisonment. In the Fifth Edition of the Treasure Hunter's Manual, I probably went to an extreme in demonstrating that to be a really successful, HONEST treasure hunter, you have to have a battery of lawyers and a complete office staff on your payroll to plot and legally authorize every move and the staff is necessary to record every written and spoken word for future court actions. I expose no secret when I say it has been proven to me that you can get by with anything if you have money at your command. If you are a wage earner or merely a name on a payroll somewhere, you've got to be careful. Now, as has always been the case, the crime is not in the act, but in getting caught.

With respect to treasure hunting, it doesn't make sense. There are billions of dollars lost and hidden and a great portion of it will be lost forever unless adventuresome fellows like you and me take the initiative and find it. Despite this, numerous legal roadblocks exist to prevent us from this pursuit, unless we are to wink at the law or else go ahead without knowledge of the law.

I could cite hundreds and probably more than a thousand examples, but let us take just a plain, simple, believable case and use it as an example of how you can innocently go beyond the pale and get something in the wringer. This not nearly so ridiculous or improbable as it will appear, because it has actually happened. Here it is:

JOHN DOE

Let us say that your research leads you to believe that John Doe amassed a substantial sum of money over the years and through distant relatives or old acquaintances you are led to believe that he had a lot of money in the basement of his home. You go to the community wherein he lived and you find that his old house has been unoccupied for 25 years, that the doors are locked, the windows boarded up, and that the barn is padlocked. The rest of the outbuildings are in ruins. Possibly you find that part of the house is being used as a granary to store wheat or corn after harvest. You find a basement window broken out, so you enter the basement through the basement window and fortunately find $10,000 in cash. As you crawl back out, the owner or tenant drives up and notices that you are carrying a lot of money. (Ever try to hide $10,000 on your person in small bills?) He demands the money and you refuse. Thereupon, he scribbles down your license plate and hustles to the nearest telephone to inform the county sheriff. You are in trouble, and the $10,000 will just about pay the bill, because your chances of being slapped with a breaking and entering charge, or a burglary charge, are just about 100%.

LOOT

Just for the fun of it, let us take another case. Let us say that a few years ago the local hardware store was robbed or burglarized, and that the burglar was caught, convicted, and sentenced without ever admitting guilt or explaining what he did with the money. Considerably later, you get interested in the case and you do what the lawhawks were unable to do: you locate and recover the money and then shoot your big mouth off to let everybody know what a mental giant you are. All the way along, the sheriff, the lawyers, and others have coveted the money, but have been unable to find it. You have put all the ingredients together for a nice stew or pickle. Everybody wants what you got, and you have just about as much chance of keeping it as a snowball in Hell. First thing you know you are either in jail, in the county attorney's office, or sheriff's office about to be charged as an accessory or accomplice. You were smart enough to tell the whole world about your remarkable discovery and now you are scared as a mouse, so you cleverly turn over what is left of the money to the authorities and expect to be released. Maybe so, and maybe not. It won't take you long, if you are as smart as you think, to learn that your fate is no longer in your own hands. I won't go on with the story, because it leaves something for you to think about. Your own city or county attorney can give you the answer as it applies to your particular state.

Actually, the problem is loaded with multiple answers. First, unless you open up and volunteer all kinds of information, the state must prove that the money you have is from the burglary loot. Second, they have to prove that you were actually an accomplice or accessory to the burglary, and don't be a bit surprised if the fellow who was convicted without confessing gets on the witness stand 'admits' that you brought the money to him and he hid it for you, and that he didn't even know where the money came from until he was arrested and then refused to 'talk' for fear of incriminating you. Third, the state must present to a Grand Jury or a court of preliminary hearing substantial evidence that you are criminally involved, and in some instances this can be conjured for a case. Finally, win, lose or draw, if you do go free, you will have learned a lesson that will stick with you for the rest of your days and you will probably have spent enough time in the pokey to learn that it does not have the comforts of home. If you still have a job when you get out, you'll appreciate it.

It is usually the case that the victim, the insurance company, the carrier (transportation company), one or more interested parties, and a few buttinski's will attempt to wrest ownership of any treasure which resulted from an illegal or felonious act. This rule will apply to the loot from robberies many years back.

RULINGS

On several occasions in the past few years, I have attempted to get a ruling or commitment from several railroads with respect to this matter, but they will not commit themselves. I have among my old treasure hunting 'junk' a couple seals which were taken in a robbery over 50 years ago. I recovered them in a cache over 500 miles from the scene of the crime and I have always been mighty curious about this particular treasure. The two seals, one all brass and the other wood and brass, are the type which were used to seal money-laden railroad envelopes with the imprint of the railroad company in wax. To me, these seals and other stuff are valuable if only because they represent an exciting event in an exciting period of our history. Because they were taken from railroad property at the point of a gun, it is possible that the railroad still has a legal ownership in them after all these years. Maybe the railroad does not want them. One way or the other, they will not commit themselves, so I'll be hanged if I'll let the railroad know I got them.

U. S. MAIL

The same confusing situation exists with respect to the mail. About 15 years ago, a friend of mine uncovered a cache of stuff near Torrington, Wyoming. In the cache were a number of opened and unopened letters and among the letters were some documents bearing the signature of A. Lincoln and Secretary of War Jefferson Davis. The fellow, now dead, was Andred Lund of San Francisco and I guess it is alright to talk about it now. Anyway, he discussed the matter with a postmaster but the PM didn't know what to do about it except write Washington, D. C. So, he wrote and nobody knows if he ever got an answer. Finally, after wasting a lot of effort and time, Lund finally gave some of the documents with historical significance to a few of his friends and sold the rest to an Americana collector in Oakland.

In a letter dated 11 July 1960 from the office of the General Counsel, Post Office Department by Adam G. Wenchel, Acting Associate General Counsel, I am informed that the responsibility of the Post Office Department terminates upon delivery of a piece of mail to the addressee. Thus, if mail that has already been delivered is located and found as a result of treasure hunting, the Post Office Department will not presume to claim possession of it. On the other hand, mail which has been taken from the possession of the Post Office Department, any of its establishments, or any employees by forceful or illegal means is still the responsibility of the Post Office Department and they require surrender of such mail to an employee or official of the Post Office Department. Of course, the big question mark here is how and who is to determine the exact legal category of any mail found while treasure hunting.

While Mr. Wenchel does not, by implication or otherwise, mention mail which has been lost from the usual mail channels, such as mail dropped from trucks or involved in plane crashes in remote areas, we can assume that such mail, when located, should be turned over to a representative of the Post Office Department. This statement is predicated on common law and Mr. Wenchel's statement "A finder or Salvor of the mail of the United States is not entitled to salvage."

Thus, you may take it as a general rule that if you find mail and mailbags which may have been accidently, unintentionally, or inadvertently removed from the control and possession of the United States mails, all of the mail and bags should be returned to or surrendered to the nearest available postmaster or employee of the Post Office Department. For your own protection, you should demand a receipt listing each and every item surrendered to such an employee.

The professional treasure hunter recognizes the primary interest vested in the mails by the United States Government, but recognizes no other interests or claims as relates to treasure trove.

So, because of human greed and the tendency of so many people to covet the property of others, it is far more sensible and troublefree to quietly keep possession of any and all treasure you find and, thereby, not become involved in legal matters or have others attempt to wrest control or possession of any treasure from you.

BEWARE

Finally, if you can not keep your own secrets, if you are inflamed by a passion for publicity and notoriety, and if you thrive on attention, then, let me assure you that the realm of professional treasure hunting most certainly is not for you and you can save yourself a lot of trouble, grief, and disappointment by suppressing any and all of your treasure hunting desires now and turning to some other interest or pursuit.

Remember this! One little fellow can't fight townhall alone. Many have tried it, many have failed.

Chapter XIV

Taxes

To my knowledge, there has never been a bona fide convention of professional treasure hunters. There have been hundreds of informal meetings at various places throughout North America and probably the World. These come about entirely by accident because two or three groups will be working on different treasures in the same area and a fellow in one party knows another fellow in another party, so they'll get together around the fire in one camp or the other at night and chew the rag until late.

BIRDS

I liken these meetings to a flock of birds getting together in the fall, because a simple statement can bring the gab to a complete silence or it can generate a condition of having everybody talking at one time.

The mention of taxes does this, especially. It is no secret that taxes sometimes cause the most painful deflation of the purse, and next to our feelings, the purse is our most sensitive spot and the longest remembered.

WELCHERS

I do not know of any professional treasure hunter who welches on his income taxes. True, he may find $50,000 worth of treasure and remove only $10,000 worth and declare it on his tax return, while the $40,000 still remains in the cache. But, he will not take the whole caboodle and not declare any of it or even part of it. I'll betcha that there are mighty few doctors, lawyers, engineers, or any of the other professions which are as scrupulous in their income tax returns as the professional treasure hunter. In fact, I'd like to find just one professional man who is as honest as most of the professional treasure hunters I know and have worked with.

IRS

A few years ago, several of us visited the office of the District Director of the Internal Revenue Service to get a 'reading' on the status of the treasure hunter and his income from the profession. I can tell you it was a pitiful waste of time because from the three tax sleuths we talked with, we got three distinct opinions. It was first humorous and then pathetic the way they waltzed from room to room looking for and through different digests and books for answers and opinions on our problems. They couldn't agree on many matters and I remember that one of them used as a precedent the case of a farmer (in Ohio, I believe) who had found a wallet containing several thousand dollars along a creek. The farmer had to pay taxes on the entire amount and there could be no deductions because he had found it entirely by accident.

I believe, and most of the tax men I have discussed it with agree, that all treasure trove that is found is taxable. By the same token, I believe that all expenses involved directly in the pursuit of treasure hunting are deductible. Most tax men will accept the 'deductible' part as well as the tax part.

Fundamentally, it goes without saying that since everything you gain from treasure hunting is taxable, so are most of your bona fide expenses deductible. The treasure hunter is in the same tax category as the prospector, and he is entitled to a wide range of deductible items.

I want to drive what has been said in this chapter by again, so there is no question. Or, rather, break it down into a simple, applicable statement. EVERYTHING TANGIBLE THAT YOU GAIN FROM TREASURE HUNTING IS USUALLY TAXABLE, AND MOST OF YOUR EXPENSES ARE DEDUCTIBLE! That's it!

DEDUCTIONS

For the benefit of those who are not tax conscious and those who have not been taking full advantage of the legal deductions, I am going to list a few of the items which are deductible and which often amount to a sizable savings in the income taxes you have to pay.

Wages & salaries paid employees	Car depreciation
Magazines pertaining to treasure	Gasoline & oil
Books (the THM is deductible.)	Small tools
Equipment rental	Supplies

It is necessary to explain these listings for those who are not yet initiated in the process of taking deductions for expenses.

Be sure to get and keep receipts for all items which you will take deductions for on your next return.

CAR DEPRECIATION: If you use your car in your activities as a treasure hunter, you are allowed a reasonable amount of depreciation each year. I know some fellows who take 33⅓% per year because they trade every year or every other year. I take a straight 20% because I never trade until my car poops out, and that might be in one year or 4 years.

EQUIPMENT RENTAL: You can deduct all funds paid for rental of equipment, tools, vehicles, or supplies. For example, if you rent horses or burros for a day or a month, be sure to get a receipt for payment and take a deduction for it. Same applies for air compressors, light plants, hoists, or anything else that is rented for your treasure hunting.

SMALL TOOLS: All of the small tools you buy and use for treasure hunting purposes are deductible. Expensive items like electric drills should be put on a depreciation schedule and written off over a period of several years.

EQUIPMENT: Large equipment like compressors, blowers, air hammers, trucks, trailers, transits, alidades, and other heavy or expensive equipment can not usually be written off in a lump sum, but must be put on a depreciation schedule over a period of several years.

WAGES & SALARIES: All fees, wages, salaries, and other payments for services are deductible when directly applicable to a treasure hunting project.

BOOKS & MAGAZINES: All of the books and magazines you buy for the purpose of helping your treasure hunting or to enhance your chances of finding treasure are deductible.

GASOLINE & OIL: All of the gasoline and oil you buy for your cars, trucks, and equipment is deductible.

SUPPLIES: All of the normal supplies you buy and use are deductible. This includes such items as batteries, flashlights and lanterns, first aid kits, snakebite kits, eating gear, rope, soap, wire, cable, and the many other supplies you will need.

On top of all these deductions, there are many others which may or may not be deductible depending on the nature of your operations. Check with your local or nearest Internal Revenue Service representative for LATEST information. Items such as tents, sleeping bags, metal detectors, and trailers (to name a few) are most usually deductible.

STATE TAXES

State taxes are a different story and you must become familiar with the state income taxes of the particular state you reside in to know for sure. Also, some states have peculiar laws pertaining to things which you would consider treasure. For example, in Florida, there is a series of peculiar laws which *are said* to require the payment of a 15% fee to the state for all treasure found within the confines of the state. I have never been able to definitely check this law or series of laws out simply because the State will not give a clear-cut edict on the matter and local attorneys look upon these laws as being contestible. In fact, one attorney advised several of us to 'keep what we find and don't say anything about it until we get into Georgia.'

When I originally started doing research on this chapter, I had fully intended presenting the applicable treasure laws of each and every state with reasonable and understandable interpretation of the laws. It didn't take long to discover that all of these laws are very confusing, not only to me but to members of the bar. Thus, the chapters on law and on taxes would supplement and augment each other. This is now impossible, because it would be too confusing.

So, with respect to the various State tax laws, learn what they are, make a reasonable appraisal of your treasure and pay your taxes accordingly. Many states will invariably contest your returns with respect to treasure appraisals, and this is why so many treasure hunters ignore all but Federal income tax requirements. It is risky, but something that many prefer to do rather than waste time and effort in hassling with the state tax departments.

Chapter XV

Research

Research is actually the pulse or lifeblood of modern treasure hunting. Yet, when you move around in professional treasure hunting circles, you find that every individual has slightly different theories and ideas about how to go about it, how to do it, and how far to go without 'tipping your hand.'

SPECIALIZATION

Most professional treasure hunters are more or less specialists in a certain line. One fellow might concentrate on treasure which is the result of criminal action. Another may concentrate on the treasure of old recluses, eccentrics, and misers. Still another might devote all of his time and energies to old or historic treasure such as you find along the old trails, in ghost towns, or old settlements. I know one fellow whose sole interest is in train robberies and he has said time and again that all other treasure, old or new, leaves him cold.

There are some professionals who do not specialize in a particular type of treasure as mentioned above, but they specialize in certain areas. I know one professional who wouldn't dream of doing any treasure hunting outside of New Mexico, Arizona, and southern California. That is his beat, and he knows it inside out. I know another who concentrates on the state of Texas and he has no other territorial interest. There are others who have became wealthy as professional treasure hunters in other states and territories such as Colorado, Wyoming, Missouri, Iowa, Indiana, Georgia, Louisiana, and portions of several of these and other states.

At one time I wondered what brought about this sort of specialization, but sometimes it is better to not ask questions. Nevertheless, by asking some questions, and by observation, and by experience, I learned that knowledge is a mighty helpful thing and that a person works best at things that really interest him. So, it naturally follows that treasure hunting will be much more interesting if you can follow a particular field that interests you to a great extent. For example, I like the Rocky Mountain area better than any other place in the world and I am literally an addict to frontier history; so when I can get involved in an old treasure in the Rocky Mountain empire I am in Seventh Heaven and what would ordinarily be drudgery is actually a lot of fun for me.

CIVIL WAR

In fact, treasure hunting in Florida and Georgia during the year 1960 was first a challenge because I had been told that treasure was almost impossible to find in these two states. When I started hitting the jackpot almost weekly, it became monotonous. To offset the monotony, I tried to study Civil War history with a view to possibly getting some leads on really big treasures, but the interest just wasn't there. I had to make work out of an activity that should have been fun. Now, had this been in the Rocky Mountains I would have really enjoyed it. In fact, I took a stab or two at Civil War treasure in Nevada (believe it or not) and also in New Mexico and I really enjoyed every minute of both projects. The trail in the records of Nevada had grown too dim and this project was a failure; but in New Mexico the story was different. Several of us joyously slaved for several days just below Raton Pass and hit a jackpot almost within sight of the Federal Highway. Both of these projects were a lot of fun and if time ever permits, I'd like to get back on the project in Nevada. Several professionals have worked on this one and lots of amateurs, and the fellow that finds this one ain't going to have to work no more; he'll have it made for good. Actually, that is not the way to say it because after a strike or two the profit incentive is relegated to an inferior position behind the challenge of locating and recovering a nice healthy treasure. Believe me, the most thrilling moments of a person's life are when you start digging, or going in for the kill, after months of research has led you to a certain spot. You get the jimmys, willies, or shakes, and sometimes some of the best treasure hunters go all to pieces when the digging starts.

You'll never realize what this anxiety is like until you have experienced it and then, after a time or two, it is like a disease. You'll work weeks or months researching a project and your big reward will be the exhilarating feeling that overcomes you as you close in for the finale. Once you have experienced this feeling you begin to realize the fantastic appeal that gambling has for so many people.

Many and many a time have I stood in the Temples of Chance at Las Vegas and watched tourists from all over the world take their gambling thrills in little doses and thought how the professional treasure hunter is so much like them except that he combines a hundred or thousand turns of the cards into one gamble, and instead of doing his gambling in public he confines his to secret places and times; all the more to make it more intriguing.

IMAGINE

I have always liked to imagine a treasure hunting project as similar to a great river. The mouth of the river or the delta being the site of the treasure and all of the little streams, creeks, and tributaries being sources of information that lead the treasure hunter on to the treasure itself.

There must be a beginning; and this must be a concrete, worthwhile bit of information. In this respect, you must remember that while you are pursuing all types of information to lead you to the treasure, you must always be alert for any information or clues that indicates that the treasure is non-existant. In other words, to be a successful treasure hunter, you have to be a pessimistic optimist or else an optimistic pessimist.

The fellow who looks merely for favorable bits of information and ignores the negative signposts along the way is almost certain to suffer disappointment after disappointment. In essence, this means that if you are not alert for or do not heed negative facts, you can continue on and on into an endless, frustrating search that can end only in disappointment.

KANSAS TREASURE

One of the best examples I know of this sort of researching is the case of Charlie Joyce in his quest for the treasure of Charlie Williams. Williams was a sort of old-fashioned horsetrader and during the winter months he worked in a livery stable in Kansas City, Missouri. Williams was killed in an accident while breaking horses near a little town in Kansas in 1872.

Charlie Joyce got a lead on a fabulous Williams treasure from some magazine in the late 1930's and he started out to locate it. As I recall, a wealthy farmer or merchant in the area of Wichita, Kansas had been robbed and murdered during the 1890's and, although not involved in the crime, Williams wound up with the loot which he hid. Joyce pursued the magazine story and closed his eyes to the significant fact that Williams had died 20-some years before the crime and therefore could not have been involved. Other facts indicated beyond a shadow of a doubt that the magazine story was 60% fiction and about 40% fact. Joyce ignored reality and pursued this treasure project for several years and finally gave up. Had he acknowledged or recognized the facts and dropped the investigation when it was prudent to do so, he would have saved himself a lot of time and trouble. Let it be said that Joyce was a more or less successful treasure hunter and he lived comfortably from his treasure hunting activities. It is obvious that he was particularly intrigued by the Williams treasure and would not abandon it even when all evidence pointed to the fact that it was non-existent. He probably enjoyed every minute of the project, anyway, and there may be many facts which are still unknown relative to his dogged pursuit of this mythical treasure.

Since I began writing and lecturing about treasure back in the early 1950's, I have been asked or invited, time and again, to embark on projects to seek famous or well-publicized treasures. In all instances I have declined and for, to me, a very good reason. Most of these famous treasures are either non-existent or else the actual facts have become so warped and untrue that it is literally impossible to pursue them to a successful conclusion. It has made some fellows pretty doggone disgusted with me when I've declined and explained to them that my joining them would not only result in wasting their time but mine, too. Most, not all, of these big treasures we read about in magazines and other stories have been pursued by thousands of fellows just like you and me. I'll frankly acknowledge that many guys smarter by far than I am have gone after some of these treasures and never found them. On the other hand, while they have been pursuing these legends, I have been tending to my own knitting and gone after the smaller less famous ones and I don't have to apologize to anybody for my record. I'm not bragging, but just demonstrating that all that glitters is not gold; or, to put it another way, it is better to have a couple small treasures in the hand rather than a great big one in the woods.

MAPS

Just like any other adventurer, I like to talk about these big ones: two, five, and ten million dollar treasure caches that we read about in the adventure magazines so often; but I wouldn't spend $10 of my own money in search of any of them. To begin with, the guys that make a business of writing about these big treasures obviously know too little about treasure hunting techniques. Then, I've said many times and I'll repeat, nobody with a fortune to conceal is going to draw up any treasure maps for future generations to follow. This is positively ridiculous. I have hundreds of genuine, bona fide, real treasure maps (?) in my collection and I wouldn't give a dime for the whole caboodle of them if I was going to use them in this business as bona fide leads to treasure.

When I was appearing on radio and television, I received many, many offers to buy authentic treasure maps at prices ranging up to $1,500. One particular map was offered to me for $300 and I bought it for $5 because it had a bullet hole through it and blood on it. I didn't tell the seller that I had the same identical map in my collection already. Lots of fellows get taken in with these map stories and some pretty well-to-do people often are sold these worthless maps at pretty stiff prices. Treasure maps, to me, are merely curiosity items and nothing more.

SUCKERS

People are still taken in by treasure maps, and I get no less than one offer per month from somebody who knows me or knows about me to embark on a search for treasure which is shown on some map they have acquired somewhere. One engineer bought a widely advertised treasure map and tried to round up a crew to locate one of the treasures shown on it. This is an example of a good education going to waste.

These maps which show the general location of a number of treasures by state or area are 'treasure maps' in name only. They give absolutely no definitive, constructive leads to any possible treasure and the few of these maps that I have been able to investigate were prepared by fellows who had done some reading on treasure and were interested in the subject, but who had absolutely no constructive or successful experience.

HOW

There are a number of treasure hunters I would like to cite as being very good examples of researching a successful project. However, due to legal and other responsibilities involved in exposing any of these, I will have to let 'sleeping dogs lie' for the time being. However, there is one very good example that I can cite and I will do it because all of the parties to the case are now beyond the Great Divide and harm can come to nobody by telling about it.

During World War II, a fellow by the name of Gust Anderson was stationed at a base near Tonopah, Nevada and while serving there he started doing a little prospecting and, at the same time, visiting with some of the oldtimers around the town. One thing led to another and he was told a yarn about a wealthy Mormon settler who migrated from England to Utah during the 1840's and concealed various amounts of personal and Church wealth along the way. His only clew to the identity of this settler was the statement that he had written and had published a book in 1855 dealing with the Mormon migration from England to Utah and that the title was something like 'From England to Salt Lake City.' This information plus a few odds-and-ends of tales was all he had to go on.

So, when he was mustered out of the service, he went to Salt Lake City and rummaged through the bookstores and libraries trying to locate the book. Through research at the Utah State Historical Society he found a copy of the book: *Route From Liverpool to Great Salt Lake Valley*, by Frederick Piercy. Actually, Mr. Piercy was not the wealthy immigrant of the original yarns, but in reading through the book Anderson was able to piece many parts of the yarn together and formulate a picture of the events as they took place with respect to this treasure.

By going back over the Mormon Trail and becoming intimately familiar with its various routes and roads, and by researching through the Nebraska, Utah, and Wyoming state historical societies, he was able to establish accurately most of the old campgrounds and rest stations along the route. He interviewed the children and grandchildren of many of the Mormon pioneers and developed further data. While studying at the library of the Nebraska State Historical Society, he was shown the Crown Collection of American Maps and from the series of maps relating to the Oregon and Mormon Trails he was able to take his notes and compare them against the maps with sufficient accuracy to locate the treasure site in the approximate area of Nebraska Centre Post Office about 150 miles west of Omaha. His research disclosed that this mail station was also known then, as it is now, as Wood River.

By further investigation of chronicles, journals, and books in the Latter Day Saints archives and in the library of the Nebraska State Historical Society, Anderson was able to accurately and definitely locate all of the important landmarks and sites in the area. This was done through reference to various emigrants guides and maps in conjunction with diaries and chronicles of the settlers, and by making local inquiry with respect to this popular Mormon rest haven and stopping place.

Finally, by going back to Utah and checking the chronicles of the captain of the emigrant company, he was able to determine the camp area. With all of his data at hand he returned to the campground and started probing for the hidden wealth. After about a week of using a probe and a metal detector, he finally uncovered the treasure and moved out of the area.

Curiously enough, Anderson removed the entire treasure to an island in the Platte River and hid it. He took enough of it with him to live comfortably for a while, and went to Omaha where he bought a new car. After a little travelling around the country visiting friends, he returned to his cache and removed another hefty load of the treasure. Thereupon, he embarked on a tour of the United States and spent almost a year visiting every state in the Union and revisiting hundreds of old friends. Finally, a few years later, he died a natural death in Los Angeles.

All of this information was related to me by Anderson's old friend and army buddy of World War I, Charlie Paulson. I believe the story is 100% factual, but a question is still constantly arising in the back of my head: Did Anderson ever go back and dig up the rest of this treasure from the island on the Platte? I discussed this with Paulson and he doubted it. This is another challenging true treasure story that I'd like to pursue, but there just isn't enough time in my lifetime to chase so many of them.

PROOF

As mentioned before, it is just as important to try to prove that a treasure does not exist as to prove that it does. When researching a treasure project, you must continually check and balance the pro and con facts against each other. Most of the readers of this book will recall a local treasure story relating to some old hermit or recluse who was believed to be fabulously wealthy, but when he died nothing much appeared to his estate. Let's face it, shyster lawyers, dishonest police officers, greedy friends and neighbors, and even not-too-honest relatives could have absconded with all or most of his hidden wealth; and it is entirely possible that local rumor and gossip grossly inflated the amount of cash on hand. This is where research can help so much and it can be discreet research, too. A little visiting with the neighbors, friends, public officials, and businesmen can often evoke a lot of information and this 'visiting' does not need to be done in a snoopy manner. Leading questions and statements will often result in more information than is expected.

OREGON

For example, a few years back, I became interested in a sort of a treasure story relating to a person who had died in a small town in Oregon. His yarn was not printed as a treasure yarn, but as a side narrative to the business story of a successful Oregon and Washington businessman who had retired. Certain figments of the story interested me and I went to the area at the first opportunity. First, I determined that the deceased man had no living relatives in the United States. Next, I learned that he had been a bootlegger during the prohibition days and had done quite well in the business. Further, he had acquired and managed some business properties in the town. And, finally, all of his relatives were in the old country and he regularly sent them money while he was alive. All of this information came from local people who had known him personally and were somewhat familiar with his life and activities.

The prospects looked good. It appeared that I might be able to recover whatever treasure existed and do it without infringing on the rights of others. So, I spent a week or so digging into further details, before I came to a dead end. As I delved into his background I found that he had maintained a close friendship with a woman in Portland. During the prohibition days, this woman had operated a cafe and rooming house. In those days, she dispensed booze by the drink or bottle, and with the passing of prohibition, she sold legal beer in her cafe. From time to time, this man would go to Portland for brief visits and then return to his own town. He engaged in various business activities on a small scale and apparently always with success.

While I carefully avoided all mention of treasure, different parties stated at different times that they believed he had hidden large sums of money in various buildings or on a farm he had owned on the outskirts of the town. These stories cropped up regularly and made the project more interesting. The part that squelched all of my hopes was the discovery that this man had never owned a single piece of property in his own name. While he had actually owned a number of business properties and several farms, each and every one of them had been recorded in the name of the lady friend in Portland or her 'husband.' This could mean only one thing: for some reason he had 'protected' his holdings by recording them in other people's names and it would therefore be assumed that he had also taken steps to deposit his cash resources in banks removed from the area under other people's names or, if he had buried money, it would be on property outside the area. The most likely area would have been the Portland area and far too many parcels of land and property change hands there to warrant much of an investigation on a purely speculative basis. His lady friend was still alive during the early 1950's and it would have been useless to 'visit' with her in an effort to gain any information. Rather than waste time, I dropped the project and embarked on another.

CRIME

With respect to the so-called criminal field, it is relatively easy to run down any rumors with respect to buried or hidden treasure since the entire story is usually spread across the public record in various city, county, and state offices. For example, information pertaining to bank and train robberies can usually be found in the sheriff's or local police offices. In some cases, you will find voluminous records which incorporate the statements of the victims, witnesses, and all of the officers involved. Notes and reports pertaining to these cases are often made and incorporated weeks, months, and even years later. In many train robberies, the local records will be greatly augmented by the records of the state sheriff or state police offices and in the offices of the railroad company's detectives.

It happened so many times that trains or banks were robbed, and the robbers killed a few hours or a few days later with none of the loot ever being recovered. In some of these cases, relatively few miles were covered by the robbers before they were confronted by the law officers. In the instances where the entire outlaw band was killed in a fight with the posse and where no loot was recovered, there are a number of possibilities. The amount of the loot could have been greatly or completely overstated by the victims, or one of the robbers could have taken off on a tangent while the rest continued on to mislead the posse, or the loot could have been recovered, kept, and divided by the posse, or the loot could have actually been concealed and never found.

Beware of accepting at face value the amount of loot involved in a crime. The victims can, and have, greatly exaggerated the amount of loot in order to cover up their own shortages or to enable them to dip their hands into the vaults themselves, or even to fortify claims against the insurance companies. In years gone by and even today, it is not at all uncommon for victims of robberies and burglaries to report losses at a high figure; then when the criminal is eventually caught and confesses he may confess to taking a considerably smaller amount of loot than the victim has reported. Actually, the victim is as big a thief as the robber and you can doggone well be sure he is up to something when he does it.

HEADS UP

In fact, one of my old treasure hunting friends (now dead) told me on several occasions that when a big robbery was reported in a small town, he always tried to drift that way so he could keep an eye on the victim and find out where he had hid the bulk of the 'loot.' This old treasure hunter had amassed a fortune at this activity. He was honest to a fault and he always complained that the prisons were 'full' of innocent men. He swore that he had never in over 60 years found an honest policeman or lawyer and he had some pretty convincing proof to offer. This most certainly does not mean that all lawmen and lawyers are not honest, as there are many men in both professions who are above suspicion. But, there are many in both professions who can't be trusted in any manner whatever.

FLORIDA

A good example of logical research is the Sebastian Inlet and area in Florida. For years, the great and the would-be famous have gone into this area with a lot of fanfare and pomp to salvage treasure from old wrecked ships. Newspapers have printed a lot of poppycock pertaining to these publicity hounds who have left more than they have taken away. Divers, dredging outfits, and others have spent a lot of dough in the area but taken out very little. So, what happens?

Quiet, unobtrusive, sensible, professional treasure hunters by the score have gone into the area and taken out hundreds of thousands of dollars worth of coin, bullion, and artifacts without as much as a word of it appearing in the papers. Not even the alleged treasure authorities have apparently been aware of this mammoth harvest which has been going on for years. This demonstrates the advantages of secrecy and research in treasure hunting. Not only has the area immediately south of Sebastian Inlet been regularly harvested, but areas up and down the Atlantic Coast have been coughing up fortunes to the silent, sensible treasure hunters who have a will and a way.

All operations are small one or two man affairs to avoid unusual attention. They are cloaked in secrecy to avoid newspaper publicity with the resulting influx of curiosity seekers, would-be treasure hunters, and others who would attempt to capitalize on the publicity.

QUIET!

Research is done quietly, and locally, when possible, but in no event is there ever any hint of experience or potential success shown. Considerable literature and printed facts are available

Relics. This old house netted a fortune in relices, antiques, and cash. The owner did not bother treasure hunters until they started digging into walls and floors. Now, nobody is allowed to trespass and it is certain that one cache of cash exceeding $30,000 remains. If you leave signs that you have been to a place, you have earned the epithet of a "flunky". Leave things as you find them.

through Government publications and private books covering the entire East Coast. This information can be bought and studied and additional information pertaining to any particular site can usually be obtained from natives or old-timers near the site. The old-timers can usually give a great deal of information pertaining to facts and legend which does not appear in the printed books or literature. By the same token, they can quite often take you to the site and show you landmarks, points of interest, and even show you exact locations where material has been recovered. The usual approach used by many professional treasure hunters is to appear as writers developing material for a story or as historians engaged in verifying or fortifying existing information.

For the benefit of those who are not familiar with this type of an operation, the material usually obtained from these sites consists of bullion, Spanish or English coin, cannonballs, parts of armament which are usually cannon, and parts of ships including anchors. The professionals concentrate on items and gear that has been washed ashore, and right here I might outfox my critics, who are in the know, by stating that considerable bullion and coin has been recovered from the beaches. This is one case where you don't have to dive for sunken treasure; you use a metal detector or rake right on the beach and backslopes.

BILL HORRIGAN

Here, too, is an instance where old books written by men (and women) in years gone by of their experience have been of untold help in locating treasure. I want to cite an example in the experience of Bill Horrigan.

Horrigan bought an old book entitled 'Around the Horn to New California' in a bookstore in Indianapolis a few years ago. It was written in 1857 by a man by the name of Bill Estes and in it he narrated his trip from New York to Sacramento during the gold rush. Their ship was becalmed off the Florida coast for several days and a few of them went ashore in a boat to explore and to just get the earth under their feet for a change. As this small party was walking along the beach they discovered a few gold coins and as they looked further, they discovered more coins. With the tide coming in and the beach cleared of all obvious coins, they returned to the ship. It was not until he had arrived at the 'diggins' in California and had become familiar with 'float' that it occurred to him that a fortune in coins may have existed on and under that beach if he would have just looked for it. All of this was reported in his book, so when Horrigan read the book, he got curious and went to Florida to find this treasure, if it really existed. It did! He quietly and calmly located the area and carefully searched the beach for miles before finding his first abraded and badly worn coin. By the time that he had finished the project, he had uncovered coins in all conditions: some in fair to good condition, some were merely thin disks of golden metal.

Horrigan has developed the information found in this old book into a profitable lifetime treasure hunting project. He works the Atlantic Coast from the Keys up to the Potomac and recovers all sorts of treasure and junk, but he has made this project exceedingly profitable and he has no timeclock to punch. Nobody is his boss but himself, and this is what so many of us wish and strive for; that free and easy life with nobody to answer to but ourselves.

THINK

This story serves two or more purposes. First, it shows what a little thinking will do while a person is enjoying some reading. Second, it shows what a little gumption and initiative will do when it is used at the right time. Make no mistake about it, there are lots of fellows who will pursue a treasure yarn at the drop of a hat. I have many acquaintances who have called me at all hours of the day and night or who have driven hundreds of miles to see me with respect to a treasure lead they had picked up. But, I want to direct attention to the difference in the sources of these yarns. Horrigan got his lead out of a book written and published one hundred years ago. It was a first hand story and not one that had been related to writer Estes; he was merely reporting his own experience. On the other hand, my acquaintainces had so often read their leads in some baloney-packed adventure magazine or had received them 3rd, 4th, or 10th handed from fellows who were merely retelling (and probably exaggerating) a yarn that had been told to them.

Along this line, I want to pass along some observations and dreams of my own. A mighty fine fellow by the name of Ed Bartholomew owns and operates the Frontier Book Company at Ft. Davis, Texas. I have never met Ed but I have carried on a long correspondence with him and he is unquestionably the caliber of fellow I like to associate with and number among my friends. You see, a 'friend' and an 'acquaintance' are two different critters to me. Anyway, this Bartholemew has thousands of old books pertaining to the wild West and everytime I go through his circulars and catalogs, I get the willy's and shakes. I'd like to buy half of these old books he lists. I think I buy my share and Ed probably wonders how I ever find time to read half the books I buy from him. I don't find time, but when I get older and out of harness, I hope to start in on these and many other books. Right now I have about two dozen books on my bookshelf here in Florida that I'd like to take time to rummage through. I have a feeling that I might find several corking good treasure leads in them, and if I did, I'd just as likely want to set writing this book aside for another year or two and get out in the sticks and start prowling. That is my life and this writing is just for bad weather when you can't or don't feel like getting out and humping it a little.

I'm not trying to sell books for this old cactus-scraper, but I do think that a lot of adventuresome fellows who don't know about the Frontier Book Company and all these old books will appreciate learning about it and might find some book they can put their teeth into, too. I've bought a lot of books from Ed and I have received better than a fair shake every time and that is more than I can say for a lot of his competitors.

HISTORY

As you most certainly must know, I'm a long-gone calf on frontier history, so my treasure interests naturally slant that way. I get a tremendous thrill from researching and locating old historical objects in treasure caches and I get more enjoyment from locating old guns, bridles, saddles, and worthless stocks, bonds, and mortgages (for example) from old bank or train loot than I do from going after the good old hard cash. Because of this, my treasure library consists more of books pertaining to history of the West and written fifty to one hundred years ago than it does of so-called treasure books. In fact, lots of fellows have asked to see my treasure library and then been disappointed to find only a few treasure books while I have several thousand old history, biographies, and autobiographies of old-timers. When I explain my use of these old books and show some of my trophies, the visitor's light usually goes on and he sees this treasure hunting under a new and different light.

Many of my leads come from books in my own library and I try to do as much of my research from my own material. Matter of fact, one room of my home in Salt Lake City is devoted to my library and office and I imagine that I could research no less than 25 successful treasure hunts without ever leaving that room. But, as they say the grass is greener on the other side . . . so I am always getting involved in some new treasure project and have to let these little pets wait for 'that day to come.'

As I have often said and it always bears repeating, I like these old books because the facts in them are pretty accurate and they are not ballooned by a lot of baloney or malarkey in order to sell the stock. These old timers just wrote the facts and let the chips fall where they may. If John Doe killed Joe Doe and made off with his livestock, the author usually put the facts as they were known in the book. Today, an intelligent writer would not dare do that because if the villain did not think of it, some shyster lawyer would read the book and get the villain to file a damage suit, and by hook or crook they'd make things pretty tough for the guy who wrote the yarn even if he told the truth and could prove it.

EXAMPLES

Just for an example of research procedures, let's take a few broad 'for instances' and show how they have been followed through by professional treasure hunters and the treasure recovered.

In his book MISSOURI TALES, Emmett Barnes gives a detailed account of the robbery of the cashier of the fair and exposition at Kansas City on September 26, 1872. Barnes was a peddler (travelling salesman) for a hardware company and because he visited Kansas City infrequently, he did not have an intimate acquaintance with the personalities and points of interest there. Nevertheless, he details the approach of the robbers to the 15th Street gate while another group created a general disturbance at the 12th Street gate in order to divert attention from the actual holdup. Barnes related the escape of the robbers down Campbell street and then off a side street, and tells how he rode down another street and watched the 3 outlaws ride into a draw and 2 come up some distance away. He searched the area and spotted the missing man emerging from an old dugout and assumed that this robber had hidden the loot from the robbery before proceeding on to meet the others.

The Kansas City Journal published a detailed article on this robbery in the issues of April 5 and 6, 1882 and a railroad man in St. Joseph by the name of Lou Hawes read the article with interest and clipped it for his scrap book. Shortly after the turn of the century, Hawe's son, Don, acquired a copy of the Barnes book and immediately reconciled this story with the one which appeared in the KC Journal and which his father had saved in his scrapbook. By comparing facts from the book with those in the article, Don Hawes concluded that this one lone robber must have concealed the loot for any of several reasons and that the robbers may have never returned for it. By the way, all accounts indicated that it was Frank James, Bob Younger, and Jesse James who committed the actual robbery while the group who raised Cain at the 12th Street gate were merely some local hellions who had been incited to harass the gatekeepers by Younger. In any event, young Hawes spent some time looking for evidence of an old dugout in the area and eventually found several which would fill the bill as far as the stories were concerned. He waited until early winter and cold weather to avoid wading into any snake nests and began searching the dugouts he had located. Sure enough, he recovered the loot where it had been secreted in the chimney shaft almost 40 years previously. It is interesting to note that the police records indicate the amount of loot taken from the cashier at the fairgrounds was between $7,800 and $8,000; the amount of loot recovered by Hawes was slightly in excess of $11,000 all in cash, silver and currency.

This story demonstrates the value of books and newspaper reports in obtaining treasure leads and in researching them. However, the reader is admonished to treat newspaper reports with respect, because they are rarely as accurate as they should be and they invariably lean toward the excessive or exaggerated side in reporting 'facts' of the news. All newsmen are horrified by such accusations, but they are never able to explain why the "extras" after a disaster will always come out with headlines saying '200 Killed in Crash,' the next extra will headline '120 Fatally Mangled in Train Wreck,' and then when the final clear facts are printed they expose the fact that only 2 people were killed and maybe 7 hospitalized. Watch for this peculiar form of factual reporting the next time the metropolitan dailies find an excuse to run an extra for some tragic event.

In one sense, this Hawes-James treasure routine was relatively simple. Yet, it took some skull work and thinking on the part of Hawes to actually find the treasure. To be sure, Hawes compared 'facts' from the book and from the newspaper article to 'verify' certain details. He must have expended some energy in searching out and locating the various dugouts in the area and he must have had some knowledge of the customary layout of dugouts and possible hiding places in them. Remember, Hawes had no books to read to tell him how to find the treasure and it is entirely unlikely that there was anybody in the area to tell him where it was concealed. Thus, we can accept the belief that he must have considered several possible locations in each dugout for the treasure and acted accordingly. We must also assume that he did not know whether or not the loot was actually hidden in one of the dugouts and also he most certainly gambled that one of the outlaws had not returned to recover the loot or that somebody else had not beaten him to it. He spent some time and effort gambling against these possibilities and won. That's what makes treasure hunting so fascinating to many people. It's gamble to the last turn of the card in most instances.

MORE OFTEN

More often than not, it is necessary to use more sophisticated and refined research to locate a treasure cache. It may be necessary to trace a man's movements for a week or so, or even a month, and it is often necessary to go back through old newspaper files and other records to zero in on a treasure cache. Local residents might have valuable information and it may be necessary to locate and interview these people without divulging what you are after. With respect to old newspaper files, the publisher of a particular newspaper will usually have copies of that particular newspaper dating back to the first issue. Also, most state historical societies will have most issues of most newspapers published in that state from the beginning. Nowadays, many of these historical societies are microfilming these old papers in order to save space, but the microfilm can be read as well (and sometimes easier) than the old newspapers. City and county records will often provide valuable information pertaining to much of the business of most subjects. This is particularly true when the conveyance of real estate, chattels, and other property is involved. Many treasure caches are the direct result of crime, violent death, and suicide, so don't forget the possibility of information on record at the coroner's office if facts you need might possibly fall into that category. It's a peculiar fact that the records of the coroner's office usually either go to extremes in detail or else they are almost entirely devoid of testimony or information other than that a person by a certain name was killed or died a natural death.

INTERESTS

I believe that to go through an exhaustive description of the procedures used on any particular treasure project would be more or less a waste of time and space as no two projects are ever alike and it is rare indeed that two of them are even similar. The most helpful information that can be passed along is the most usual and convenient sources of information that will cover the history of a particular community. Since my forte is treasure concealed before the turn of the century, if I were to go through one of my projects and tell exactly how I worked one of these projects out to a successful conclusion, it would probably be highly interesting to people with interests such as mine, but it would be sheer boredom to those who are interested in some other category. I know doggoned well that a fellow who is interested in kidnapping or bankrobbery treasure in New Jersey will not particularly appreciate reading page upon page of information on thumbing through old newspapers in Grants Pass, Oregon, and then searching page after page of deed transfer records in the county courthouse and then looking for Sadie Chamberlain through eastern Oregon, Washington, and finally finding her in California. This plus hundreds of other peculiar operations and searches before the actual POSSIBLE location is determined.

TAPED TALES

Over the past several years, I have used my tape recorder to tape the intimate details of about a dozen really big and successful treasure hunts by some of the nation's most successful treasure hunters. This taping has all been done on the premise that I would not divulge the details for a certain period of time. Time is running out on some of these commitments and, in fact, I have already started to rough out some of these yarns for small $1 books that I want to print one of these days so that other fellows can share in the wild, crazy experiences that some treasure hunters encounter in their struggle for wealth. My object in this venture is most certainly not profit, but it is actually to provide actual, honest, concrete facts for those people who seriously want to share in all of this lost and hidden treasure that is total waste unless somebody takes the initiative to search for and find it.

HAMMOND

In line with this chapter on research, there are several professional treasure hunters I would like to write books about. Bill "Hardrock" Hammond of Los Angeles, California, packed a good four lives into his one. If Hardrock had written an autobiography and told nothing but the truth, nobody but his close friends would have believed it. Hardrock was in about everything: an oldtime, longtime aviator; an educator; a race driver; a writer; a miner; prospector; a financier; an aeronautical engineer; a civil engineer. Oh Hell, I'd like to know what he hadn't been. Even took a guy's appendix out in Mexico once, and the poor guy lived and got healthy again. I rode the river a lot with old Hardrock, and his word was his bond. I've seen the time when he could have fattened his purse without anybody else ever knowning it, but he was too honest, and he shared his wealth as he believed he should. We shared tepees together in a hundred places, romped and rollicked together, and almost died together. We drank booze from the same bottle and worked shoulder to shoulder deep in the bowels of the earth drilling blasting holes and setting powder to push a tunnel or shaft farther and farther up, down, sideways, and otherwise. The guys that knew him take their hats off to this old bull, and I do, too. When God created Bill Hammond, he threw away the die.

MILLEN

Old Charlie Millen is another 24 karat character that there ain't many more around like anymore. Charlie hales from Orlando, Florida; Portland, Oregon; Springfield, Illinois; and Durango, Mexico and anywhere else they'll let him hang his hat. Charlie is a flannel-mouthed friend who'd slay the devil if ol' Satan said anything against you. I believe that Charlie knows the accurate and absolute locations of more treasure than any man alive. He once told a little group of us alleged treasure hounds that he believed he could put $10,000,000 to $15,000,000 worth of gold bullion under one roof in 30 days if it were necessary and legally possible.

This little squirt has a natural ability of scaring the hell out of his best friends. While I was living in an apartment in Santa Monica, Charlie came in one night and asked if he could leave some junk in the spare car in my garage and I told him OK. Next afternoon, I was piddling around in the garage for some reason and happened to look on the floor of the car and there was a small washtub with a blanket over it. You guessed it; it was two-thirds full of gold coins of every description. It scared the Holy Smokes out of me because I could imagine the FBI, the Secret Service, and even Ike himself visiting me with a valentine worth 40 years in the hoosegow for 'possessing' proud metal such as this in such huge quantities. Anyway, we locked the stuff up in the trunk. If you've ever lifted a small pouch of gold coin you know how heavy it is. Knowing this, imagine my poor aching back trying to rassle this small tub of coin from the front seat to the trunk of the car. Charlie showed up in a week or so to pick up his 'junk' and when I lit into him about the matter, he shrugged it off by saying that nobody would give a second thought to this scrap-metal. That's Charlie Millen.

GORMLEY

One of the most talented and wealthy treasure hunters I have ever known was John P. Gormley, now deceased. Gormley was a prominent civil engineer under another name and he was a partner of a large engineering company. Actually, the story of his life was diligent, successful treasure hunting and he became wealthy by virtue of his treasure hunting activities. During the years of the depression his large firm was barely able to make ends meet, but he sustained it by doling money out to it from his treasure hunting funds.

Gormley's peculiar field was that of crime. He evolved a highly successful procedure for maintaining up-to-the-minute information on the comings and goings in the criminal world in Omaha, St. Joseph, Kansas City, St. Louis, Chicago, and other points. Although he was apparently never involved in the racketeering activities, he did have a thorough and apparently accurate knowledge of what was going on and what was about to happen. Thus, in many instances, when a criminal was 'rubbed out,' Gormley was able to cruise around and pick up the cash resources of the individual wherever they were concealed. While

I am not familiar with this particular element or field, I find in my notes a comment of Gormley's to the effect that when a man by the name of 'Kubek' was killed, Gormley drove to a barn where there had been a clandestine distillery and uncovered over one-half million dollars in currency. I do not know who Kubek was or where he was from and I have never taken the time to investigate, but I am sure that if the records were checked, there would be a Kubek show up in them somewhere and the records would show that he was slain in a gang activity.

I am not too familiar with Gormley's history or activities, but since crime and politics often waltz along hand in hand, it is logical to assume that Gormley might very well have been one of the men who pulled the strings in the political world and, in consequence of this, had an unusual knowledge of the criminal activities in various communities. If this was the case, it is obvious that the research took place before the fact rather than after the fact. There are a lot of questions and curious facts that surround this man but his peculiar realm of activity indicates to me that I should 'Keep Off' and I do.

FAMOUS NAMES

There are a number of well-known and prominent people who are engaged in treasure hunting and most of these people merely plot the research and hire other people to run down the facts which are fit together much like a jigsaw puzzle. There are several people who are independently wealthy from mining, pertoleum, banking, and industry who engage in treasure hunting with the same fervor and industry as others from these ranks engage in gambling or other activities. It is a diversion to them, or a profitable hobby. Most of these prominent people engage in their treasure hunting activities under an assumed name or an alias. So it happens that if you spend much time in the field, you might occasionally and unknowingly break bread or have a drink with a tycoon or industrial giant. Lest I be misunderstood, I mention the activity of some of these 'wheels' merely to show the number and variety of people who engage in clandestine search for treasure. I have met and discussed treasure projects with people from all walks of life and it has been my impression that some of these so-called 'wheels' are merely greedy pipsqueaks while others are men of the first water and fellows I'd enjoy associating with anywhere and anytime.

WHO'S BEST

On several occasions I have been asked the very significant question: Who makes the best treasure hunter, educated fellows or the uneducated? I'll probably be criticized for my belief, but I'll blurt out my opinion anyway. From my observations and I've made a lot of them, the best all around treasure hunters are from the ranks of the wage-earners and the low middle-class. They seem to have a natural aptitude for researching in the right direction and, in general, they have a feeling for properly analyzing information. The better educated treasure hunters are usually more capable at organizing a project, but they flunk horribly when it comes to digging up the important information or when it comes to moving in for the 'kill.'

To give an example, a few years ago I was involved in a well-bankrolled treasure project near Lake Baldwin in Southern California. The guiding light and bankroller for this project was a real estate man from Los Angeles. This fellow retained me in an advisory capacity and since advice is what he wanted, advice is what I contributed. It didn't take me long to learn that his success in real estate had made him blimp-headed, if you know what I mean, so I gracefully backed off from the project and suggested that he carry on alone. With success in business and a large bankroll behind him, he thought it a good idea and my services were dispensed with. In the final analysis, this mental giant dropped a lot of cash into the project and never recovered as much as one rusty washer. However, months after he had thrown in the sponge, several of the fellows who had worked for him on the project as paid researchers got their heads together and decided to resume the project with their own time and money. This they did and in about 6 weekends they made the discovery. They merely used common sense and did not rely on the belief that money can buy everything. They reaped the harvest.

This is merely one of many examples that go to prove that it doesn't take a lot of money to engage in treasure hunting or indulge in the research that leads to success. Practically all of the records that are customarily used in treasure research are public records and they are available without cost. The most usual costs in this respect is in having copies made of certain records so that they can be referred to frequently and conveniently witout travelling to the courthouse or city hall or other depository as the case may be. Historical files and libraries of various city, state, and county governments are usually available without cost of any kind. Many private business firms also maintain historical archives and these can usually be consulted without any charge of any kind. So, as so often happens, if some wheeling-and-dealing bigshot barges onto the scene of a suspected treasure and begins squandering money right and left on a project, you may be sure that unless he eases up on the reins and lets the peons, who actually hold the key to success, do the research on their own initiative without interference, the treasure will remain for some wiser person to discover. It just works out this way all the time.

I like to compare this high powered, expensive treasure hunting with deer hunting. It's an indisputable fact that more deer are bagged every year with cheap rifles than by the more expensive rifles; and these $250, $500, and $1,000 rifles would not even be fired at a deer if it wasn't for the talented guide who usually takes the owners of these expensive rifles by the hand each fall and shows them where, how, and when to shoot. Same idea works in treasure hunting, only double.

So, if you are fighting the wolf from the door, don't let it discourage you. You will probably be twice as smart in this treasure hunting business as your mortgage-bound, wealthy, sickly cousin from the city. It never fails to be this way.

CHAPTER XVI

Disposition of Treasure

Shortly after the Fifth edition of the Treasure Hunter's Manual was published, I received a telephone call from a hook-nosed jewelry dealer in Chicago and he threatened me with all kinds of lawsuits and even made up his mind to send 'some of the boys' down to see me. All of this because I had written that jewelers, not always, but almost invariably, are the fastest but most dishonest outlets for unloading gems, gold, and other forms of jewelry found in treasure caches. Why this little runt presumed that I meant him, above all others, I do not know, but there are many others like him around the country and I imagine that Chicago is lousy with them, too.

Anyway, it is true that jewelers were once the most certain outlet for valuable treasure, but times have changed and they, in general, are not so 'certain' anymore. For some curious reason, many jewelers figure that all treasure is 'hot' and that you'll settle for what you can get and let matters got at that. This sometimes happens and honest, legitimate treasure is sold for 10 or 15% of its actual cash value simply because the treasure hunter is scared into believing he has a lion by the tail.

Among professional treasure hunters there are five principal ways of disposing of treasure, and these are: dumping, peddling, circularizing, advertising, and publicizing. Each of these are explained as follows:

Dumping is merely the process of taking an entire lot of treasure cache and selling it to a dealer or a party who will take the whole caboodle at a reasonable price. This is a practice which is commonly used when a treasure consists of a variety of items such as old money, guns, heirlooms, and other assorted valuable items.

Peddling is the practice of selling treasure items out by the piece or item to individuals, dealers, and others. In fact, some antique dealers are actually treasure hunters who became peddlers and then opened their own shops so that they could legitimately warehouse and sell their treasure, along with other items, at a more profitable price.

Circularizing is essentially nothing more than mail order peddling. Some treasure hunters seek and find, seek and find, and build up a nice inventory of treasure items and then circularize a known list of buyers and dealers and invite them to buy from the accumulated stock they have on hand. This is a relatively common practice but it is not well known outside of the treasure hunting and antique fields.

Advertising is just what the name implies. A treasure hunter advertises his current stock in a series of unobtrusive classified and display ads in a number of appropriate publications such as Collector's News, Antique Dealer, Frontier Times, Guns, and other magazines. Very rarely do you see a big list of items in a single advertisement, so suspicions are not aroused.

Railroad Loot. A portion of a cache recovered in Kansas. Seals are from 'B&M RR Co.' Silver dollars were cleaned and polished. Spike was probably robbers' trademark.

Publicizing is nothing more than giving a good story to the newspapers or sending out press releases and letting the buyers come to you. Very rarely does the true story get into print and even less rarely does the amount or value of treasure ever become known. These stories are usually couched in the happy theme of an unsuspecting man inadvertently stumbling on a small treasure cache. Wise collectors and buyers know what the ad means and flock to the advertiser to spend their money.

Actually the mechanics are not so simple as explained, but these headings pretty well follow the practices at present. Times are constantly changing and so the manner of doing business must change with the times. There once was a time not so long ago when deals could be made over the telephone and both parties would honor the deals. This is no more. Treasure hunters are still a pretty honest bunch but a diseases known as 'Greed' has infected so many dealers that the guy who now has some treasure to sell does it with almost total distrust of everybody involved. Too bad it has to be this way, but it is.

WHERE & HOW

You now know how most treasure is disposed of, and you need to know where or who. Generally speaking buyers or dealers of treasure will fall into one of the following categories: individuals, banks, antique dealers, collectors, investors and speculators, and celebrities. These categories are explained as follows:

Individuals are the casual buyers who will buy an odd or unusual piece of gear just to have it around the house, or they may buy to satisfy a particular whim, or for some other reason. You would be surprised at the pieces of treasure which are hanging over backbars, fireplaces, in dens, or other conspicuous places and now have the most fantastic stories associated with them by the present owners.

Banks are not good buyers except in certain instances. Banks will buy old or rare coins for the account of others and some banks will *offer* face value for valuable coins and what happens to them after that is a matter of question. In many instances, old money, bullion, and other numismatic items will arouse the interest of bank personnel and they will often consult a customer or client and handle the transaction as an agent. Lawyers will do the same thing. Essentially, banks are usually a poor outlet for treasure material except in instances where bank personnel will contact potential buyers among their customers. Banks do nothing for free, so you might get stuck with a stiff fee.

Collectors are good buyers and some of them are 'plungers,' that is, a few of them will pay premium prices to get certain items. The professional treasure hunter soon learns to assemble

Confederate Money. A portion of Confederate money found in a field near Ft. Davis, Texas by Ed Bartholomew, well known treasure author. The money was interleaved in a book to protect it, but, through the years, weather had deteriorated it.

a 'mailing list' or 'contact list' of collectors so that he can get in touch with them whenever he finds something of interest to them. You can get in touch with many good collectors through small ads in almost any of the many collectors magazines and newspapers which exist around the country. Some collectors cover a lot of territory and you will learn that a small ad in a coin collectors paper, for example, will sell guns, old typewriters, coffee urns, and even mustache cups. Collectors are a funny breed of people, but you'll have to admit that they are pretty doggone honest and nice to do business with.

Antique Dealers are good buyers, but mighty shrewd, and I'll even go so far as to say that a lot of them are downright dishonest. Some of them are mighty fine people to do business with despite the bad apples in the barrel. I'm going to stir up a hornet's nest in saying this, but you might as well know. There are a lot of female antique dealers and with some of them (not all of them, mind you) will use every ruse, wile, and trick in the book to get something away from you if they want it. Tears, anger, sweetness, winsome smiles, and even downright bullying are part and parcel of their business procedures, so **Look Out!** I have a lot of antique dealer friends who I think the world and all of, but when I take into consideration all the antique dealers in the country, their manner of operation, and everything else, I'll have to say that this category is certainly not my first choice for doing business with. In your own case, you'll have to let experience be your teacher.

Investors and speculators are a class of their own. Somewhat like collectors, they will pick up an item at premium cost and think nothing of it. On the other hand, they'll buy as cheap as possible, as therein lies their profit. Some people in this category do not buy with the idea of making a profit, but to syphon off money from their business or profession. Doctors, lawyers, salon-keepers, contractors, shopkeepers, and businessmen engage in buying antiques and treasure items of unquestioned value so that their cash will be tied up in merchantable items. It is not at all uncommon to find an office or den packed with old guns, spears, arrows, old jewelry, coin collections, and other material. This represents an almost liquid investment to the businessman and, at the same time, it provides interesting diversions and conversation pieces for the client or customer. The surest way to get to these guys is through their trade or professional papers with small innocent-sounding classified ads.

The Celebrity is often a sucker for anything old, unusual, or out of the ordinary. I don't care whether a person owes his fame to sports, entertainment, women, outlawry, or to any other cause, once the 'bug' bites they invariably want to keep their name in print and want people to gawk at them on the street. As so often proves true, fame most often strikes the lesser deserving person and, consequently, this person will go to no limit of ends to keep their name in print and the public's eyes popping at them. Thus, anytning out of the ordinary is for them. For example, in the entertainment world, look at the ridiculous clothing that is worn only for the sake of attracting attention, or the phony fights that were planned maybe weeks or months before, or any of the other artificial events that were written up as press releases before they happened or were alleged to have happened. All of this hokum makes the celebrity a natural customer for any type of treasure material. They'll buy it, put it on display in their homes, and at a later date you are quite apt to see the merchandise you sold show up in some magazine in a picture with your customer and find a story relating how he adventurously came into possession of it. If you have treasure items which you believe would interest the celebrity, your best bet is to contact his or her business manager, rather than hitting the celebrity head-on yourself. These types of purchases are never discussed in public and the celebrity is always in public.

MAGAZINES

For the benefit of those who are not familiar with magazines and periodicals which often carry advertising for buyers and sellers of treasure trove, antiques, and artifacts, I will list the following few for example. There are many others, but these are my standard reading and most of the more important periodicals exchange advertising so you can pick up most of the others as time goes on.

Newsletters and Magazines of interest to treasure hunters:
American Gold News, P.O. Box 427, San Andreas, California 95249
Antique News, P.O. Box B, 262, W. Front Street, Marietta, Pa. 17547
Antique Trader (The), P.O. Box 388, Kewanee, Illinois 61443
California Mining Journal, P.O. Drawer 628, Santa Cruz, California 95060
Coinage, 17337 Ventura Blvd., Encino, California 91316.
Coin World, P.O. Box 150, Sidney, Ohio 45365
Collector's Den, P.O. Box 5525, San Antonio, Texas 78201
Collector's News, P.O. Box 156, Grundy Center, Iowa 50638

Eastern Antiquity, 1 Dogwood Dr., Washing, New Jersey 07882
Flea Marketeer (The), P.O. Box 140, Lathrup Village, Michigan 48075
4x4 and Dune Buggy News, 10644 Sepulveda Blvd., Mission Hills, California 91340
Lost Treasure, National Reporter Publications, Inc., 15115 S. 76th E. Ave., Bixby, Oklahoma 74008.
Northwoods Call, P.O. Box 318, Charlevoix, Michigan 49720
Prospector's Gazette, Ames, Nebraska 68621
Research and Recovery, P.O. Box 20652, Houston, Texas 77025
Search International, P.O. Box 3007, Garland, Texas 75041.
Southeastern Adventurer, P.O. Box 446, Lehigh Acres, Florida 33936
Treasure Hunter (The), P.O. Box 188, Midway City, California 92655
Treasure Magazine, Subscription Dept., 9420D Activity Road, San Diego, California 92126.
Western & Eastern Treasures, Circulation Dept., P.O. Box 253, Mt. Morris, Illinois 61054.
Western Antique Mart, P.O. Box 2171, Eugene, Oregon 97402
Western Mining News, North 1220 Division St., Spokane, Washington 99202
Wildcrafter's Publications, R.R. 3, Box 118, Rockville, Indiana 27872

Chapter XVII

Use of Instruments

I know a fellow who is literally (and actually) loaded with instruments of one sort or another. The trunk of his car looks like a machine shop. An outside estimate is that he has over $5,000 wrapped up in treasure hunting and prospecting instruments. To my knowledge, this fellow has never found anything more than a few horseshoes, cartridge cases, and some other old junk. He is in the same boat as a lot of fellows; he just won't take the time to master one instrument.

A good instrument adds considerably to your odds in treasure hunting, but you have to master the instrument. By the same token, a good instrument can cause you a lot of useless digging. You've got to learn to interpret what the instrument tells you, and this isn't hard to do. Some of the best instrument men I've seen were practically illiterate, but they knew how to make a detector talk and talk and talk.

Maximum success in the use of the metal detector is vested entirely in the compatability of the instrument and its operator. There are no two ways about it . . . the operator has to know how to use the instrument and how to interpret its indications and reactions. This 'know how' comes from practice and experience.

Unfortunately, too many instruments have been sold by manufacturers and dealers on the assumption that the instrument would almost automatically find anything that is buried. You've seen a lot of these ads where the instrument will search to so and such a depth and detect gold, iron, copper, water, and I shall not be a bit surprised when a couple of these manufacturers even claim that their instruments will detect air or even fruit juices. It is unfortunate that some of this advertising is misleading. There was a time not so far back that I'd write some of these manufacturers and ask them questions that would really zero in on the weak spots of their instruments. I'd use a phony name and since I'd do this when I was out in the field some place, it would all add up to the manufacturer as just another live one lining up to take the bait and invest some money in their outfits. However, never in my life did I ever see such fancy grammatical foxtrotting as these dudes would go thru to avoid answering my questions. Oh yes, I'd always get the envelope full of literature, but I'd never get a direct answer to my questions. Didn't take long until they got wise to me and quit sending me all this baloney when I'd ask for it.

Most of the instruments on the market today will do a pretty good job for you if you learn to use them, but don't you ever believe for a minute that an instrument will automatically snoop for buried treasure while you just mosey along watching the meter or listening to the tone. If they'd do this, the manufacturers would no more think of selling you an instrument than they would of using their ears to fly. They'd be out themselves automatically finding a lot of this treasure or they'd have bonded crews using their instruments as their own employees and they'd keep the gravy and give the drippings to the crews. I'm not criticizing or defaming the manufacturers, but I'm trying to pound some reasoning into your heads so that you will not believe all of the malarky you read in advertising.

So, an instrument, be it good or bad, does not insure success. If an instrument did assure success, there would be no manufacturers of instruments. It takes practice to develop instrument skill, and you can develop this skill yourself by practicing and while actually hunting treasure.

GORDIE HOWELL

I would say that a skilled operator is much more important than a good instrument, and Gordie Howell of Renton, Washington is a good example. He uses a little two tube outfit he made at home and he is a sight to behold when he starts working over and scanning an area. He has become so adept with his home-made instrument that he passes over most junk and usually has to dig only for worthwhile items.

CIGARETTE PACKAGES

Cigarette packages and beer cans are notorious 'bamboozlers' of beginning treasure hunters who use instruments. Both of these give unusually high indications on the instrument and they are scattered everywhere. Cigarette packages, in particular, will send an instrument wild and it is here that your experience and

L. L. "Abe" Lincoln proudly displays a portion of a cache recovery he made in Idaho. He reported that seven years' research and on-site investigation work was necessary for successful location of the cache.

Townsend Mosley and W. W. Mosley are specialists in locating Civil War relics in Arkansas. This is only a small portion of the total quantity of Civil War battlefield relics they have found during the past year. The Mosleys now use Garrett Master Hunter VLF/TR Deepseekers exclusively in all their searching.

your knowledge of your instrument will begin to count. With a good stable detector and a working knowledge of how to use it, you can almost 'read' what is below the surface of the ground.

INTERPRETIVE DETECTION

When you start to first use a detector, you will get a lot of thrills . . . and just as many disappointments when you pass over empty cigarette packs, beer cans, and other trash. So much of this can be avoided, and here is how.

The foil in a cigarette pack is what upsets the field of a metal detector and produces such a violent reaction. Since these packs are small and usually near the surface, the instrument will give a very high indication over a very small area. It will not take an operator long to learn to recognize the indication for various metals and objects with reasonable certainty. In fact, some fellows are so good with their instruments that they can identify the brand of beer that went into certain cans merely by the reaction of the instrument. They can also sort out a few brands of cigarettes in the same way. The way they do this is to learn or memorize the different indications from different containers. You see, manufacturers specify different requirements for their containers and, in consequence, the containers for two different brands are rarely alike.

Just as gamblers practice continually in handling and dealing cards, so do many of the professional treasure hunters practice with their instruments.

PRACTICE

To test your own capabilities with a metal detector, have somebody hide a regular size pack of cigarettes and a king size pack in your yard. Then, try to locate them. If you can't locate both of them with your instrument, you have a long ways to go. If you do locate both packs, do not uncover them but try to determine which is the king size and which is the regular size pack. You can do it; it is relatively easy! It takes practice, but it can be done.

When you have mastered this test, start planting various items of different composition, size, and weight around your yard. With a good instrument, and developed skill, you can pretty well determine the size, metallic content, and depth of a buried object. To start with, use a variety of items such as a railroad spike, a beer can, cigarette package, a piece of pipe, and a wad of wire. Actually, you can use any assortment of items, but keep them all different in size and composition so you'll have a good strong difference in instrument indication to compare. Use different metals to start with, and as you improve, refine your skill by learning to recognize similar metals in various sized objects and at different depths.

As you develop your skill, start burying your test pieces in different kinds of soil and note the difference in indication. Black dirt, clay, sand, and other soils will react slightly different and it is a good policy to learn the differences as you progress with your instrument.

BEACHES

If you are going to search the ocean beaches, as so many do, you will find that the beach sand gives an entirely different indication than does the common sand that you find inland or, for example, in the sandhills of the Great Plains and the West. Furthermore, you will find that different areas of beach will give you a different indication as you move up and down the coast. A good instrument man will find a difference between the beach at San Francisco and that at Los Angeles or Santa Monica. Likewise, instrumentation will react differently at Key West than it will at Jacksonville. In so many cases, the difference in indication will be relatively insignificant or unnoticable, but to a good instrument man there will be a decided and noticable difference.

VARIABLES

There are several variable conditions which will affect the use and operation of a metal detector. Some of them have already been mentioned, discussed, or hinted. Some of this difference is due directly to the type of circuit used in the metal detector or to the components used.

SOIL — The type and condition of soil will often greatly affect the reaction of the detector and you will find that the same identical soil will react different to the instrument when it is wet than when it is dry. You can check the extent to which your instrument is affected by making a few simple tests. First, push or drive a half-dollar or large washer into hard, packed soil and note the indication. Then, spade up the same soil and bury the object to the same depth and note the different indication. Repeat this test with damp soil and note a completely different indication in each case. Actually, you can run the dry test first and then run a sprinkler over the area for a half hour and recheck the area with your instrument and readily note the difference. You can repeat these tests in different kinds of soil and get just as many different indications. Don't let this confuse or confound you!!! As you get more and more experience with your instrument, you will become adept at instinctively making adjustments to the instrument to compensate for different conditions.

TEMPERATURE — Changes in temperature will often greatly affect the reaction of your detector. Changes greater than about ten degrees Fahrenheit will cause most detectors to drift or change their tuning. After about five to ten minutes, well-designed detectors will stabilize to require only very infrequent and very minor readjustments during use. Most metal detectors will perform reliably up to 110 or 115 degrees Fahrenheit and at higher temperature the operation and indication may become erratic and uncertain. The only important difference in operation which is caused by cold weather on most metal detectors is the pronounced decrease in battery efficiency. For this reason, some professional treasure hunters carry the batteries in a vest or other garment in cold weather so that their body will heat the batteries and maintain higher efficiency. Of course, this procedure requires special leads from the battery pack to the instrument, but this is easy to arrange.

HUMIDITY — Humidity and moisture will change the ground capacitance and thereby affect the reaction of your detector. It may also directly affect the circuit of certain types or designs of detectors. Some types of search coils are affected more than others by humidity and there are a few designs which can not be used in early morning or late evening because the dew which collects on the search coils disables the entire system. There are some instruments which are worthless in damp areas and the sensitivity to moisture of one instrument is so great that it is practically worthless anywhere except in the desert. Only instruments with 100-percent Faraday or electrical search coil shields will operate satisfactorily in damp areas.

ALTITUDE — Altitude usually has little appreciable effect on metal detectors. There are some circuits which are pressure sensitive, but only to a minor degree. It will usually be found that altitude variations up to 7,000 feet will be unnoticeable. This matter of altitude-sensitivity is mentioned here only to alert those instrument owners who find that their instrument apparently goes haywire in the mountains or high plateaus. If this does happen, check your tubes or transistors at the first opportunity and you may find that you have a defective tube or transistor in the circuit.

COSMIC REACTION — Now and then you will find an instrument that operates entirely different at night than it does in the daytime. Some of this can be attributed to temperature and humidity, but ofen it is a direct result of 'light-sensitivity'. A similar, but certainly not identical, affect is the background count on a Geiger counter. Electronic engineers who are familiar with metal detector circuits and theory have a multitude of their own theories pertaining to this phenomena and they can discuss and argue for hours on end about this reaction existing and why it takes place. Nevertheless, it does. This reaction is mentioned here so that you will be aware that

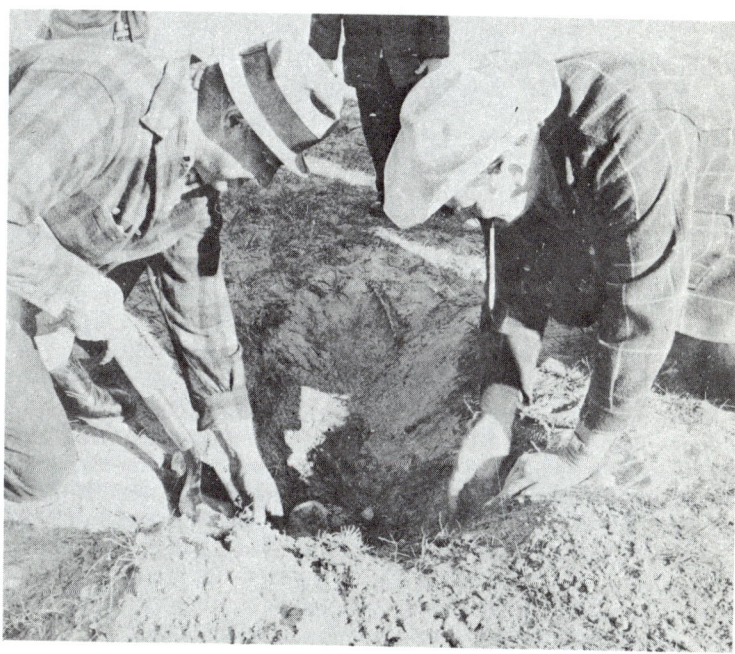

Florida Jackpot. Bill Reynolds and von Mueller dig out a rotted and deteriorated pouch of treasure near Titusville, Florida.

this phenomena does take place in various instruments and that up to now it is apparently a normal reaction with some circuits.

WARBLING — This is a reaction that does not properly belong here, but it is a relatively common reaction that puzzles many instrument owners and, in some instances, has been mighty expensive to repair because the repairman apparently did not immediately recognize the cause. 'Warbling' is a term used to denote the rise and fall of the tone at frequencies that may vary from as high or higher than 300 cycles per second to as low as one cycle per second. This reaction denotes a distinct malfunction or flaw in the metal detector and it must be eliminated before the instrument will function properly. Warbling is most generally caused by one or both of two things: a loose search coil or a loose coaxial cable which connects the search coil to the electronic box (oscillator). Either trouble can be repaired by securing or gluing the loose wires into proper position or by tightening the coaxial connectors and securing the coaxial cable into its proper place. Loose wires or parts in the box may cause warbling or it can be caused by a defective tube or condensor. However, it is unlikely that a defective part will cause this condition.

If loose parts or wires are the cause of the trouble, the instrument will warble whenever it is moved and the frequency of the warbling will be in relation to the speed of movement. For example, if the instrument is moved slowly, a low-frequency warble will result. If it is moved rapidly or bumped sharply, a high frequency warble will result. A good test for loose parts or wires is to set the operating instrument on the floor or ground and listen or observe for diminishing frequency of the warbling.

PLACER GOLD

The metal detector has been used with varying degrees of success for locating placer gold deposits and for tracing rich float to the lode. It has been my experience that, for me, some well-known metal detectors are absolutely worthless for this purpose while one or two have proved to be very helpful. For the most common placer searches, you need a very small search coil and this is something that most instruments are short of and should have.

Only the Beat Frequency Oscillator, BFO, should be used for this type of searching. Transmitter Receiver or Induction Balance detectors have the inherent characteristic of producing positive audio sounds on BOTH metal and mineral. Small mineralized hot rocks will produce positive metallic sounds at various positions on the bottom of the TR and IB search coils. Thus, to search for nuggets in dry washes and stream beds, you may dig up all the hot iron mineral rocks that Mother Nature put there. BFO instruments DO NOT produce positive metallic sounds on these iron rocks, only negative mineral sounds. Any positive sounds you receive with a BFO will indicate the presence of conductive metals, never non-conductive iron minerals. You won't find any knowledgeable and successful prospector with anything except a BFO.

ACTUAL USE OF INSTRUMENTS

As is the case with almost everything, you just never learn all there is to know about treasure, and all its manifest problems and challenges. One thing that distresses any professional treasure hunter, and particularly a good instrument man, is to see somebody searching a field or location at random. This means that they weave and wave around with the instrument with no plan or pattern, like a hound searching here and there for the track of a rabbit.

In professional treasure hunting, all chances of failure must be eliminated to the greatest possible extent. This rule applies even to the use of any form of instrumentation. So, when the professional treasure hunter has tracked his treasure project down to a definite area or locale, a farm yard, for example, he will carefully and systematically search every foot of the area with his instrument. There are many ways to do this, but the most common is to lay the area out in grids or quadrants and search every square foot of it in much the same fashion and sequence as you would plow a field or, in that matter, mow your lawn.

It is necessary to plan to search an entire area because it is entirely unlikely that you will outguess the fellow who originally hid the treasure you seek. He intentionally and deliberately hid the treasure in a spot where he believed was the least likely to be suspected and found.

A good example of this is a treasure which was found in an

old apple orchard near Jacksonville, Illinois a few years ago. Probably more than a hundred people had searched this farmstead and orchard after a well-to-do farmer had died. Instruments, probes, shovels, and about every other device was used to uncover the old man's treasure. Finally, the lucky finder resorted to a systematic search of the orchard with a treasure detector and he located it not at the foot or roots of one of the trees but between three trees and in perfect alignment with the chimney of the house and the pipe at the windmill. No telling how many people had walked over the spot or run probes into the ground within a few feet of the treasure. It took a systematic search to find it.

BUILDINGS

A lot of would-be treasure hunters seem to have a mania or desire to tear buildings apart or, in general, to destroy property. Modern instrumentation makes this absolutely and entirely unnecessary. By using a metal detector with a large search coil, you can search the ceiling, walls, and floors of an entire house, granary, barn, or other building in a jiffy. In fact, with a good instrument, you can start at any wall switch and follow the conduit or just plain wiring from there to the meter without trouble or failure. You can locate and count the nails that hold wallboard in place. You can learn a lot about any building with a metal detector if you'll just master the instrument. The walls and floors of basements can be searched with certainty and ease just as can the walls and ceilings be searched. Stairways and window and door sills have always been popular hiding places for the family wealth and you can check these locations with a metal detector in less time than it takes to tell about it.

A few comments about stairs are needed. When treasure has been hidden in or around stairways, it was almost always slipped into the hiding place from the underside or backside of the stairs. Only in rare cases was one of the stair treads lifted to deposit the treasure. Since the area or compartment under the stairs in most houses was almost always used as a closet, pantry, or storage place, access to and from the under side of the stairs was relatively convenient.

When searching a stairway that has a newel, it is not necessary to tear the thing apart. Merely run your metal detector throughout its entire height on the outside and be particularly alert for any indication at the bottom and about six inches from the top. It's that simple. Newels were usually built on the first step, so search the first step carefully with your metal detector for anything that might be hidden underneath.

Some sharp-eyed and experienced instrument men will notice and challenge my particular reference to the use of large search coils, and they are justified in so doing. The use of large or small search coils is purely a matter of personal preference. I like, and recommend, the large search coil because it allows me to search a wall in 1/3 to 1/10 the time necessary with a small coil and it precludes a great deal of false indication from nails, wire, and any other small hardware that might be affixed to wall studs. Opposing me in this preference are several professional treasure hunters who go over a building with small coils and literally 'read' the inside of the walls.

Further comment is needed regarding concrete and brick walls. I have had 'experts' tell me that you can not search a concrete or masonry wall with a metal detector. Nothing can be farther from the truth. Anyone with fair capabilities can go over a masonry wall and locate every tie-wire, nail, or foreign metal object with very little trouble. You can even ascertain the depth of the object by taking an oblique shot all the way around it. Of course, this is getting into some fancy operating, but it can and is done with a great deal more accuracy than we would like to believe.

In summarizing the use of metal detectors, I want to point out that by no stretch of the imagination do I believe that a metal detector is absolutely necessary to successful treasure hunting, nor do I believe that a metal detector is much help unless you master the instrument you use. On the other hand, a good metal detector is the primary instrument and it can save a mighty lot of work and effort if you will just learn to use it. Last but not least, don't believe for a minute any of these advertisements or claims that any certain brand of metal detector will, by the wildest stretch of imagination, find any treasure whatever for you. The instrument is merely a medium YOU use to locate the treasure. If you do not have the time or patience to master the instrument, you are wasting your time and money in buying one. If you will take the time to master it, it will probably be one of the wisest investments you ever made.

BUYING

When you do decide to splurge for a manufactured instrument, choose wisely!!! Don't accept advertising claims at their face value. Snoop around a little and learn what the professionals are using. Don't beg, borrow, or steal enough dough so that you can buy a 'Sooper-Dooper Moolah Skooper' just because it has a fancy name or because everybody you know has one or talks about them or because the manufacturer sent you some eye-banging advertising literature that says it will penetrate the earth 400 feet and allow you to sort needles from pins at that depth merely by reading a meter. Ask questions of the manufacturer if you have no way of checking on what instruments the professionals are using; it's his instrument he is trying to sell you, make him prove his instrument will do as he claims. Save your money if you can't be convinced!!!

PROXIMITY COILS

One of the most amazing treasure hunting instruments I have ever seen was a sort of proximity coil which was manufactured for a short time by the National Electronic Police Devices outfit at the Santa Monica airport back around 1954 or 1955. This device was essentially on air-core transformer and for searching the walls, floors, and ceilings of frame buildings, it was almost fantastic. However, it had two disadvantages: (1) it was almost worthless for masonry walls and for ground searches, and (2) it was not powerful enough to probe into walls which were over 3 or 4 inches thick.

The theory behind this instrument was that the field from the battery-energized coils was picked up by an adjacent set of coils and an indication appeared on a meter. If a small metal object was passed through the field, it would be indicated on the meter by a fluctuation, one way or another. With one small model of this instrument, you could actually count the number of nails used to affix the laths to a wall stud, but you had to master a peculiar, but simple, technique to do this. You could pick up coat hangers and nails on the other side of a door.

This instrument had unbelievable possibilities, but its disadvantages were overwhelming and the manufacturer honestly mentioned them in its advertising literature. Another disadvantage was the high current consumption which required frequent replacement of batteries. Someday, I want to publish a series of

$1 or $2 books covering various phases of treasure hunting and one of these books will certainly cover this little instrument: what it is, how to use it, how to build one, and what has been

In the top photo Bill Mason of Red Wing, Minnesota, reenacts a treasure find. He located the cache of coin-filled jars at the corner of this old building with one of the original Garrett Hunter detectors. The bottom photo illustrates coins which were part of the cache shown in the top picture. There is no question but that BFO instruments have found far more than their fair share of treasure caches. Today, however, cache hunters are changing over, almost exclusively, to the new VLF and VLF/TR instruments like the new Garrett Master Hunter VLF/TR Deepseeker detector.

done with some of those which were sold and made their owners wealthy.

ULTRA VIOLET LIGHT

Some years back, I mentioned the use of ultra violet light in several different articles which appeared in as many different magazines. Somehow, this is a mighty ticklish subject with some people and I really heard about it. Nevertheless, I have used UV light successfully on several occasions and I know several fellows who have, too. In fact, I wouldn't be without one and I have several of them stashed around in strategic spots so that when I need one, it is not very far away. Likewise, I do not know of a single successful treasure hunter who does not own a UV light, or two, and I know they are used quite often.

The UV light is particularly useful in searching the walls of adobe buildings for holes which have been dug to plant treasure and then sealed up again. In so many cases, the plugs will show up as big as the moon when you flood the area with UV light. Even plastered walls in frame and masonry buildings can be searched with a UV light, but so often the holes or patches have been covered over with wallpaper and you can not locate or distinguish them.

To digress a minute, one of the most curious treasure hiding places, and not at all uncommon, is what is known to the professional as 'wall pendants'. This is a clever form of secreting treasure in building walls and here is how it was done. A fellow with a bundle of money to hide would cut a small hole in the wall of his house. He would wrap his money tightly in oilcloth and then hang it on the end of a 6 to 15-inch piece of baling wire, and push it through the hole in the wall and hang it from one of the exposed lath so that a very short tab protruded from the surface. Then, he'd replaster the spot so that the little tab protruded about 1/16 to 1/8-inch from the surface. After this, he might repaper the wall and the only evidence of the cache would be a small bump on the wall which he could locate in a minutes notice. Caches such as this may be found with a UV light under the proper conditions, but it is a lead-pipe cinch for a metal detector or proximity coil when properly used.

The UV light has also been used to detect and locate caches in caves, out-buildings, and even out-of-doors, but it takes some ingenuity to use the light in so many cases but anybody interested in treasure usually has a lot of ingenuity, and this might be an instrument you can use often and well.

SEARCHING BUILDINGS

It seems that every successful treasure hunter develops a technique of his own in almost every operation. Actually, while many of these techniques are radically different, they are all fundamentally alike in one way or another.

For the benefit of the uninitiated, I want to pass along some time-saving tips on building searching. I'll list them at random and you can dig out the ones which are applicable to any immediate projects you have in mind.

When searching floors, walls, or ceilings with an instrument, carefully cover every inch of the area just as you would a yard or other area. Remember what I said about doing it as you'd mow your lawn. The fellow who hid the treasure was trying to outsmart fellows like you, so he did his best to hide it where you couldn't find it.

Don't follow the joists, beams, or studs on your first pass. Go at right angles to them. For example, if you are searching a wall, make your passes horizontal rather than up-and-down.

For floors and ceilings, you can easily determine which way the joists run by following the indication of the nails. You'll get a constant indication as you follow a joist due to the nails, so when you have determined the direction of the joints, make your search in passes at right angles to the joints. Now, note this and remember it, as you pass over each joist you will usually get an indication from the nails and you can ignore these indications, but when you get a considerably greater indication, TAKE HEED. Something is on the other side that is not kosher. However, don't expect riches every time.

I remember so well one time when we were searching an old, abandoned barn in the haymow. We were doing just as I instructed above when we got a terrific indication. Upon rechecking the area with the detector, we found there were several. Since the barn had been ceiled, we had no way of knowing what lay underneath, so we proceeded to take up one of the boards. Nope! We found no treasure there. All of this indication came from several swallow nests. No telling how old they were, but we guessed that they'd been there for many years because the ceiling had been put in the barn a good many years before and the nest had to have been there when the ceiling was installed.

It doesn't always turn out this way, and this is what adds a little ginger to this wonderful gamble of treasure hunting.

THINK

Fundamentally, the use of instruments in treasure hunting is a great boon to success and nobody, regardless of how experienced he is, can ever tell you of all the different techniques used by those who make treasure hunting their business. No two projects are ever alike. Sometimes similar . . . yes! But identical . . . Never!

So, learn to think and reason, don't rush. Use your head to save your back. Buy or make a good instrument and then master it. Learn to enjoy practicing with it and using it, and you'll find that it will add a lot to your pleasure and also multiply your chances of making a big strike.

Chapter XVIII

Gold Dredging

Gold dredging on a large scale dates back well over a hundred years and the principle of suction dredging was apparently first used in a period of around 1898 or 1899. The first mining reports that I have been able to find so far favor the State of Washington with gold production by the suction dredge method being reported in 1900 and 1903.

LADDER DREDGES

The big ladder, or bucket, dredges of which we are all aware have been used with varying degrees of success in every western mining state and, of course, around the world. However, the cost for one of these large dredges and the operating costs put them well beyond the means of the average person or group. Too, their efficiency has never been anything to brag about.

Unquestionably, the suction dredge is the most ingenius, labor-saving, and profitable mining device that has ever been used and it is really "a poor man's bigtime mining machine."

The cost of the cable, alone, on an average ladder dredge would pay for 25 to 50 small suction dredges. The cost of one bucket on a ladder dredge (and some of them use as many as 50 or 60) would buy one suction dredge. The barge used on a ladder dredge would equal the cost of 50 to 1,000 suction dredge floats.

Despite all of the cost for the ladder dredge, the same amount of money invested in suction dredges would produce from 25 to 1,000 times the return per dollar. There are many locations that the ladder dredge can and will operate in where a suction dredge cannot, but there are also many places that the suction dredge can be used where the ladder dredge would be worthless.

JET-TUBES

The jet-tube or suction tube is the heart of the suction dredge outfit. As mentioned in my "Gold Dredger's Manual", the earliest suction dredges simply sucked water and gold-bearing gravel through a suction hose or metal tube into a large pump, similar to modern gravel pumps, and the pump discharged into a sluice box arrangement.

How and where the modern underwater suction tube was devised is difficult to determine since at least a dozen people claim to have invented the principle. The design and efficiency of the underwater tube leaves much to be desired and credit for its invention is not a world-shaking credit. Despite its inherent inefficiency, some manufacturers continue to manufacture, recommend, advertise, and sell this antique device and unknowledgable would-be placer operators continue to buy them and become disillusioned. The first known use of the surface-type tube that I have been able to determine was in the mid-twenties in Central America where some Marines and U.S. Sailors used a Navy fire-fighting nozzle as a jet-tube to suck gold-laden gravel from streams in Panama and Nicaragua and dump the material into sluice boxes. Later, hydraulic bilge pumps were used for the same purpose.

Until the early 1950's, Central America was the scene of most of the suction dredging and then the practice caught on in California, where it was highly publicized. When outrageously fictionized stories appeared in various periodicals the rush was on, and some operators made fortunes while other simply lost their shirts. The distressing fact was that nobody took the time to investigate and report the technical aspects of dredging and most operators went about their business, blindly, and learning all they were to know about dredging by experience.

Not until 1960 did anybody take the time to test and then tabulate test data so that the efficiency of different types of suction dredges could be compared. The efficiency of standard production suction dredges into the late 1960s was so low that 4,000 feet altitude was just about the maximum at which they could be efficiently used, and even at this low altitude most commercial outfits were unsatisfactory.

Suction dredging at higher altitudes simply was not feasible and most manufacturers were inclined to admit this point. Nevertheless, Darrel Vialle was experimenting with dredging equipment in northern Colorado and later developed the High Country dredge. In southern Colorado and New Mexico Exanimo Establishment was testing modifications of commercial units and developing new high performance devices for use at altitudes over 5,000 feet.

One commercially available brand of suction dredges, which had been developed by Herman Fiedler of San Francisco, was found that would operate efficiently in the regions of 9,000 to 10,000 feet, and even higher. As the Exanimo Establishment tests and experiments progressed, a few other manufacturers swapped information and advise. The result was the development of a genuine, high-altitude dredging procedure that was reported in a series of issues of the National Prospectors Gazette. Plans for building a suction dredge, in the same paper, were adopted by several manufacturers and poor copies of the plans were made and sold commercially by a few opportunists.

The impetus of suction dredging, especially away from the coasts and at higher altitudes, resulted in a number of inexperienced dealers; some of them completely without experience and in locations hundreds and thousands of miles away from suitable dredging areas. This is all well and good, but suction dredging, while simple in principle, can be a very complicated and expensive activity if the experienced counsel is not available when it is so badly needed. The important point, here, is to remember that a nonproductive dredge is a worthless piece of property, a senseless investment, and an inefficient dredge is not only a waste of money to begin with, but, it will continue to pyramid expenses while producing negligible amounts of gold in the sluice box.

There are several types of jet-tubes and each type has an inherent advantage in certain types of operations. The straight-thru type is the universal type that can be used just about anywhere under almost all operating conditions. Despite the universality of the straight-thru type, different variations of the bent-tube type are far more efficient in many applications and, by the same token, they are practically worthless in other applications. What all of this amounts to is that a genuine working knowledge of hydraulics and pneumatics is absolutely necessary to design and recommend the proper jet-tube for a particular application. Strange as it may seem, very few dealers and, remarkable as it may seem, most manufacturers do not have the necessary knowledge. The fact that several manufacturers, with years of manufacturing experience, modified their designs to correspond with the Prospector's Gazette designs is significant evidence that these few are fabricators and not designers. These few facts are presented for the information and protection of the beginning dredger and most certainly are not intended to criticize or malign the dredging industry as a whole. The fact is self-evident that, like any other industry, there are some fabricators and dealers who will peddle anything to get your money.

THEORY

A suction dredge operates much like an ordinary vacuum cleaner. Instead of air, water is the vehicle, and instead of a bag, the sluice box is used to catch what is carried to it. However, in a dredge the object is to retain the gold in the riffles and to allow the water and the dirt and gravel to go on through. This is accomplished through an ingenius set of riffles and other gold-retaining devices that are located in the sluice box.

The nozzle of the suction hose is directed over the bed of a stream or lake and around boulders much like the vacuum sweeper nozzle is managed over the floor of a house and around the furniture. As the water is sucked into the hose, it carries with it varying amounts of dirt and sand, which are naturally mixed with particles of gold if gold is present. This dirt, sand or gravel, and possibly gold mixture is conveyed through the hose into the jet-tube and then discharged into the sluice box.

It is in the sluice box where the magic of separation takes place. If the sluice box is poorly designed or improperly situated, practically all of the solid material that is borne by the water will pass on through and be discharged back into the water. However, if the sluice box is properly designed and built and if it is properly positioned, the gold and heavier components, such as black sand, will drop into and behind the riffles while the lighter rock and sand is carried on through the sluice box in the flow of water.

This does not end the dredging operation. Most of the gold should be caught in the upper third, or at most the upper half, of the sluice box. When it gets so loaded with gold and black sand that the gold accumulates in the lower portions of the sluice box, it is necessary to take the gold and the associated black sand and other heavy components from the sluice box. This operation is commonly known as the "clean-up".

The "clean-up" results in an accumulation of gold, black sand and assorted other heavy components. After the "clean-up", the material that was taken from the sluice box is usually put in a storage container and the dredge placed back in operation. The material which is removed at each clean-up can be concentrated and the gold content removed at the end of each day, at the end of a week, or it may be accumulated and worked at the end of a season. There are a number of methods of removing the gold from the concentrates. Among small operators panning or chemical treatment is most often used, but various applications of vibration, gravity, centrifugal force, and electrostatic principals are used by some small operators and most larger operators.

PROFITS

Small scale dredging is one of the most profitable mining and outdoor activities that a person can engage in. To be a successful dredger and reap the maximum profit from a minimum investment, the operator must have good equipment to begin with and he must have a reasonable degree of common sense. Suction dredging is no more foolproof than driving an automobile or raising a garden. Problems do arise and the successful operator must be able to reason the problems and evolve a suitable correction. Dredging is, fundamentally, a very simple activity and for every trouble or fault there has to be a solution, and the solution is usually extremely simple.

If you start out with inefficient or poorly designed and built equipment, you are destined for disappointment to begin with. Poor equipment is unprofitable to start with and you can, and usually do, compound your problems with poor management.

As any experienced miner will tell you, $1.00 dirt (placer material that contains approximately $1.00 worth of gold per cubic yard, is practically worthless for all mining operations. Yet, with a suction dredge of the 3-inch size, an operator can work between 5 and 10 yards of placer material per hour. If he manages to save 75% of the gold in this material, and assuming that he works 6 yards per hour, he will recover or save approximately $4.50 worth of gold per hour based on $35.00 per ounce. Assuming that he works $10, $20, or even $40 per yard gravel, he will multiply his hourly recovery accordingly. For Example, $10 dirt should produce $45.00 per hour.

Everything would be wonderful, if it averaged out this way, but it usually does not. First of all, some placer material is richer than other. Extremely rich placer ground can lie alongside almost complete barren gravel. In fact, some unfortunate scamps have operated for weeks in marginal gravel that was located just a few feet from extremely rich gravel. In good placer material, a suitable metal detector can be used with considerable success. In fact, a good detector can pay for itself in one hour, but we will deal with this later. You must also reckon with overhead costs: oil, gasoline, repair parts, food, camp equipment, transportation and, among other things, clothing. Consequently, in relatively poor, or marginal, placer material you can figure on breaking even or, at best, making a clear profit for about half of your production. When you get into rich placer material, the percentage of expenses becomes smaller so that it can actually amount to only about one-tenth of your productions.

You can actually get into rich gravel and still have your production inhibited due to having to work around boulders, slide areas, and other impediments. By the same token, you can work down to bedrock and do a marvelous job of removing gold from crevices with an efficient dredge. In fact, a suction dredge is one of the better devices for working around boulders and other obstructions where high concentrations of gold do actually exist, even though under certain conditions boulders can and do present problems.

As the dredge operator gains more experience, he naturally becomes a more efficient operator and, consequently, his dredging operations become far more profitable. To begin with, a good operator can manage the suction end of his hose and from the feel of the hose and sound of the engine he can tell pretty well what is going on in and around his dredge. With experience, the dredger learns to operate in the richer parts of a stream and he also learns to set up his dredge for a maximum recovery rate. It is unfortunate that not a single dredge manufacturer or dealer in the United States provides his customers with comprehensive instructions on prospecting and operating a suction dredge. The Exanimo Establishment does provide adequate instructions with their Spartan Dredges and the Fiedler Manufacturing Company provides their customers with better than average instructions.

METAL DETECTORS

There are many short cuts, tricks, and specialized tools that will help the dredge operator achieve a higher recovery rate and very few of these have ever been put in print. There are a number of dealers who advance the particular detectors they sell as being "perfect" for dredging and placering activities. Actually, there are two detectors that are head and shoulders above all of the other detectors on the market when it comes to suction dredging and placering activities. These two brands are the Garrett and Spartan metal detectors. It has been my pleasure and misfortune to test just about every brand and model on the market for dredging applications and it has been a mighty disappointing experience. The pleasure has come from confirming that my name has not been associated in recommending any of the unsatisfactory detectors.

For dredging, a metal detector must be absolutely waterproof and it must be practically drift-free. I have tested several expensive metal detectors with names that imply that they were designed especially for prospecting. Every one of them became completely useless within no more than 10 seconds after they were dipped into cold mountain streams. I have had experts come to my dredging operations with fantastic boasts about what they could do with their metal detectors and every one of them has left with his tail between his legs when he found that, actually, his expensive detector was absolutely useless in rich placer ground, due to the erratic operation.

In my own placer operations, I use a Spartan 175 and a Garrett Hunter exclusively because I can depend on them and because they are convenient. I prefer the Spartan 175 because I can stick the control box in the bag of my breast waders and, when necessary, work ahead of the dredge in depths up to 5-feet of water, and this is sometimes necessary. For ordinary dredging, I do not mind the size and weight of the Hunter and it provides a convenience that I do not have with the Spartain 175, and this is that I can lay it on the stream bank without undue delay. The search coils on both of them are adjustable so that they can be used anywhere and if it is necessary to adjust the search coil to a 45, 90, or 180° position, it takes about 3 seconds to retune the detector.

Probably the most important feature of both of these detectors as far as the dredger is concerned is that there is absolutely no confusing drift or malfunctioning due to the cold water. It is not necessary to set the search coil in the cold water for a half-hour or so to let it "age" to avoid excessive drift.

For placer operations, a metal detector is not an absolutely necessary device and this is particularly true if you are a part-time dredger or engage in dredging for the pleasure of it. If you are a full-time dredger, the metal detector can actually multiply your production and profit. Here is how you use a metal detector properly.

Set the detector for either METAL or MINERAL indication and at a relatively slow beat. Go back and forth across the stream in about 3-foot swaths and look for rises or falls in tone, and mark each one of these. Then all you have to do is operate the nuzzle-end of the suction hose in those areas where you get a positive or negative indication. This is all there is to it, although there are some refinements of this practice which need not be discussed here.

The reason you observe both high or low indications is that you want to locate the stringers of gold or black sand. These deposits are rarely spread evenly across a stream or pond bed, but usually occur in stringers, irregular deposits, or in pockets, where they have been carried and deposited by water. In very few cases, you will locate these deposits that consist almost entirely of coarse and fine gold, but in most instances you will find that the gold will be associated with black sand and other heavy minerals, but most often with black sand.

By using the metal detector procedure, you can avoid dredging the entire bed of a stream and will need to dredge only those areas where you get an indication. This will allow you to work ten to

Upper Left

Roy Lagal using his newly-developed, patent pending, gravity trap gold pan to examine a pocket of magnetic black sand (see back cover), discovered when searching for gold nuggets in the famous Salmon River in Northern Idaho.

Upper Right

Charles Garrett searches for gold nuggets in a dry wash.

Lower Left

Even though an area may have been worked for years by the old prospectors small gold nuggets can still be found with the aid of small detector search coils and careful exploration with small crevassing tools.

Lower Right

Wet or dry nugget shooting can be readily accomplished with 100%-Faraday-shielded BFO nugget search coils.

twenty times as much stream area per day, and often you can work more. If you are working on or near bedrock, you can instantly determine which crevices are gold-laden and which are not. It is usually assumed that all crevices are gold-laden but this is not always true, so a good metal detector can be used to save time and effort to locate the loaded crevices as well as the richer areas of a stream. In many instances, the Spartan and Hunter have recovered their entire cost in less than a day. These instruments are as much at home in the water as out.

Dredging can easily be a one-man operation, but if you are going to use a metal detector it is a lot better for two men to do the job. One man handles the suction nozzle and the other man operates the metal detector. The man with the metal detector should stay at least 3-feet away from the nozzle and work back and forth across the stream. When he gets a good indication (here is where earphones are better than the meter or speaker), he merely indicates the spot to the nozzleman and then continues on across the stream. The detector operator, can work across the stream at least 5 to 10 times faster than the nozzleman, so all he has to do is go about his business, always working across and upstream, and signaling the nozzleman where he has received a signal. After 15 minutes to an hour of this, they can change places, because operating the nozzle is hard work and the detector operator can easily get far ahead of the nozzleman.

A 5 or 8-inch search coil is best for this purpose, although some operators prefer the 12-inch search coil. Earphones are usually a must because gold-bearing streams usually require the operator's full attention in avoiding falls on loose and slippery rocks. The noise of the stream and of the dredge engine often drowns out the speaker and, of course, it is not always possible to keep an eye on the meter. Actually, good prospecting detectors could very well be equipped with earphones only and the experienced operator would care less. Big meters, big boxes, and big search coils have absolutely no place in prospecting or placering. An adjustable search coil is an absolute must for prospecting streams. The old fixed search coils and big boxes are 10 to 15 years behind the times and they are proof of unknowledgeable and absolutely thoughtless engineering. It is relatively simply to eliminate the drift in metal detector circuits without inhibiting the sensitivity and two manufacturers have accomplished this. In prospecting and placering, drift and large size are unwanted and either or both of these conditions can diminish or completely eliminate the advantages of using a metal detector.

BUILD OR BUY?

There is always the question whether to build or buy a suction dredge. A man with a little technical knowledge can easily build a very good unit at relatively low cost. On the other hand, if he does not have the technical knowledge and the ability to reason technical problems out, he can easily invest far more than the cost of a good manufactured outfit in a dredge that provides mediocre performance. The engine, pump, and the jet-tube are the components that provide the moving-power to get the gold-bearing dirt to the sluice box and a flaw in either one of these can goof-up the entire system. The magic that takes place in the sluice box, where the gold is dropped out of the material, is easily designed and built by a person that knows how, but it can be disastrous for the man who does not understand or know what he is doing.

The hose is one of the biggest problems for builders. If you know what you are doing, you can save up to 50% on the cost of your hose and still get the right hose. Some dredge manufacturers, unfortunately, use the wrong hose on their dredges and reduce their product's efficiency through this medium in order to increase their profit a few dollars. This, of course, is foolhardy.

If you are not a mechanic, then your best bet is to buy a complete unit that will meet your requirements. The size and type of unit is dependent on where and how you are going to work. THERE IS NO ONE DREDGING OUTFIT THAT WILL WORK AT MAXIMUM EFFICIENCY EVERYWHERE. If possible, get the counsel and advice of experienced dredgers who are located in gold country and who have a minimum of 5 to 10 years experience before you buy and this advice will save you a lot of money and trouble. There are dealers located in several states where little or no dredging has ever been attempted. It is not difficult to rationalize that these dealers selling gold dredges are about like implement dealers in Alaska selling cotton-harvesting equipment.

Herman Fiedler of Fiedler Manufacturing Company, San Francisco, is fully qualified to recommend and build a dredge of any size to meet your requirements. Darrel Vialle of High Country Dredge

Company at Commerce City, Colorado is qualified to recommend and build dredges in the 6-inch size and larger. The people at Exanimo Establishment, Segundo, Colorado, are qualified to answer your questions, and they have the facilities at their command to solve any of your problems and recommend the proper type for your intended application. Either of these three companies can custom-build a unit or a jet-tube for unusual requirements. It should be noted here that all good dredge manufacturers always have a backlog of orders and delivery dates may run anywhere from 30 days to one year after receipt of your order. They do very little advertising and most of their business comes from recommendations of their old customers.

There are, perhaps, a half-dozen other manfacturers of dredges who can provide immediate delivery and there are, perhaps, about 25 dealers who can deliver from their store. However, I do not know of a single instance where you get a suitable dredge and satisfactory answers to your technical problems after you buy one of these. Nobody can become an expert in this business in a few weeks or a few months. In fact, you never cease learning more about the business and the more you know, the more you realize that there are lots of money and trouble saving tricks to the trade. While it is not at all uncommon for beginning dredgers to go out and strike it rich in their first season, it is not the majority that manages to do this. Most of them do make expenses and come out at the end of their first season with a healthy profit, but some beginning dredgers are destined for failure from the very start. This can most often be attributed to inadequate equipment and lack of knowledge and is compounded by their absolute refusal to learn what they are doing.

Many beginning dredgers want to start out with the largest dredge they can handle and this is, in itself, foolhardy. About the smallest size I would recommend for a beginner is a two-inch dredge and the largest would be the three-inch dredge. Anything smaller than a 2" is actually a sampler or prospecting outfit and its inability to handle large volumes of dirt will drive you mad. Four-inch and larger dredges are for the experienced dredger only, and as the size increases, more horseposer and larger volumes of water are required.

Size of the dredge has a close relationship to the amount of water available and this becomes increasingly important when it is late in the season. In many applications, there is a scant flow of water and in rich dirt it is often necessary to dam an arroyo and form a pond to work in. Here, the 2 or 3-inch unit really pays off.

PORTABILITY

Much has been written and more has been said about the portability required for a suction dredge. This is mostly misleading. If an operator was to dredge here for an hour, and then two hours somewhere else, and 15 minutes at another place, the matter of portability would be important. This, though, is not the case. Generally, a dredge is assembled on location and left there for weeks, months, an entire season, or for several years. In fact, some old-time dredgers remove the engine, drain the pump, and carry their dredges back in the trees a ways, turn it upside down, and leave it this way for the winter. They will pack their engine out and have it overhauled during the off-season, and that is all they do.

I have helped design some of the radically new units that will be forthcoming from the Exanimo Establishment under the trade name of "Spartan" and "portability" has been relegated to secondary importance. The amount of production and the recovery rate has been given primary consideration. And, this all makes sense. It is usually possible to drive a pickup or pull a trailer to good placer gold areas, so the matter of size and weight has been given too much attention, in the past. In fact, in some cases, the efforts toward miniaturization of gold dredges has become ridiculous since actual production has been sacrificed in smaller dredges for no justifiable reason. Anybody who will be satisfied with 50% recovery, or less, is perfectly welcome to invest his money in these midget units, but you will never find an experienced placer operator wasting his time or money on them.

Portability boils down to one important fact; if the operator is willing to sacrifice covenience in operating and profits, then good portability is fine and dandy. If he is dredging for profit and for a living, he should look first to suitable equipment without undue interest in size or weight.

SUPPLIES AND EQUIPMENT

The acquisition or purchase of a suction dredge, or any other kind of placering equipment is just the start of the investment for the average operator. Not a single dealer in the United States, to my knowledge, will advise you of the auxiliary equipment that is needed, with the exception of Exanimo Establishment, Fiedler, and High Country and of these, only Exanimo is stocked to supply you with some of the hard-to-get items.

First of all, and probably the last thing to be thought about until you get ready to test or float your dredge is a common tire pump.

During 1970, I received calls from at least 25 new dredgers who complained about not being advised about this fundamental piece of equipment. Although a tire pump is almost as necessary as gasoline for the tube-borne dredge outfit, Exanimo is the only dealer and manufacturer who makes it a point to tell customers about this one item.

Another extremely important item is a gasoline container. I have a personal aversion to the plastic gasoline containers for a number of reasons. First of all, they are easily crushed and they can spill gasoline into and over your other supplies and completely ruin most of your food while in your vehicle. Next, they are easily punctured and therefore are a constant hazard. Third, the threads are easily damaged and can cause the container to become worthless with the first use. In this respect, if you must use plastic gasoline containers, be sure to get those with the steel, threaded insert for the cap. Fourth, gasoline contracts and expands considerably with the differential between day and night temperatures, especially in the mountains. The unwary and unknowing user can fuel his equipment at night when it is cool and be surprised to find that the sealed can has ruptured before noon the next day. He has not only lost the gasoline, but he has ruined a container, too. The military-type jeep-cans, even the low cost, low quality imported, are far better than the plastic-type cans, and they can save a lot of trouble. Be sure to get a filler hose connector when you buy your first jeep-can so that you will be able to empty it into your tanks without a loss of gasoline.

Even though you may be dredging in water ten-feet deep, a shovel will be one of your most valuable tools. Speaking of tools, you should have a couple of good screwdrivers, a set of open-end wrenches and a set of socket wrenches up to 3/4-inch, at least.

Camp equipment, if you are going to rough it, should include the basic storage, mixing, and cooking equipment. The cast-iron griddle is one of the most valuable camp items you will every buy, so get a good one and be sure it is large enough. A gas camp stove is handy, but it can never suitably replace the fireplace and griddle for day-in and day-out use, and it never wears out. It actually gets better with use.

A sleeping bag with extra blankets is usually necessary unless you are going to live in a trailer, camper, or cabin. Even then, you will occasionally need the sleeping bag. A good tent is a dandy item to have for protection from wind, rain, and snow, and you will never really appreciate a tent until the first time you need it. Tarps and

Dredging. High-altitude suction dredging has opened up new fields for profitable adventure. Two years ago, few dredgers operated above 5,000'. Today, Exanimo Placers has one placer operation at 12,000' and another at 9,000' using an old principle in a new manner. In this picture, Hardrock Hendricks and Karl von Mueller are using Hunter and Spartan detectors to find stringers, while Wally MacLaren operates the suction hose. Jim Sasser, is tending the dredge. A drift-free, waterproof metal detector is a valuable adjunct to placer operation. Most detectors do not perform properly in the cold mountain streams.

ground cloths are not absolutely necessary, but they are handy and often worth their weight in gold.

Plastic rope or cord is one item that not a single prospecting dealer in the U.S. stocks or recommends, except for Exanimo, and this is an absolute must in any camp and in any dredging operation. The 3/16 or 1/4 inch size is the most versatile and you will use it to moor your dredge, to control the location of your dredge, as a clothesline, to raise and lower supplies to difficult areas, to hold and guy shelter cloths and plastics sheets, to suspend food supplies out-of-reach from tree limbs, and for dozens of other camp purposes.

Boots and waders, believe it or not, are items that are often overlooked by beginners and all mountain streams are simply to cold for people to wade around in for any length of time. You can get low-cost, good quality breast waders for about $15.00 or high quality waders for about $30.

Extra batteries for your flashlights and lanterns are often overlooked until needed. The same applies to extra mantles for Coleman-type lanterns. These gasoline lanterns are valuable in camp and if you get one of them, be sure to get a flint-lighter for it. The cost is low and you will never be without one of these lighters once you have used one. They install permanently to your gas lantern and you can light the lantern in high winds, rain, or snow, and this is something that is hard to do using matches.

Some other important tools and supplies that are not usually considered and not stocked by all dealers are the following: Tweezers, and be sure to get long ones. Magnifying glass, at least 10 power and preferably 15 or 16 power. Gold pans, in the 6" and 14" or 16" size. A bucket or tub, two buckets for cleaning up and also for carrying camp water are desirable. Plastic bottles or bags, to be used to store your gold and concentrates. Pocket knife or hunting knife, be sure to buy a good one. Don't try to save money on your knives as this is one frugal mistake that you can make. Axe or hatchet, you should have both, but, if you want to save money or weight, get a good axe. A good saw for cutting firewood and props; a bowsaw which costs only $3 or $4 is dandy for this purpose. Plastic sheets, such as painter's throw-sheets, in the 9x9 or 12x12 size, can be used as ground cloths and for a number of other purposes such as protecting equipment and people from rain and snow. They also make good tarps to catch rain water, when necessary. A good compass for direction finding, mapping, and claim staking. It is a good idea to buy a good compass and then have several cheap ones that you can take with you at all times. A snake-bite kit, even though you may never see a poisonous snake around your camp or placer operation. A prospector's field test kit, if you are going to get seriously involved in placering and prospecting. Gold scales, and you can get very accurate scales for less than $10.

These are some of the key supplies and tools that you will probably need every day you are in camp. It is a good idea to take along an assortment of nuts, bults, and screws, as well as nails, and a couple of extra hose clamps may save you some time looking in the stream for any that you might inadvertently lose. A good metal detector operator can usually find any clamps, bolts, or nuts that he drops into the water, if he has a detector that will perform in the cold water.

One item that almost all beginners forget to get is a suitable water container. Here is where a plastic container is alright. If your camp is some distance from the placer operations, you will want to carry water for drinking during the day, unless the water in the stream is satisfactory for drinking and it usually is.

FINALLY!

For most people, dredging and placering cannot be beat for outdoor activity. It is relatively inexpensive and it can be profitable. Most of your success will depend on you, but one of the most important points in getting started is to get good, experienced advice to start off with. If you are a city-dude, it might take you a week or so to get into the swing of things, but once you get the bug you will begin to see the total insanity of urban life as we know it today. When you sit in camp in the evening, you will revel at the quiet, the peace, and the serenity. If you have a crew, you will get more enjoyment from the bull-sessions around the campfire. Believe it or not, I have swapped lies with my pardners, Hardrock Hammon, Montana Larry, Wally MacLaren, and others, through the night until 4:15 AM, and been able to get up and get operations going on time the next morning. I have also sat around campfires and heard some of the biggest fakirs, fourflushers, and liars in the world spin their stories and make complete fools of themselves without realizing it. It is around these nightly "lie-fests" that the men are separated from the boys and where the self-styled experts are usually baited and shot-down by their more experienced and knowledgable brethren.

I have seen big-time operators with Mickey Mouse equipment fold up and quit without turning a wheel when the experienced help needed to get their comical outfits into operation showed up. I have seen first class opportunists lose their fannies when they did not have the know-how and gift of gab to back up preposterous pretentions. I have seen famous authors and book-educated miners fail

Karl von Mueller and local treasure hunter, Cal Clifford, checking for gold in Karl's high-altitude dredging equipment which was set up at the Oklahoma City Treasure Show at Shepherd Mall. (Editor's Note: Karl is known as the "old man" of treasure hunting. Most treasure hunters believe he has contributed more to the entire field of treasure hunting than any other man. He founded the original PROSPECTORS GAZETTE which is the oldest treasure hunting and prospecting publication in the world. His unbeatable TH-ing books are the standards of the industry. His "Exanimo" detector and prospecting equipment outlet in Segundo, Colorado (formerly of Weeping Water, Nebraska) has placed more correct equipment in the hands of the treasure hunter than any other equipment outlet. Karl's high-altitude dredging equipment opened up many formerly unworkable, high-altitude placer mining locations. His persistent efforts to see that the man in the field gets a fair shake are common knowledge.)

totally and completely when it came time to apply their presumed and second-hand knowledge in a practical manner.

On the other hand, I have met, worked with, and enjoyed the companionship of the finest people in the world in treasure hunting and mining activities. Many strangers have stopped at my camp and we have become fast friends. I, too, have stopped in strange camps and usually found my new acquaintances to be exceptional people. You simply do not find these types of people in roadside campgrounds, and you never will. Many of these people are fugitives from the timeclock, incredible taxes, and abnormal urban routines. They are the last remnants of the type of people who made America great.

I cannot and will not encourage you to engage in prospecting or mining, but, having lived in many cities, I will tell you that urban life is in my past and I would not and could not enjoy myself in the city anymore. I become distressed and saddened when I see sleek, regimented people rushing, unhappily, toward nothingness. Another example I see in the city is the huge, expensive church; yet I live and work in a cathedral; a fallen tree trunk is my pew, and the murmur of a stream, the chatter of the wild-life, and the tree and flower-studded slopes around me tell me and show me all that is holier than all of the churches and missions in the world. This is the life, and you'd better believe it.

This extremely valuable 5,000-year-old bronze statue was found by Pat Diamond of Chicago. For obvious reasons, Mr. Diamond won't give the location of his find. Two books which give tips on techniques for researching treasure locations and which should be in every treasure hunter's library are Karl von Mueller's TREASURE HUNTER'S MANUAL #7 and George Mroczkowski's PROFESSIONAL TREASURE HUNTER. These two authors have been successful many times because of their study, research, and detector and equipment handling abilities, coupled with untiring persistence and the desire to succeed. Their books are so interesting that it is difficult to put them down once you start reading them.

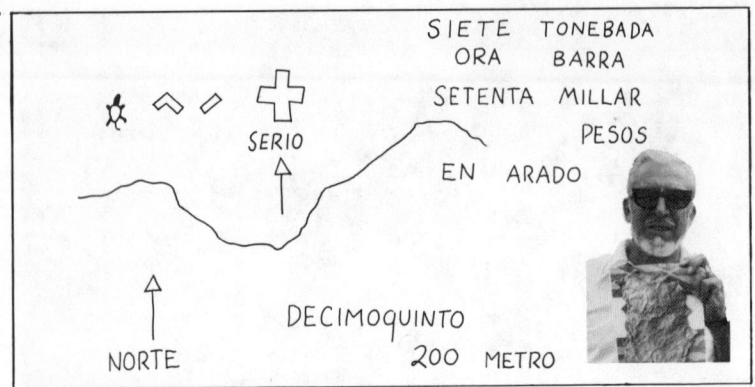

Bill Mahan, one of the earliest electronic explorers and professional treasure hunters of Padre Island, Texas, fame, displays a picture of an animal skin which contains a map believed to give directions to a large Spanish or Mexican treasure. The skin was found tacked on the underside of an old Mexican chest of drawers. The outline of the map is apparent only when illuminated with a long-wave ultraviolet light.

This treasure map was drawn on the skin in the above picture approximately 70-100 years ago. The bends in the river and other landmarks were found to be accurate according to today's maps. Since the treasure has not yet been located, the map as presented above has been changed, and many important details have been omitted. In the event the cache is located, the complete story will be told.

This ship's compass was found by Robert Hokr of Ellsworth, Kansas. Note the compass points are reversed. Thought: how did the ship's compass get to Kansas?

Chapter XIX

Maps

For several years I spent considerable time touring the country visiting with treasure hounds, miners, prospectors, and other people who liked to get out into the fresh air and really live. Since everybody seemed interested in treasure, I framed my talks around the subject and used protions of my library of color slides to put a little zip into these lectures.

REAL McCOY

Invariably, there would be somebody at each lecture who would confide in me that he had managed to get his hands onto a real, genuine, honest-go-gosh treasure map and that he might need some help getting the treasure out and he'd be tickled to death to have me in on the deal because I'd done a little treasure hunting myself. At first, I was naturally interested but one look at the map was all it would take to convince me that I had the same lousy map in my own library.

Believe me, although there have been thousands of treasure maps sold for prices ranging from as little as ten cents up to prices that I know of in the range of $220,000, there are very few bona fide treasure maps in existance, if any.

Let's look at the idea with our eyes open and with no greed to blind us. It just doesn't make any sense at all that anybody will go out and hide any treasure of any amount and then survey the site and draw a map of it. To make an even less ridiculous example, it is entirely unlikely that anybody would bury even a small amount of money and draw a map to show where it was hidden. I know in my experience I have never seen any treasure recovered through the use of treasure maps. Yes, I have heard of it, but I just have never been able to find the guys who made the big discovery.

So many of these stories get started by the 'natives' BS-ing the tourists and then when the tourists get back to their homes they started talking about it, a little item shows up in the newspaper and all of a sudden the little piece of baloney has become a full-fledged factual story.

SHORTY HARRIS

The immortal desert-rat and prospector, Shorty Harris, filled a Los Angeles reporter full of malarky many years ago and it has grown into a full-fledged lost mine story. What Shorty didn't tell in the story, the reporter did, and so we have hundreds of people every year traipsing around the desert looking for something that isn't there. And, a lot of them will fight you at the drop of a hat when you try to explain to them that it is all a lot of bull. Nosiree, Boy, when some of these educated idiots get to believing something that is absolutely preposterous, you just can't change their minds. They read about it in the newspapers, and they believe it. With respect to newspapers, did you ever notice in a calamity that the extras will come out with ten to 100 times as many people dead as it actually winds up to be. So much of the 'news' that newspapers print is pure hogwash that you can take any newspaper item with a grain of salt. This has nothing to do with maps, but even newspapers print inaccurate maps.

Anyway, when you have the opportunity to buy a treasure map at any price, don't be taken in. My advice to you in NEVER buy a treasure map for the purpose of using it to find the treasure. You'll be wasting your money and time if you do.

I buy treasure maps! I have several hundred of them, but I buy them only because they are interesting to me and I like to compare them, occasionally. You'd be surprised how many of these maps are merely redrawn copies of others. Misspelled names, mislocated towns, out-of-place mountains and rivers, and even trails where none have ever existed are few of the common defects that are passed from one original treasure map to another original treasure map. The 'original', of course, applies to the paper and ink, not to the map.

So, the idea is to not buy treasure maps for the sake of finding the treasure they allegedly show the way to. Buy them as curios, but let it end there.

A TOOL

Maps are a very important tool in treasure hunting and they can save you considerable time and trouble if they are properly used. If not properly used, they can be a waste of time and money, so it is up to you.

GOVERNMENT MAPS

Unless you have done some mining or prospecting with an

A. M. Van Fossen shows several samples of highgrade silver which he discovered electronically at a mine location. Van is an active TH'er/prospector, as well as an avid research historian who is presently working areas in South America.

This handcrafted buckle was found by W. W. Mosley of Camden, Arkansas, on an old Civil War military road near Jenkins Ferry on the Saline River. The buckle is gold and silver plated over brass and measures 3 1/16-inches by 2½-inches. It is valued at $750-up. Mr. Mosley and his son, B. T. Mosley, are experts in Civil War battlefield searching. They have located (and thoroughly cleaned out with their BFO and VLF instruments) many battlefields. Drop by to see them if you are ever in Camden.

experienced partner, you are probably not familiar with the quadrangle maps' which are distributed and sold by the Geological Survey. These maps show every town, road, hill, mountain, stream and other geological feature of the area they cover and they can be exceedingly helpful in running down treasure caches which are related to local treasure stories or even some historical caches.

These maps cost in the neighborhood of $1.25 to $2 each, and you should get one just to see what they are like. For complete information write one of the following addresses: (areas east of the Mississippi), Branch of Distribution, U.S.G.S., 1200 S. Eads, Arlington, Virginia 22202; (areas west of the Mississippi) Branch of Distribution, U.S.G.S., Box 25286, Denver Federal Center, Denver, Colorado 80225. Request a price sheet. To begin with, order a map to cover the community where you live. The maps may not be available for all portions of the United States, but the chances are that you will be able to get one of your area.

RAILROAD

There are actually thousands of sources of maps in the United States. Of course, we are all familiar with the road maps of the oil companies. The railroad companies almost all have railroad maps for sale and you can occasionally buy old railroad maps which show things as they were 50, 75, or 100 years ago for certain railroads. If you are interested in railroad maps, write to: Association of American Railroads, Transportation Building, Washington 6, D. C. and ask for a copy of their booklet 'List of Maps Showing Railroad Lines'. It is free and lists sources and addresses for thousands of maps by state, area, and by railroad lines.

Most of the departments and bureaus of the Government publish maps and many of these are not only detailed but quite accurate. Some of these are available to show where towns, trails, roads, railroads, and other significant features for certain years as far back as the late 1700s. Among the Government departments and bureaus are: Department of Agriculture, Department of Interior, Department of Defense, Department of State, Postoffice Department, Coast and Geodetic Survey, U. S. Geological Survey, Department of Commerce, and even the executive

A complete outfitting for a prospector's weekend gold recovery operation. Left to right: two "Gravity Trap" gold pans, tarpaulin, 2½" nozzle and hoses, rubber gloves, chest type waders, a detector designed for prospecting, wire support frame, Briggs and Stratton engine with pump, truck-type inner tube, sluice box, gas can, and miscellaneous detector searchcoils. Notice that the frame is equipped with a ¼" wire mesh sieve. The wire mesh was installed so the operator could use the dredge to facilitate recovery of coins and jewelry lost in shallow swimming areas.

branch of the Government (The President's Office) has issued maps.

ARMY MAP SERVICE

If you are a map collector, or if you seek a particular map of a certain area for a given period of time, the Defense Mapping Agency, Topographic Center, Washington 20315, may be able to help you.

If you are in a scribbling mood, write to the Superintendent of Documents, Washington, D. C. 20402, for Document Number 102 (Maps, U.S. and Foreign) or Document Number 183 (Surveying and Mapping). First check with your local library to see what Government Printing Office publications they have.

YOUR LIBRARY

This leads us up to your local library. If you live in a big city, the chances are that they have one section which contains nothing but maps. And, if you are a map fiend, you can go raving mad in this section as they have about everything under the sun. If you live in a smaller city or village, there is still a chance that your library might have a surprising number of maps on hand in the form of atlases, bound collections, and simply loose maps. It always pays to investigate these libraries.

Other sources for maps include your local or county surveyor, the state engineer, your historical societies, the Governor's office, your county and state clerks and treasurers offices, and, if you have a state land office, it is possible they may have a lot of interesting maps for you to choose from.

MAKE YOUR OWN

Sometimes it is incumbent on a treasure hunter to map an area for himself and this is a problem that invariably leads to disappointment if certain precautions are not taken. If the map is being made for immediate use, such as within a few weeks or next spring, the use of movable and destructible landmarks is permissible. However, if you do not know when you'll get back to the area, you had better use permanent, natural landmarks.

The requirements for a map are so widely different that it is difficult to discuss them with any justice in the small amount of space available here. For the uninitiated, however, I will give a few brief examples of how maps are made and used.

My first treasure hunting experiences were at Fort Kearney, Nebraska and when I started probing the area there were still a few landmarks left to help me find the camp grounds and sites of old Government buildings. Despite the fact that I had government maps available to me, I could not always find the particular sites I wanted, and so I resorted to making my own maps and comparing them with the maps in the historical society museum. By using the mounds of the old stockade as a turning point and a compass to orient myself, I was able to draw a pretty good map of the area as it existed in the late 1920's. Of course, fences existed then, and I drew them on the map exactly as they were. Then, I'd take the map to town and compare it with the Government maps and I managed to locate most of the campgrounds in this manner.

Left
The loot shown in these two pictures was found by Gene Rolls of Forest Ranch, California. The rings in the upper picture were found around various swimming pools. The coins and keys in the lower photo were found in different coin hunting sites.

Right
The Civil War relics shown in these two photos were found by Mr. and Mrs. Stanley Frank of Natchez, Louisiana. If you are ever in Natchez do not fail to go by to spend a while in the Frank Museum. It is truly a rewarding experience. All of the items in the Museum were found at historical sites and Louisiana Civil War battlefields by the Franks.

In another case, we were working on a treasure project in Idaho and inclement weather was closing in. In other words, the weather was about to drive us out, but we had enough encouragement to want to come back. Stakes, markers, and other identification points could not be depended on to remain through the snows, so we mapped the area. Here is how we did it: Using only a compass and a table top for equipment, we set the table up at the point of a little butte which jutted out into the area. We used another butte across the valley as a landmark and established it on the original blank sheet of paper. Then, we established NORTH and SOUTH on the paper. The point of the butte from whence we mapped was drawn in and we had our minimum landmarks established. From this point on, we would sight down the straightedge directly at important points in the treasure area and then pace off distance, and mark them on the map. When we got thru, we had a crude, but usable, map; and when we got back to the area the following summer we had no difficulty whatever in proceeding from where we had left off.

A few of us were interested in an area between Palmdale and Victorville, California a few years ago and we tried working the area. This was during the great landboom and when we'd get a few items of equipment going, somebody would invariably stop to see what we were doing and to visit. Didn't make any difference what day of the week it was, people were always flocking by and too many would stop. So, we mapped the area using an old alidade we bought in an army goods store and an old drawing board. Our stakes and markers would be torn down overnight quite often, but we got the area mapped and went on with our treasure activities with less meddling from the outside. We never got anything from this project, and I cite it only to show that we did use mapping as a means to an end.

Twelve hundred strong line up around the perimeter of this competition hunt site. These treasure hunters have come from all over the world to attend and compete in the International Championship Treasure Hunt sponsored by Search International. Search is an organization of treasure hunters dedicated to the advancement and protection of treasure hunting and electronic prospecting. For information, write Search International, P.O. Box 3007, Garland, Texas 75041.

These are a few of the participants who recently enjoyed themselves at one of the field trials sponsored by the Northwest Treasure Hunters Club of Spokane, Washington. There are several dozen such field trials, sponsored by various clubs, held each year at various cities all across the United States.

CHAPTER XX

Photography as a Tool

Depending on how you abuse, use, or handle it, photography can be a very valuable tool in treasure hunting. Improperly used, it can be a very expensive and confusing device and can often spell the difference between success and failure. It is probably most frequently used to establish landmarks in their relationship to building or caches, or vice versa.

FORT STAMBAUGH

An interesting, but fruitless, example is one of my experiences and I shall pass it on for the benefit of those who might later be confronted with similar circumstances.

For a number of years, I had occasionally read about some peculiar characteristics and activities of the sutlers at both Fort Laramie and Fort Stambaugh. From these stories, I smelled treasure. Fort Laramie is a national monument and, therefore, off-limits for any treasure hunting activity. Fort Stambaugh is another story; it lies exposed and yet hidden on the slopes of the Rockies at the periphery of famous South Pass on the Oregon and Mormon Trails. Although a much young fort than Fort Laramie, it is in complete ruins and almost never visited by the public.

So, in the late Fall of 1957 after the tourist season, I drove from my home near Santa Monica back to Nebraska and did a little further research in the archives of the Nebraska State Historical Society in Lincoln, and then headed back up the Platte River valley toward my goal. Following the old Oregon Trail, I did as much research as possible by visiting with members of local historical societies and talking with personnel at the Scottsbluff National Monument and Fort Laramie National Monument. At Casper, Wyoming I accidentaly hit paydirt when a service station attendant suggested that I see 80-year old Jim Phillips for information on Stambaugh. Phillips had a wealth of information on the area from personal observation and from hearing his folks talk about it. Phillips information was exactly what I needed to complete search. Treating him to a bottle of 'corn-juice' and a box of cigars, I thanked him and went on my way.

Arriving on the site of old Ft. Stambaugh at mid-morning the next day, I immediately attempted to reconstruct, mentally, the old fort and then locate the sutlers store. By referring to an official army map of the fort and using picket pins to mark the corners of buildings, I was able to relocate various buildings with reasonable accuracy and mark their locations with pins. However, the sutlers store just couldn't be located where the map showed it was suppose to be.

By dark, I was pretty well along with my survey and also pretty well confused. I spread out my bedroll, fried my bacon-and-beans, and lay back to watch the evening fireworks in the wonderful Wyoming sky. Later, using the North Star and a flashlight for triangulation points, I marked the site for true north so that I could establish landmarks.

The next morning, I established a turning point in the center of the site and marked the four true directions from the turning point with ribboned stakes. Then, I proceeded to photograph the site by setting a tripod with panoramic head and Rollei camera directly over the turning point and shooting pictures of the entire site in 60-degree panoramic increments. This means that I would shoot one picture, then turn the camera 60-degrees and take another picture, and so on, until I had photographed the entire area just as you would see it if you faced north and looked, then turned almost east and looked, and then turned east-south-east and looked, and so on.

When the photographic chores were completed, I resumed working on the puzzle of where everything had been. By mid-afternoon, two facts were assured; the map of Fort Stambaugh that I had did not match the scene as I found it, and the weather reports indicated that a snow storm was sweeping in from the northwest and I would have to get out of there. So, pulling my pins and marking key spots with unobrusive rocks, I departed.

Upon arrival at Fort Bridger (another historic and treasure-ridden area), I discussed the history of Fort Stambaugh with the Widdups who were then caretakers of the state-owned and maintained Ft. Bridger and one of my suspicions was confirmed. The layout of old Fort Stambaugh had been changed several times during its relatively short existance.

I spent a good share of my spare time during the winter of

1957-58 studying the history of the old fort and getting various maps of the fort and the area surrounding the fort. A new map was created of the old fort and the photographs I had taken were used to properly orient the map and to locate the picket-pins in their proper position on the new map. By late Fall of 1958, I was certain that the treasure could be located in a very short time. Weather and other circumstances prevented a return to the Ft. Stambaugh site until August 1959.

During the late Spring and early Summer of 1959, I accumulated more data and facts on Fort Stambaugh from persons in the Ft. Bridger, Green River, and Lander (Wyoming) vicinities. Enough positive information was on hand by the end of July to assure locating the old sutlers cache. Al Miller, Fred Irons, and I left Salt Lake City early on the morning of August 29th for South Pass. By evening we had established a camp and made a preliminary survey of my old landmarks. Everything was in order.

Early the next morning, we replaced all of the picket-pins in proper locations and by checking against my new maps and existing landmarks in the area, located the sutlers store. A few quick and precise measurements located the old fireplace, and a few more measurements located the calculated spot for the cache. A few spadefuls of dirt uncovered ashes and coals, so we were sure we were right. At a 2-foot depth, we drove a leach toward the estimated front of the old fireplace and hit rocks and some old tins. This indicated that somebody had been there before and refilled their diggings with rock and debris; the trade-mark of a professional. Nevertheless, with trowel and crowbar we carefully excavated the area, but found nothing. We were too late! We refilled our excavation, carefully landscaped the immediate area so it looked as it did when we arrived, and drove on up to South Pass City and enjoyed a bottle of beer with the honorable mayor of this old ghost town before returning to Salt Lake City. Thus, an interesting treasure hunting project came to an end at a total expense of probably 5,000 miles of driving, a hundred hours or so of research, and few dollars for grub. But not all treasure hunting projects turn out this way; sometimes you hit a winner.

In a sneaky and roundabout manner I have used this as an example of the value of photography. The photographs were used, together with the old official maps and my own map, to establish the exact location of the sutler's store and of the fireplace. The treasure represented the sutler's (trader's) bank account and his bank was a shallow pit directly beneath the bed of the fireplace.

You, the reader, will unquestionably wonder how I ever got a lead on such a kind of treasure in such a location. The answer stems from being curious about buried treasure and being observant for leads and clues. An old cowhand and rancher by the name of Hicks gave me the first lead back about 1952 when he related how he and his brother (who had ranched in the Jackson Hole area way back when) had, years ago, hired an old ranchhand and this fellow had told them a yarn about there being a good many thousand dollars worth of money and dust buried beneath the old sutlers store at Stambaugh. The Hicks brothers had given little credence to the old-timers yarn, but it tickled their curiosity and they had planned a trip over to Stambaugh to look around for years, but they put it off from year to year. Finally, the one brother died and the other settled at Mountain View, Wyoming. Later, he moved to Ft. Bridger and that is where I got acquainted with him. We had more or less agreed to go this trip together, but as with the Hicks brothers the years went by and we never got around to it. Finally Hicks died and only I was left.

Early in 1957, I read a letter in an old TRUE WEST magazine which, without mentioning any names, dates, or places, pointed a finger right at this treasure. I corresponded with the letter-writer for some time, but he could provide me with no further information than his father had told him about an old miser or skin-flint who ran a military trading post and was killed. His father always claimed there was a fortune buried but he never said where; didn't even mention the fort. With this scant, yet valuable, information, I hustled back to Lincoln, Nebraska and spent two days digging through their library for further information. There I found definite leads which triggered the unsuccessful search.

Even though nothing was recovered, the value of photography in this particular project is that without the photographs to pinpoint and analyze the site, I could very well have spent days or weeks, and a good many hours of back-breaking digging, to finally locate the cache. Photography, in this case, payed off by eliminating work and lost time and effort.

PHOTOGRAPHS

Nothing is so down-right objective, critical, or definitive as a photograph. You can run a very simple test by yourself and be convinced. Take a picture of an area or a subject with which you are either intimately familiar or totally unfamiliar. Your main street in town, or a group of people in the city park, for example. Immediately after taking the picture, closely scrutinize the area which you photographed and observe for unusual conditions or circumstances. When you get the print back for this picture, look it over and count the number of things you missed in your original observation. If the picture was taken of your main street, notice how the hardware store sign is starting to sag, and how you can hardly see some of the traffic signs (you should have noticed this before because you drive over this street several times a day), and that the globe on one of the street lights is broken, and that the lines on the pavement are getting awful dim in places, and so on, ad infinitum. This is an interesting and amazing test, and you can even try it on pictures you have already taken and have in your album.

You can use this critical and unforgiving characteristic in many of your treasure hunting projects. By the same token, many thoughtful prospectors are now using photography as a tool to determine prospecting and mining procedures and to establish proof of priority or of development work.

LOST DUTCHMAN

Tom McDonald used photography to blow the Lost Dutchman Mine myth to hell a few years ago, and it is unfortunate that he did not publish this entire record with all of the wonderful photographs in book form. Tom is a total disbeliever of the Lost Dutchman myth, as am I, and to prove to himself, as much as to anybody else, that it was a myth, he armed himself with a couple cameras, a tripod, some grub, his bedroll, and a .22 pistol for snakes, and set forth into the Superstitions. You can understand this was quite a fete of bravado considering the fact that hundreds of people have allegedly been murdered in these famous Superstitions without a single felon ever being brought to trial. Anyway, Tom sallied forth into the fearful mountains and spent two weeks photographing the entire area around the Weaver's Needle without having anybody take a shot at him. He met and visited with several parties of prospectors and vacationers (probably looking for the old Dutchman's bonanza), and none of them had reported any trouble or any unusual incidents.

Anyway, Tom got his pictures and when they were processed, the prints were closely analyzed and then compared with the many myths and legends that have been written and printed in the past 25 years. In no instance did any of the books precisely report the terrain, the geology, or other conditions in a manner which would correspond with Tom's photographs. Some interesting facts were evolved or revealed in this project. The photographs in one popular book had obviously been retouched to match the fictional exploits of its author. Photographs in another book were obviously of such poor quality that they 'apparently' substantiated misleading facts as reported therein. A pamphlet dealing with the Lost Dutchman myth contained a photograph of the Weaver's Needle which indicated the author had either taken the photograph several thousand years ago before nature had reduced the Superstitions or else the Needle had been transposed to a photograph with an Alpine background.

Thus, the proper use of photography again exploded one of the myths of treasuredom.

REFERENCE PHOTOS

It will often happen that libraries, museums, and archives will not let you borrow or copy maps, charts, or other material. Here again, photography can be your tool. You can shoot pictures of the objects, areas, or items you want to compare or check, then bring them to the library or museum and use them. I have had to do this a number of times and it has, on occasion caused me to drive back miles to shoot the pictures for comparison purposes. Now, as a matter of habit, I shoot pictures of any and every potential treasure site and process the film into negatives myself. This means that I have a photographic record of the location; and if pictures are needed, all I need to do is make the necessary pictures and then process them.

In fact, in my negative files, there are probably 50,000 frames of negatives of potential treasure sites alone. Very few of these have ever been printed, and it is entirely unlikly that I will ever see the day when even half of these negatives have been made into prints. The fact remains that in a matter of a few hours I can have photographs before me of potential treasure sites from border-to-border and coast-to-coast, plus Canada and Mexico, and not even have to leave my home. All of these negatives have been exposed over a period of about 25 years and were taken with the knowledge that they might or might not be used at some future date.

TAKING PICTURES

There are certain techniques or practices that should be followed in taking your pictures. First of all, there must be a purpose behind the project, and then you must shoot your pictures accordingly. A big book could be written on how to use photography in treasure hunting, but we have neither time nor space for this type of treatment in this book. However, as briefly as possible, I want to give some of the more important information on photography in the pursuit of treasure.

First of all, the very basis of photography is light. The proper use of light is what makes many pictures good and others simply lousy. Usually, in treasure hunting, we take pictures to reveal something unusual. For example, a bulge in the wall of a building, or an almost undistinguishable mound in a field, or to show where the shadow of a butte or mountain falls at a certain hour of a certain day of a certain season of the year.

In the second place, we can use the camera as a 'memory-tool' to record precisely what we see or what conditions were at a certain time.

I think an experience by Buelah Guthrie is a good example of one use of photography. She became interested in treasure hunting by listening to the unusual experiences of some close friends in Kentucky. She went with them on several jaunts but, like all true adventurers, she yearned for a project all of her own. She found one, right in her own family.

Her grandfather had been an early-day farmer, stockman, businessman, and sportsman in the Clinton, Kentucky area. The family never did figure out where he had hidden all of his money, so after he passed on and the estate was settled, the whole doggone tribe became a pack of moles. They searched nearby caves, attics, cellars, outbuildings, and even tore some of his furniture apart looking for 'you know what'. Some of his concealed money was found, but it was a family opinion that they had barely scratched the surface.

It finally dawned on Beulah that she had been born and reared right in the center of an interesting treasure situation, and she began to investigate the different tales of different factions of the tribe. Through discrete questioning and discussion, she finally decided that her first try at fortune should be in the basement of the old family home. It had a dirt floor and, although the house had been searched from roof to basement, nobody had given much thought to the basement floor. Digging the entire basement up would be a hard, dirty, time-consuming task, so Beulah had to figure out an easier way. She did; she decided to photograph the floor by using a bright sidelight to determine any and all irregularities in the surface. Here is how she got the job done without any special equipment. She set her camera up on a little crock in one corner of the basement and then located a flashgun at floor level about half-way down one of the walls and so it would throw its light at right angles to the camera. Then, she took a picture. By changing the location of the camera to all four corners of the basement and changing the location of the flashgun so that its light would illuminate the floor from a different angle, she managed to get some pictures that showed every high and low spot in the entire basement.

By assuming that any digging and filling that was done after the basement was dug would naturally become a low spot, she potted out the largest, most prominent low spot in the basement and dug. Jackpot! On her first effort, she located the grandsires money-nest right where everybody had walked time and again. She told no one else in the family about it; not so much because of greed, but because she believed that several lawsuits would ensue.

An interesting observation was made by Mrs. Guthrie and it is passed along here to show how sometimes the most obvious is the best concealed. She said that an old-fashioned porcelain insulator, such as was used in early-day wiring, was nailed to the floor joist immediately above the cache, and that if somebody would have suspended a plumbob from this insulator to the floor, it would have hit the cache dead center.

FARMYARDS AND TOWNSITES

Practically the same idea, but on a much larger scale, can be used to ascertain the location of old building sites, basements, cellars, and other improvements in areas where the buildings have been removed. The sun provides the light in this instance, and the pictures are shot as soon after sunrise as there is sufficient light to expose the film or just before sundown. Old adobe ruins which have 'melted' in the sun, wind, and rain will be emphasized by shadow. The depressions left by basements and cellars which are not at all discernable during the normal daytime will show up clearly in light and shadow on film when the picture is taken of buildings at high noon, or shortly before or after, will often expose irregularities in the walls, patches, and other changes in the structure.

MULTIPLE USES

These and hundreds of other uses can be found for the camera in the serious pursuit of treasure. It takes a little originality and imagination to use pictures to save time, work, mileage, and trouble. Every treasure project requires a different application of photography, if photography is to be used, and this is one of the decisions that must be made by the treasure hunter.

CAMERAS AND FILM

Everybody to his own liking. No two people will agree, exactly, on cameras, film, techniques, and application. My choice of film and cameras is the result of long experience and is predicated on the equipment that will best suit my requirements and still be convenient. I am going to briefly list my equipment and supplies and explain why they are my choices. Let me emphasize that my selection of these items will not agree with the selections of others with every bit as much experience or knowledge as I have.

My number one choice for a camera is the Retina IIIC. This is a 35mm camera which is equipped with a fast f/2 lens and also has a coupled rangefinder and exposure meter. Here are the reasons I prefer this camera: It is light and convenient. I can shoot 36 pictures from one roll of film. The Xenon lens is just about the best that money can buy. It has a self-timer feature which permits me to get into the picture for the record, if necessary, or allows me to hold an object which is to be photographed. The list price for this camera is around $189.50, but it can be bought NEW for around $100 in many Los Angeles, New York, and Chicago camera shops by mail.

My first choice for film for this camera is Eastman Plus-X film. While this film is rated at a film speed of 80, I rate it at 160 to 200 and get perfect pictures for my purposes. Since most of my pictures are printed in the 4x5" size for reference purposes, I get good results from the camera-film combination. When critical or larger detail is needed, I enlarge the pictures to 8x10" size on glossy paper and still get all the sharpness and detail I need.

My second choice for a camera is the Rollei. It is an expensive, heavy camera, but like the Retina, it is equipped with a fine lens (Xenotar) and produces superb 2¼x2¼" negatives which invariably produce sharp, crisp pictures. Actually, on the job, I prefer the Rollei but its weight and limitation of only 12 pictures to the roll of film is sometimes distressing. I have taken many almost impossible pictures with it in the late evening by opening up the diaphragm to a full f/2.8 and shooting Verichrome film at f/300 or f/400. The film is normally rated at 80.

For lighting inside buildings, caves, mine tunnels, and other poorly lit or unlit locations, I prefer the speedlight for a number of reasons. First of all, it is completely self-contained and you do not need to burden yourself with a lot of extra flashbulbs, filters, and other accessories. In the second place, it produces light which is practically the equivalent of daylight, so if color film is to be shot you need not worry about filters for the different films. And, most important of all, once you have acquired a speedlight you do not need to continue buying flashbulbs. You simply use the same old lamp, time and again, until you have shot 10,000 or more pictures and the chances are, even then, that it will go on indefinitely.

If you are going to shoot pictures outside in the daylight, all you need is a camera and film. Any camera or film will usually do, but when you have hit paydirt a few times and get a few dollars to spare you'll invariably start thinking about finer working tools and you can do a lot worse than those items I've mentioned above.

When you shoot pictures in poorly lit areas, you are going to have to start thinking about a better camera and a speedlight. You can get pretty good pictures in pretty dim light with almost any camera by using Tri-X film, or any of the other super speed films.

Speedlights are no longer impossibly expensive as they were a few years ago. Some pretty good units can be purchased for as little as $25 new. If you do splurge for a speedlight, wait until you really need it, and then be sure to get one which either uses 110-120 volts ac-dc or can be used with batteries. If you want to go a little deeper into equipment, buy one of the new transistorized units with a monitoring circuit which cuts off the power consumption when it is fully recharged. This feature costs less to operate and is especially important when you are taking pictures in remote or difficult areas and need to get as many pictures as possible from each set of batteries.

Study and ponder the matter of photography as a tool. It can be helpful. Someday, maybe somebody will publish a low-cost book on photography in treasure hunting which will illustrate and tell all.

These treasure hunters are in search of a buckskin bag cache buried during the Nez Perce Indian wars. The Idaho hunt was organized by Bill Inghram and Roy Lagal. Left to right: Charles Garrett, Dee Miller, Bill Inghram, Roy Lagal. Photo by Duane Alderman.

CHAPTER XXI

History

When I was a brat in school, English and history were, in my estimation, the dryest, least interesting, and most unneeded subjects they had to offer. And, they didn't just offer them. You had to take gobs of both subjects. How well I remember how I suffered through these classes and I believe that mathematics was just as nauseating. In fact, like almost every other kid, school was just about the worst torture that man ever created and teachers were unbearable. If I'd have had my way, my schooling would have ended in the first grade.

Now, I realize how much I missed in school and for the past 25 years I have attended school of some sort in that never ending pursuit of knowledge.

Fortunately, my interest in history was aroused while I was still in school and this interest was prompted by early activity in treasure hunting. As time has moved on and I have become acquainted with more and more really successful treasure hunters, I have found that they have been, without exception, well-versed authorities on American history. Charlie Millen is one of the best informed authorities on western gunmen. Eddie Brutz has an intimate knowledge of railroad history that is amazing. Bill Hammond has a fantatstic knowledge of old mines, desert rats, mineralized areas, and ghost towns. Eddie Dammitz is a military specialist who can quote names, places, and dates pertaining to the Army with precision that is exceeded only by textbooks and he knows a lot that isn't in the textbooks.

Knowledge of history will help you immeasurably in the pursuit of so many treasure caches, and as you study history you will often pick up leads that will steer you right into a treasure hunt.

As the tempo of your treasure hunting activities pick up, you will find yourself devoting more and more time to reading and studying history. By the time you have 3 or 4 successful recoveries under your belt, you will come to realize that you have been waltzing around with a lot of history in your head and that you are beginning to habitually pick up figments of history day by day.

This applies to the treasure hunter who seeks treasure which was hidden a few weeks or years ago as well as to the treasure hunter whose interests are only in treasures beyond the turn of the century. Any way you look at it, every treasure cache is bound up in local, territorial, state, or national history. Even the old recluse that lived on the edge of town and concealed a small fortune on his acreage is bound up in local history. Maybe he didn't neighbor with a soul and hardly talked with anybody; he's still part and parcel of the community and his story is entwined in the history of the area.

So, if the records, the gossip, the old newspaper, and the local history are of no interest to you, you'll find that researching treasure will be a drudgery for you; that will lead only to failure. There simply is no two ways about it.

On the other hand, the pursuit of sudden wealth in the form of treasure can stimulate the interest in history no end. In fact, the fantastic knowledge of history of some of the successful treasure hunters can be attributed only to the 'need to know' or never ending pursuit of historical knowledge as a means of becoming or being a successful treasure hunter.

There are those who have challenged my attitude in this respect but, I must add, these challengers' success has been marked by mediocrity, a few old guns, an accidental discovery of a treasure cache that has stimulated the search for more and greater treasure, or the mere acquaintance with a successful treasure hunter.

A wholehearted interest in and curiosity about history is part and parcel of the success story of any treasure hunter. The interest in and study of history follows the old admonition: You scratch my back and I'll scratch yours. This means that you study pertinent history on a particular treasure and it will invariably lead you to facts and figures on another treasure. It may be unbelievable, but the successful treasure hunters who make their livings and fortunes in the pursuit of treasure invariably have more irons in the fire and more treasure projects in process than they can possibly take care of at one time.

I think a wonderful example of history and treasure hunting is bound up in the books of Hubert Howe Bancroft who subsidized so many history books on the west. I have a priceless

Upper Left

This cache was recovered in Northern Oregon. The Garrett and White instruments were used during the recovery. The story was originally published in DISCOVER, a manufacturer's publication issued by Kenneth White, Sr. Photo courtesy Duane Alderman.

Upper Right

These coins and artifacts were found by the members of one family during a short period of time using the White instruments and the Metrotech TR shown in the picture.

Lower Left

Don Lewis of Raydon Electronics, Farmington, New Mexico, photographed this fantastic find. The silver bar weighs 85 troy ounces; the silver cross weighs 19 troy ounces. The unusual spear-point-like objects are parts of Spanish armor which were found in New Mexico. The bar and the cross were found by Charles Haskin.

Lower Right

These Spanish bars are part of a large cache found in one of the Western states.

copy of his book RETROSPECTION wherein he projects his theory on mankind and history and in this one book are no less than one dozen leads on buried treasure in San Francisco and central California. Bancroft was too busy writing history and making money to pursue the many treasure caches he knew existed in the West, but he mentions them and their probability many, many times in his various books.

However, this does not mean that we are to presume that innumerous treasure leads are intentionally bound up in the history books. We do know that references in history books frequently are the clinching facts that motivate the professional to continue or abandon a treasure project. And, we know that some references are the seed from which successful research is inaugurated that terminates in the recovery of a treasure cache. And, we know that quite often the only available facts may be found in some obscure history books simply because all of the human sources of information are deceased or can not be located.

Thus, you will find that every successful treasure hunter harbors a growing library of history and fact books pertaining to his particular realm and that he is a first-rate customer at various public libraries. In effect, this means that the successful professional whose forte is treasure hidden, lost, or abandoned by the pioneers of the last century will invariably have a substantial library of books pertaining to the old West and particular to the area and period of his interest. The professional who is interested only in the treasure caches of racketeers, criminals, and outlaws of the present day will have a library that could be taken, for all practical purposes, for the library of a detective or lawyer. The treasure hunter who is interested in the loot which was taken, but never spent, from old train robberies will invariably have a good reference library pertaining to railroads, their personnel, and railroad crimes.

All of this discussion does not imply that it is necessary to invest a lot of money in books. To the contrary, if you are not a bookworm, you can generally get all of the books you need from the local library. Not only this, publications like TRUE WEST, FRONTIER TIMES, and the publications of the various historical societies can offer you a lot of information for a little bit of money.

Watch your local auction sales for fantastic buys in old history books pertaining to local and state history. It is not at all unusual to buy collector's items for as little as a dozen books for $1. Rummage sales often offer doggone good history and local reference books for little or nothing.

And, while we are on the subject of books, dont' overlook the value of books which have been written and published locally by early day residents pertaining to the history of the community. A fellow by the name Clem Houdershledt used one book on the history of Clay County, Missouri to locate seven different treasure caches which were buried by early well-to-do farmers and business men and Clem has lived comfortably in Mexico City for the past 25 years on the proceeds from leads provided by this one book.

You don't need to know history like a professor to get along in this treasure hunting business, but you doggone well better be able to enjoy courting history like a farmer's daughter if you want to make any headway in the business.

Spanish Landmark. This is a typical Spanish pointer. Thousands of these are known to exist in an area extending south from Salida, Colorado to Central America. In various areas, when certain combinations of these markers are coordinated, they locate, exactly, Spanish mines, smelteries, and caching sites. The Spanish never smeltered the ore at the mine. This explains the large smeltery near San Francisco Peak and another at Ft. Sumner.

Chapter XXII

Buried vs. Sunken Treasure

For my money, sunken treasure is beyond the reach of most amateur and professional treasure hunters. It is either too far at sea, too deep, or it takes too much money to get it.

I think a classic example of the futility of sunken treasure hunting is the experience of a very good friend of mine. Thirty years ago, he was well beyond being a millionaire and so he 'retired.' Today, he is not quite penniless, but he lives a very quiet, inexpensive life and he does not have the wherewithal to splurge occasionally. Where did all this money go? Into sunken treasure hunting!!! In May 1960 I had a long visit with him at Key West and when we got down to brass tacks about his affairs, he told me that he had bought enough boats, gear, equipment, and paid enough wages to support a Naval demolition squad. He figures that he has spent over 2½ million dollars in the past 30 years without ever recovering anything but a few old anchors, ships hardware, and some cannon. He claims it took him 5 years to see the futility of the program, but like a disease his urge to 'win' carried him on and on and on.

When I mentioned that others were carrying on and 'apparently' doing OK, he said it was all being done on other people's money and that a lot of the success was 'just show.'

I have always maintained and I still swear that it takes money to seek sunken treasure. On the other hand, essentially, it doesn't take a dime to do a lot of good, successful buried treasure hunting.

You can buy charts that will show you exactly where a ship went down at sea or along the coastline, and a little research will inform you as to what was aboard the ship. Discounting any probability that the ship has shifted miles away from its point of sinking, you still can't walk to the spot and probe the area or salvage the ship without cost. It just can't be done, that's all there is to it.

With buried treasure, you usually don't have to travel miles to get to the site, and you can probe at your leisure. If you want to invest money for instruments to make your job easier, you are free to do it; but you don't have to. You need no boats, no diving gear, no crews, and you have none of the normal hazards of diving.

As I mentioned earlier in this book, my first treasure hunting didn't cost me a dime. I used a tailgate bolt from a lumber wagon to probe the ground and it payed off for me. I couldn't do this today, or then, with sunken treasure.

I am prejudiced toward buried treasure and I have never yet found a good argument against my prejudices in this respect except the adventure angle. Even then, if I want the adventure of the sea, I can still buy a boat and sail to some of the islands which have coughed up buried pirate treasure and satisfy my whims.

In the profit column, I do not know a single sunken treasure hunter who has ever made any money to speak of directly from his discoveries. I do know several who have done quite well for themselves through the device of using other people's money to finance their 'hunts' and making a nice profit from this business. This, however, is not treasure hunting, except in name only.

Since I am not 'gone' on sunken treasure, it is possible that I do not know all that I should about it and its activities. There will unquestionably be those who will offer instance upon instance of my errors. I stand ready to be corrected and I still say that for every person who became wealthy directly from sunken treasure hunting there has been no less than 10 people who have attained great wealth from buried treasure hunting and that they have done this at a fraction of the cost and effort.

For me, sunken treasure makes interesting reading when the stories are kept within the limits of reasonableness. But, I have read stories of men who have salvaged millions from the sea floor and one of them, in particular, owes me money which I will probably never see. The reason: the true (?) story was a complete hoax!

I will stick to my buried treasure and I will continue to admonish all others who are interested in making treasure hunting both interesting and profitable to stick to the treasure that is within their reach.

If you can't get to it, you are wasting your time, energy, and money working on the project. This applies even to buried treasure, but especially to sunken treasure.

Chapter XXIII

First Aid, Life Saving, and Safety

This is the most important chapter in the entire book, but I'm not going to *waste* much time on it because 9 out of 10 readers will pass it by anyhow. Nevertheless, I'm going to pass along some age old advice and let you fry in your own fat when the time comes that you need to know this information, and don't.

If you are going to bang around at treasure hunting, prospecting, or just simple exploring out in the great open spaces, don't ever get the idea into your head that you can meet all emergencies and contingencies that *could* arise with the abundant knowledge you now have. I learned while lecturing that it is possible to literally scare the sox off a greenhorn by relating some of the problems that arise in the field. Actually, these problems are no graver than those confronted by the city-dude in his natural habitat, but they are different and, without exception, they require a cool head and commonsense.

I'm going to treat these matters more or less informally but I'll inject as much good, helpful information as possible along the way. Don't let any of these things scare you as thousands of people are braving them everyday with greater safety than they'd confront the dangers of city life.

FIRST AID

Entire books have been written about first aid so it would be useless to try to cram an entire first aid course into this chapter. I would suggest that you get a copy of Dr. John Henderson's book of First Aid; in fact, get two of them and keep one around the house to study now and then and stick the other one in your glove compartment, or under the car seat, or pack it in your 'warbag' so you'll always have it available when you need it most. Dr. Henderson's fine book can be bought at most bookstores or found on most paperback bookracks in stores all over the country. Price is 50¢ and it is worth every cent of the price.

When you get this book, or any good first aid book, learn how to bandage, to treat insect bites and snake bites, and study the sections on broken bones. As soon as you have had a chance to read and understand the book, start to accumulate your first aid supplies.

While it is literally a toy in comparison with what my outdoor first aid requirements could be, I carry in my car at all times a 'First Aid Travelkit' which is assembled by Johnson and Johnson for the AAA. My good friend, Paul Walker of the Utah affiliate of the AAA, gave this kit to me a couple years ago and I would not be without it. However, while this little kit is far better than nothing at all, it does not have all of the first aid materials that are needed for gadding around in the mountains and deserts. Again, it is small but it will help in a pinch. There are other first aid kits which are assembled by Johnson and Johnson and other manufacturers which are much more complete and this is the type that you should buy or assemble for your excursions. My big field kit measures about 6"x6"8" and contains everything, except splints, that I could conceivably need for an injury in the field. The only thing lacking is a snakebite kit, and I carry that in my pocket.

SNAKEBITE KITS

There are a number of snakebite kits on the market and most of them are real good. However, some of them are so large and cumbersome that they can not be conveniently carried on the person or even in your warbag when you are hiking or packing into the back country. I have bought and used about a half-dozen different brands and there is something to be desired in all of them. Some are complete, but too large. Others are large, but incomplete. My personal preference is the one known as the COMPAK and it is manufactured by the Cutter Laboratories of Berkeley, California.

The most important feature of this kit is that it is small enough to be conveniently carried in the pocket. In fact, I like to be on the safe side so I have a half-dozen of these Compaks and I keep them stored handy as follows: One is always in the glove compartment of my car. Another is in my sleeping bag. I keep one in my warbag, one underneath the driver's seat, and two more in the trunk of my car. When I get out of the car to do some work, I take one of the two in the trunk and stick it in my pocket. If several of us are going into an area away from the car, I take two of them with me.

I want to tell you a little about these kits. They all have a knife or blade for making incisions over the fang punctures and a tube or vial of antiseptic for sterilizing the area before and after the incisions. Also included is a tape or cord to be used as a tourniquet, and some form of suction device for sucking the venom from the bite.

Snakebite treatment goes something like this. You open the kit and immediately apply the tourniquet between the fang marks and your body. Then, you sterilize the fang marks and make small cross-shaped incisions over each of the fang marks. Following this, you apply the suction devices to the incisions.

Don't worry about the snake until you have administered first aid to yourself. Then and only then, if you feel up to it, you can kill him, but worry about yourself first and don't get panicky. Take it slow and easy, and you'll get things done faster than if you try to rush.

Make local inquiry about the poisonous snakes and their habits. A good place to do this is at service stations or local stores. The habits of snakes vary with the areas, so find out. For example, during the hot summer months, the desert is a pretty dead place during the hot daylight hours but it becomes alive at night. Anybody who has camped on the desert at night is quite familiar with the sounds of the desert at night: the rustle and whistle of birds, the squeal of a rodent when caught by a fox or snake, the whisper and squeaks of small rodents as they scavenge for food and the crash of the creosote bush as it is collided with by the pursurer or the pursued in the everlasting hunt which makes up the law of the wild. Thus, for example, sidewinders are rarely seen on the desert during the hot days, but comes the night and they thrash about looking and listening for food When they hear man or beast clomping through the brush, they recoil, ready to strike without warning, and they often do. So, if you are not familiar with the area, whether it be mountains, desert, or plains, ask somebody who does know so you'll have some idea of what to expect.

While on the subject of areas, any wilderness area is a dangerous place to be, alone. True, thousands of men and women have travelled the wilderness areas from one end to the other for lifetimes without trouble, but these people have known what they were doing, knew intimately the ways of the area, and they knew what to do in an emergency. They were self-sufficient.

If you have not yet enjoyed the good rugged living that comes with prospecting and treasure hunting, you have missed a lot. Sometimes it is extremely difficult to adjust your mode of living to the coarser outdoor living, but once you are adjusted you will find there is no comparison for really enjoyable living.

This often means dispensing with camp stoves, chairs, tents, and all of the other niceties of 'civilized' living, but it is fun. In fact, for example, a camp stove is a cumbersome, unnecessary piece of equipment except in areas where there is little or no firewood or other fuel. Once you get accustomed to cooking over a fire, you will find that nowhere can you get the flavor or the nutrition that will equal it. Likewise, most of my fondest memories go back to days when I ate with my back to a big pine or a large boulder and without the convenience or comfort (?) of padded chairs and overloaded tables. Just like my old friend Boison has said so many times 'Tables and chairs are for people who have ulcers.'

SLIDES AND FALLS

Don't take unnecessary chances and never make the mistake of thinking you are younger or more agile than you actually are. When hiking or working in the mountains or around ravines or other places where you can slip or fall a good distance, exercise great care that you have sure footing all of the way.

If you are packing, under no circumstances should you mount your pack in such a way that it can not be immediately jettisoned in the event you start falling or sliding down a slope or grade. If your hike or travel is such that you must go up or down a slope or grade on your hands and knees or in a sitting position, remove your pack and pull it up or down with you. Remember, it is possible to go back down a slope and pick up your pack, but if you tumble or roll any distance with a pack on your back, you're almost certainly in for a broken or injured back. Falls also account for a great number of other broken bones, especially arms and legs, but I have a horror of broken backs and that is why I particularly mention it here. A man with a broken arm or leg can usually be taken to a doctor or hospital in some fashion or other, but the fellow with the broken back is in for a pretty rough time before he ever sees a doctor because he can't be forked across a horse, or carried between two other men, and he can't be put in a car and rushed to medical help. It's got to be a stretcher trip; nothing else will do.

SUNBURN

All of you sun-worshippers, nature-boys, and would be nudists can have the time of your life rollicking around a million miles from nowhere on your treasure hunts and you can suffer for it afterward. I've seen desk-jockeys from Los Angeles have the time of their lives scampering through old diggings, ghost towns, and old camps in senseless pursuit of treasure on weekends, naked from the waist up. Come Sunday morning they were as red as a hereford bull and by evening they were raw on their shoulders and back and puking like a geyser. This doesn't apply only to Los Angeles but to dudes all over the country. The moral to the story is to protect yourself from the sun and keep burn ointment or suntan lotion in your 'get-well' kit. You can't undo a good sunburn; you just have to suffer it out while you're being skinned alive.

While on the subject of the sun, don't forget to take your sunglasses with you and don't be bashful about using them.

So that you may know, if you are not informed, protect yourself from the sun in the mountains, on the desert, and on the beaches or coast. Because of the characteristics of the air in these locations, the sun is more intense both in summer and winter and you can actually get a painful sunburn on a foggy overcast day.

THORNS

I've taken the liberty of lumping all of the botanical hazards under the heading of thorns. I've had some pretty painful relationships with thorns, so I mention them in particular. However, poison ivy, poison oak, yucca, and hundreds of other plants provide natural hazards that you must look for in the field. In some localities, you will find grass that has blades so sharp it will literally butcher you unless you are toughened up. In New Mexico and Florida, I have had nearly new shoes and boots cut and slashed by the native grasses so that they were worthless for wearing where I wanted some form of waterproofed or water-resistant footwear. Some of the native plants in the Southwest and in Florida have leaves that are like spears and if you should accidently hit them just right while walking, they'll go through your hand like a dagger or spear. I mention these things not to scare you but to warn you about them so you'll be alert for all of these natural hazards.

ANIMALS

Animals are relatively harmless and usually if you leave them alone, they'll leave you alone. The major exception is bats, and even they will try to get out of your way and away from you. My only experiences with bats have been in a few old buildings and in caves. I've never had one attack me, but I have had them fly into me and cling to my clothing a moment and then hasten off. Some people have been bitten by them, and it is a good idea to get to a doctor if you are bitten.

A few animals are as cantankerous as I am and it pays to steer clear of them if you possibly can. I'll name a few of them so you'll know.

The Javelina, or wild boar, in the Southwest is the most unpredictable critter I know of. You may be walking up one of the old dry washes in Arizona and go around a bend and run into one of several of them. They may stand their ground, or they might take off like a herd of wild cattle; but this doesn't necessarily end matters. Just as often they may charge off, then turn around and attack you. My experience with them has been so confusing I just can't tell you much about them except you can expect anything from them. As I recall, they are about the size of a medium size dog, but the more I think about them, the bigger they seem. It also seems to me that they are a relatively fast moving animal; yet, when I look back at a race I had with one to my car, it seems like I outran him, and I'm no antelope. Anyway, I beat him to the car and he was pretty doggone mad about it, so he took it out on my left front wheel and what he did to the hub cap shouldn't happen to anything.

Wolves are said to be pretty mean critters. I don't know. I've been around a lot of them in the open spaces and while they'll come down and hang around the camp at night, I've never been afraid of them. However, on one trip into Mexico with a group, we had an experience that kept me awake a few extra winks one night. We were camped at about the 8,000 foot elevation about a hundred miles south of the border and my old friend, Bill Hammond, who is one of the swellest guys in the world and at the same time the lousiest cook that ever hit a mining camp, fixed the grub. We were sitting around eating after dark and seeing who could 'sell' the biggest lie when we noticed a necklace of glowing eyeballs around the camp. I don't mean just a pair or two, but there must have been a hundred pairs of eyes watching us. I was neither afraid nor brave; I just sat there slurping up the awful grub twice as fast and hoping the eyes would go away. Frank Nova, who knows his way around in Mexico as well as the next guy, was familiar with the situation, so he picked up a rib of the deer that was providing the banquet and threw it out into the darkness. All of the 'beads' disappeared at once and you've never heard such a racket as they set up while fighting for this rib. A few minutes later, things quieted down and the necklace began to form again a few eyes at a time. They didn't bother us that night, but I'll betcha they'd have liked to came in for a closer visit and maybe had a banquet of their own.

Bears are the doggonest critters that God ever put on this earth. They are unpredictable, and I'll have nothing to do with them. Guys like Al Miller of Hastings, Nebraska and Floyd Nash of Salt Lake City tell me that a bear is harmless, except for a mother with cubs. I know that a mother will slap the socks off of anybody or anything that gets near her young 'uns, but I got knocked on my can once by a two-thirds grown bear just for trying to hand him some fig cookies. Usually I don't back away from a fight when I don't start it, but I'll have to admit that sometimes I am a coward. Up in Montana a short jaunt from Gardiner, I had a grizzly chase me once for absolutely no reason at all and I outran him, but I wouldn't bet on it the next time. So, my advice is to let all bears go their way, and you go yours. If they decide to go your ways you'd better go faster than they do; and don't you believe this old malarky about bears not being able to run down hill.

Rodents, to my way of thinking, are harmless little natural toys. They'll scamper like hell to keep out of your way. They won't bite unless you get hold of them or corner them. Whenever I'm camped out with somebody else, I always like to sleep head-to-head. If there is just two of us, we spread out our sleeping bags or balloons so the heads are about a foot apart. If there are 3 or 4 of us, we form a kinda of a star or cross with the heads of the sleeping bags toward the center. Well, a few years ago, I was camped out with somebody and it seems like it was Johnny Pounds of the Associated Geographers and I'd just fallen asleep when I felt a jerk on my hair. It woke me up. Just as I was going to sleep again, I felt another jerk. I thought Johnny was joshing me a little, so I got hold of my flashlight and lay waiting for him. Sure enough, it happened again and I shot the old light out and Johnny was still asleep, but I did see a couple of kangaroo rats hopping away. What they were doing was swiping a few of my remaining hairs to line their nests, and I got quite a bang out of it when I finally figured out what was going on.

Lizards are relatively harmless. In all of my experience, I've had only one crawl into my sleeping bag with me, and I never knew it until the next morning when I found I'd crushed him. On the desert or in the mountains, you'll hear things all night, but you'd never get any sleep if you let these sounds bother you. I've had snakes snuggle against the outside of my sleeping bag while I was in it, but I just layed still and let them rest. If they'd have tried to get inside with me, it would have been a different story, believe me, and I'd have vacated in a second.

If you are ever bitten by any of these things, administer first aid right away and then get to a doctor. Don't trust to luck that you won't be infected or get sick. Just play safe and get to a doctor.

ARTIFICIAL RESPIRATION

Learn to administer artificial respiration. It may not only help you save somebody's else's life, but also your own. In fact, I think the very best book for anybody interested in prospecting, treasure hunting, mining, hiking, or any other outdoor activity is, of all things, the Boy Scout's Handbook. It costs only 75¢ and it has more common sense and outdoor lore than any other book I know of at any price. You can find a copy of this book under my car seat any time and I wouldn't be without it. I have several copies and I keep them handy.

RESCUE AIDS

If you do much banging around you'll eventually get into a 'pickle' that you can't get out of alone. This may be having your car bog down in a swamp, or stuck in the sand, or hung up over a boulder, or maybe just a discharged battery. Whatever the cause, you may someday find yourself in a jam and not know what to do. Here's a few tips, remember them!

SAVE BATTERY

If your car won't start, DON'T RUN THE BATTERY DOWN TRYING TO START IT!!!!! Save what is left of the battery for signalling at night with the headlights. Three blinks, three shots, or three of almost anything that can be seen or heard is a distress signal that is known around the world. So, save your battery for night-time and give three blinks of the lights to any cars you can see miles away or to any planes overhead.

STAY WITH CAR

Above all, don't leave your car and try to walk for help. More lives are lost this way than any other way I know of. On the desert, the whole area is alive at night with every form of wildlife and it can be literally suicide to cross the desert at night afoot. Then, if you are lucky and make it through the night and still are not back to civilization, you have a blazing sun to contend with. Stick to your car and signal for help!!! Let help come to you because the chances are that you can't get to it.

WATER

Go easy on the water, wherever you are. Save it as it might take days for somebody to discover you. Same goes for food. When I'm going out on the desert, I always stick a few cans of peaches, tomatoes, and other high liquid foods in the car to have just in case my water poops out on me. If you should be near a spring or stream, don't forget that you have a lot of water conveyances with you: hat, hub caps, your jacket, and even the air cleaner, to name a few. These canvas water bags are the greatest and you can roll one or two of them up and stick them almost anywhere in the car to have them on hand when needed.

Above all, don't get panicky and don't give up hope. It is practically impossible for an automobile to go unnoticed for a very long period on the desert or anywhere else. A parked car in any remote area is often spotted repeatedly by unseen prospectors, miners, foresters, rangers, and others, so if you hang a shirt from the antenna, you'll give a signal requiring an investigation.

When I speak so often of the desert, forgive me, because it is my first love. Next to the desert, I am happiest in the mountains. Nevertheless, my business as a writer and adventurer takes me into all varieties of communities and the safety comments I make are almost universally applicable.

If you depart from civilization and get out into the sparsely populated areas very much, the time will come when you will find yourself 'over a barrel.' You can almost bet on this happening, and as sure as it happens you may be sure that there is a relatively easy way out. Panic and fear will be your greatest hazards. On the North American continent, it is literally impossible to get completely out of communication. You can get into wilderness areas that are really supposed to be wild and untamed and still occasionally run into a prospector, hunter, ranger, mountie, or a rancher. Night and day, overhead, you will see and hear airplanes. All of these represent *help* when you need it if you know how to get it and maintain your senses. So here is some more advice in addition to that already given.

SMOKE

Your automobile tires are ideal tools for signalling help. Burn them, but start with the spare or poorest tire. Let the air out of the tires before you ignite it. You do not need to burn it on the wheel, but just take the wheel and tire out a safe distance from the gasoline tank. You can most easily get the required gasoline by hanging on to one corner of a hankerchief or other rag and poking the other end down into the filler tube and sopping it up. Then, hustle over to the tire, squeeze the gasoline onto the tire and light it. Don't use the gasoline-covered hand to do the lighting; use the dry one.

TIRES

About using your tires, if the day is perfectly still so that the smoke will rise straight up, your smoke signal will be seen for miles and somebody will investigate. If the day is windy, look around the area during the daytime for a high point, or lookout, that can be seen from a great area. Then, at night, roll your tire to the top of the high point and light it. Think! Use daylight and darkness to your advantage. If planes fly over regularly, try to attract their attention with your fire. On a still day, you can even increase the volume of smoke sent up by dumping some oil onto the blazing fire. In fact, if you carry extra oil in the car like I do, you can often use a plain old wood fire for smoke signals by tossing about a cup of oil in the fire occasionally. Again, if planes fly over regularly such as the scheduled airlines or military planes, you can send up the well-known 'three' signal by building three fires about ten feet from each other and then throwing a cup of oil on the first one at the first sight or sound of a plane, and when the smoke begins to diminish you can throw a second cup of oil on the second fire, and so on for the third fire. Thus, you'll have three balls of black smoke in the air at the same time different altitudes and a short distance apart.

White is a good color to protect you from the heat and sun, and it is also a good color to attract attention. When you are signaling during the daylight hours, hang a white shirt, sheet, or anything else white on a tree limb or drape it over your car, or get it into a conspicuous place somehow. This is so that your location can be pinpointed from the ground with field glasses or from the air. All commercial and military planes are equipped with radio gear and they can report your signals and position immediately if they can spot you. When this is done, emergency procedures go into effect and you'll have the Civil Air Patrol, rangers, sheriff's officers, or the highway patrol looking for you in a jiffy. This requires that once you have began issuing distress signals in any form or manner, you also keep vigilant and altert for help so that you can signal them further to help locate you.

SPOTLIGHTS

A flashlight or spotlight is a valuable aid at night. You can signal airplanes, automobiles, and people around distant lights. I carry a flashlight for handy portable use and, under the driver's seat in my car is a spotlight with a long cord that plugs into the cigar lighter. It is a sealed-beam affair and in a pinch I could use it to shoot a beam directly at any planes in sight at night and also give the intermittent 3-blinks. By the same token, I can use it for signalling on the ground and the light is powerful enough so that it can be seen for miles and miles. In fact, in Mexico we used it to signal 17 miles across a valley and the light could be seen clearly and distinctly.

MIRRORS

If you live in a town or city that has a department store, or other shop, that stocks Boy Scout supplies, you can probably get them to get you one of the signal mirrors that was packed in rescue kits during the late war. Thousands of these mirrors were sold, later, thru surplus stores and in camping equipment stores. The mirror works on a geometric theory that enables you to reflect sunlight at an object on the ground or in the sky. Positive aiming is assured by a sighting principle and the reflected sun rays can be seen for miles. There is nothing to wear out, so you can use one of them at night with your auto headlights by standing in front of the car with the lights on and aiming it at possible rescuers miles above, beside, or behind your car. These gimmicks did cost 65¢ and they are worth their weight in gold when you need them.

STUPID

When you get off the beaten path with your automobile, don't be stupid!!! If there is the slightest doubt that your old hootenanny won't get through, you'd better think twice. Don't let all this modern advertising mislead you with respect to what your car will do. All of this horsepower they try to sell us is 90% baloney. Let's look at it this way. An old Model-T Ford had something like 17 horsepower and would go 50 miles per hour, and this was over the old dust and gravel roads. Now we have cars that crowd 300 and 400 horsepower and they have one hell of a time going 125 miles per hour over these glass-smooth roads. Twenty times the horsepower to go 2½ times as fast; now just who do you think is trying to kid who.

These oil and gas eating monsters we fork out a couple thousand bucks for today are built for city and highway driving, and they just don't work so well on dirt. My 1958 Chevrolet rides like a cloud on the highway and it is a pleasure to drive on paved roads, but it has its disadvantages. It has burned a quart of oil per tank of gasoline since the day it was new and it has caused me no end of mechanical trouble. The Chevrolet company went through the motions of trying to fix it but once the dealer gets your money you have a fight on your hands getting any service, so it continues to drink its ration of oil and I continue to complain to everybody about it. It leaked from one end to the other (water, oil, grease, and gasoline) when it was new and I had to threaten to drive it through the dealer's show room window to get the company to do anything. They kept the junker in the shop a week and managed to replace the oil seals in both rear wheels in that time.

This isn't to complain about Chevrolet, but to point out some disadvantages of modern cars in the backwood. First of all, they are built so low that rocks and stumps can easily tear the pan off of the engine. They stick out so far in front and back that the slightest gully or ridge can hang you up so you need help to get out or off. These new tubeless tires are a nightmare in rocky areas as they'll blow out in a jiffy from the pounding they take from the rocks and bumps in the road. These automatic transmissions can be literally cooked from the overloads and resultant heat that comes from the repeated and constant changes of loads and speed which is required in the backwoods. Finally, all of these windows and glass in the late cars is wonderful for sightseeing, but it can make your car feel like a furnace on the desert in the summertime.

These new cars are wonderful in the city and on the highways, but you'd better think twice and know what you are doing when you start cross country in one of them.

Speaking of cars from a safety point of view; the American cars are for the birds as far as I am concerned, and this includes the so-called compacts. A year ago I was stalled at night clear out in the center of creation in this new-fangled rear engine compact that Detroit so thoughtfully birthed to pester mankind. We danged near froze that night near Greys Well, California and not a single car came along the highway. Along about daylight we got it fired up and got the dealer in the next town out of bed to fix it. Nothing wrong with it except a lousy engineering job, and the mechanic so told us.

I am mighty fond of any of the small foreign cars for desert and mountain travel because they are built better than the American cars, for my money, and they stand up while their American brothers are foundering.

All of this should have been in Chapter XII (transportation) but this matter of reliable transportation is ofen a matter of life and death and I have taken the liberty of pointing out some of the facts and fallacies relative to automobiles.

BEES

Ever so often, you may run down a treasure that is located in the walls of an old house and find that the walls are infested with bees. Or, you may have a swarm surround you in some of the old ghost towns or just about anywhere. A word to the wise is sufficient: bees don't like smoke, so build yourself a camp fire while working under these conditions or else have a couple kerosene-soaked torches ready to fire up with your cigarette lighter if you work around bees. Your best bet, actually, is to get a bee-smoker and quiet them before working around them. At the very least, bee stings are painful and they can be fatal if they really clobber you.

THINK

Be a coward!!! Don't take unnecessary chances. Use that big fat noodle on your shoulders to keep you out of trouble and difficulty. Think!!! You rarely hear of the old desert rats getting into trouble and this is because they know the consequences and avoid unnecessary risks.

I like to work with and be around these old characters and I always get the impression that they slowly get things done fast. In other words, they methodically putter around and get a day's work done. You never see them flirting with danger because, you see, they carry too many scars to remind them of reckless bygone days.

LET LIVE

If you must live dangerously, do it so that you endanger only yourself. Don't ever be responsible for injury or death to others because of foolish conduct. Don't ever forget that you can so easily cause hardship for others by irresponsible conduct. Unfortunately, the idiots who bring disaster to themselves do not suffer alone. So often others are injured with them and it always requires the services of other people to rescue the unfortunate fools who manage to get into the most distressing circumstances in the damnedest places.

Always think twice and use your old noggin so that you can be one of those that feels sorry for the victim, instead of being the victim.

Chapter XXIV

Legends and Myths

The dictionary tells us that a legend is a story which has been handed down from the past and is not necessarily verifiable. A myth is also a story which has been handed down from the past, usually to explain or support a belief, a rule, a practice, or a phenomenom. Essentially, as we accept them today, a legend is questionable fact, while myth is logical fiction.

History is sprinkled with both, and this is especially true of American history. The Walzers, Crocketts, Fremonts, Cody's, Earps, and many of the other well known American heroes are covered with legends and myths. Even in the lives of the great and famous General Fremont and Col. Buffalo Bill Cody, there has been so much poppycock and fiction written into their lives by themselves and others that it is almost ridiculous to read and believe anything about them.

My pet peeve is the Lost Dutchman Mine. For many years, I have said and I still say that there never was a genuine Lost Dutchman Mine as it is associated with the Old Dutchman. I say the Lost Dutchman Mine is a myth, and I say the Old Dutchman (Walzer) is a legend. There is no question that he lived and that he intentionally contrived many tales to divert his greedy acquaintances from his way. This, we know. But, over the years, writers and yarnspinners have created the fantastic Lost Dutchman Mine yarn and, although disproved, it continues to lure thousands of greenhorn treasure hunters to the Superstitions every year. Television has even done its part to publicize the hoax and dupe the public into accepting it as gospel. I personally resent the perpetuation of these kinds of stories because of the great number of inexperienced adventurers who come from all parts of the country and seek to find the LDM. Many of these get lost, snakebitten, and suffer unnecessary hardship in pursuit of this myth, and they never learn.

There are hundreds upon hundreds of these questionable treasures and lost mines today and nobody knows how many million words have been written about them and how many billions of words have been spoken in gabfests among adventurers. Neither does anybody know how many millions of dollars and hundreds of thousands of hours of wasted time has gone into the pursuit of these questionable Eldorados. I am familiar with several hundred wasted, dangerous, and misguided trips of many greenhorns and others in the pursuit of these fictional bonanzas and I really and truly feel sorry for anybody who embarks on these speculative treasure hunts without first determining beyond a shadow of a doubt that the treasure actually does exist.

For many years, I have maintained that with very few exceptions there has never been such a thing as a lost mine, and I am

Vallecito Treasure Myth. Karl von Mueller and Hardrock Bill Hammond loiter before Vallecito monument. Fictional article brought hundreds of men here to seek non-existent treasure.

just as much convinced today that there is no such critter as I was back in the early and mid 1930s. It is positively preposterous to believe that such a thing as a full blown mine can be lost. Yet, my contempt for lost mine hunters is tempered by the fact that a few old, experienced prospectors and miners have spent years in search of certain old lost mines.

I look at it this way. To begin with, I can not conceive of anybody going to all of the time, trouble, and tremendous effort to dig a mine shaft or tunnel and then, for some of the ridiculous reasons given in these stories, lose its location in the twinkle of an eye. I have done a little bit of mining and I know so well the amount of work and the time in running a 40-foot tunnel with the help of explosives and modern tools. I know damned well that I could find my way back to any of the mines I have worked in or around and I have been gone from some of them for 10 years or more.

Next, these old characters who allegedly lost all of these mines, you can be sure, were far more experienced and informed about geology, botany, astronomy, and the other sciences than we are today. In fact, I maintain that all of us city dudes today are little more than educated idiots. Yes, we know how to read, write, drive cars, find our way to the next town by following the highway, mix lousy belly-scorching whisky with flavors to kill the taste, and so many of us know how to break every one of the Ten Commandments without losing a wink of sleep. But, just how many of the 180,000,000 residents of the United States today could survive for two weeks without our civilized conveniences? I have seen several of my sophisticated city brethren get deathly sick and wretch from merely watching the slaughter, butchering, and cooking of a deer in a mining camp. Now, just how in the hell are guys of this caliber going to find a mine which was lost by some old prospector or miner who really knew how to live, how to read 'sign', and always managed to get 'there' and then get 'back'. You can believe this stuff; but it's not for me!

Finally, the clincher is that so many articles and stories have been written and published telling exactly where certain lost mines are located, yet of the thousands of fellows who go in search of them not a one of them is successful. This means something. Too, the writers who invariably pinpoint the location of these lost mines and treasure are the writers who have neither the proverbial pot or window to throw it out of.

I have no argument with a writer or anybody else making an honest buck, but I do resent anybody who generates these fictional versions of history and causes untold expense and hardship to the suckers who read and believe it, and I most certainly despise the editors of many adventure type magazines who insist that articles be jazzed up to give the reader something to talk about. I do not write for any of the magazines anymore, nor do I subscribe to the hogwash they publish as the 'Real McCoy'.

In any event, the serious amateur treasure hunter will do well to stay completely away from any of the fabulous treasures which are published in any of our present national magazines. To begin with, the odds are more than even that the story is more than 50% fiction. Then, you may be sure that thousands of greenhorns have already read the article and are already planning to make their own search for the treasure, and many will be there before you get there. And, finally, in 999 cases out of 1,000 you'll be wasting your time because you won't find anything anyway. I have always maintained that if a bona fide treasure exists and if a writer can garner enough information to make an interesting story, he should be bright enough to find the treasure. Treasure hunting most certainly is not so difficult that given the facts a person can't tie up the loose ends and make the discovery and recovery himself. It's done everyday by men who often have less than a high school education, so why can't the men who have suffered through high school and college do it.

I have said before and I'll say again that legends and myths make good reading, exciting stories, and are often wonderful entertainment, but they have no place in the successful pursuit of buried treasure. Read and listen to them only for the entertainment they provide and don't believe a word of them and you'll save yourself a lot of time, money, grief, and hardship.

Chapter XXV

Gold Isn't Everything

Looking back over my little more than 30 years of treasure hunting, and drawing on the experiences of several of my associates and friends, and then just sensibly trying to stack the odds in my favor whenever legally and morally possible, I am inclined to believe that the following few paragraphs might be the most important part of this book insofar as financial success is involved.

As I have stated or implied at various points in this book and, I believe, in all of my lectures, there is no question in my mind that there is enough buried and lost treasure remaining as such in the United States to make every person who will read this book a very wealthy person. Treasure hunting is an adventuresome, healthful, profitable avocation or full-time activity. Whoever you are, wherever you live, or whatever you do, opportunities in treasure hunting are all around you.

Treasure hunting is an extremely profitable and successsful activity for a few hundred men that I know of, and, at the same time, others who are just as diligent, intelligent, and resourceful have only medocre success. I can not explain this away as plain luck, because I have an almost parallel situation with respect to hunting and fishing. Literally, all I have to do when hunting is load the gun and shoot and I get my game. On the other hand, I could drop a grappling hook into a tankful of big fish and never catch a one of them.

RESEARCH PAYS

Most of the unsuccessful treasure hunting activities that I am familiar with are a direct result of improper application. In other words, fellows have gone after known treasures in good faith, but they have failed to exhaust the sources of information that are available to them or, in so many cases, they have failed to exercise common sense. Usually the amateur or inexperienced treasure hunter tries to do everything the hard way or the impossible way.

To many adventurers and would-be adventurers, there is no other treasure than *gold*. Many writers have written millions of words about cargoes of gold on the floors of the oceans, and in the bottoms of rivers, and on the beaches of a hundred countries. Yes, to many people, there is no treasure but gold. Yet, as I have shown throughout this book, there are many treasures other than gold and I have carefully avoided mention of many of them so that you, the reader, can get your think-tank into operation and start thinking for yourself.

ODDS

This chapter is to show you that gold isn't everything and its fundamental premise is to help you compound your opportunities; to help you get several irons in the fire; and, more especially, get the odds of financial success as much as possible in your favor. If you want to be a really successful treasure hunter and count your dollars only from the treasure you will recover, then read no further. I have already given you all the tools you need to assure success, and more.

I like to make every trip a profitable one and I most certainly enjoy the possibility that each trip, in addition to resulting in a treasure discovery, will also lead me to one of natures' treasures. By this I mean a mineral deposit with commercial possibilities. In other words, I try to make every treasure trip a prospecting or business trip, too, and I look forward to the success or failure of these activities with almost the same fervor and anticipation as I do toward a treasure recovery.

LEARNING THE HARD WAY

In the years gone by, I prepared myself for the role of at least a mediocre prospector by investing my time in learning about minerals, deposits, and the whole world of geology. Believe me, I did not learn it all and in the beginning it was a mighty dry study. Members of many gem and mineral clubs throughout the west will recall me as being a member of their club or a periodic guest at their meetings. The more rockhounds and prospectors that I met and the more I learned about mineralogy and prospecting, the more intriguing it became. So, when the farcial uranium craze came along, I was in the uranium rush up to my neck. Then I got into the gem material prospecting business, and then into gold, tungsten, and the rare earths.

BOOKS

How does this affect you? You can do the same thing! And, it doesn't need to cost you a fortune either. For example, Dr.

H. C. Dake has written or published a small library of good low-cost books on just about every phase of gem cutting, mineralogy, and prospecting. These books average about $2 each and you find them on many newsstands or if you write to the *Mineralogist Magazine, Portland, Oregon*, they will probably send you a catalog. Get a copy of the *Handbook for Prospectors* by von Bernowitz. The book price is $7.50, or maybe more now, but it's worth every cent of the cost as it covers just about every phase of prospecting and mining and it does it in simple language. You may find all of these in your local library, and many more.

Learn a little about geology, join a local or nearby gem, mineral, prospecting or geology club, if possible, and learn how and why some of the little holes you see in the desert have coughed up millions of dollars in wealth.

Write the *Bureau of Mines, Department of Interior, Washington 25 D. C.* and get on their mailing list for their publications. Get their catalog and pick out a few low cost publications.

One of the best sources for mining and prospecting information is the *California Division of Mines, Ferry Building, San Francisco, California*. You can write them and ask for a catalog of their publications. I do not believe that there is another State bureau or Federal bureau that has publications that will compare with those of the California division. They are not only comprehensive and clearly written, but their illustrations are clear, precise, and informative.

Prospecting is an interesting avocation. It can lead to perpetual riches in the form of rich strikes and subsequent valuable mining properties. Hundreds of Sunday prospectors (employed people who get out only on weekends) have struck it rich and thereafter been relieved from the shackles of the timeclock. You can do it, too. It doesn't necessarily take a lot of money to prospect. You can equip yourself with all of the ridiculous modern camping equipment and go out and *suffer* the life of Riley, or you can go out and rough it and really get to enjoying the kind of life that gives more than it takes. It is up to you.

Naturally, you can not prospect all over the United States. If you find a deposit on private land, you have to work out an arrangement with the property owner, and you are usually at his mercy. So, most prospectors do their prospecting on public lands, stake their claims, and take a sensible coarse from there depending on what the requirements might be.

SPECIALIZE

Start out by specializing in one mineral such as gold, cobalt, tungsten, copper, or a gem material. Learn all there is to know about that mineral and prospect for it in its most likely geological location. As you read, study, discuss, and prospect, you will learn more and more about all of the other minerals. This progress

Checking the Pannings. Karl von Mueller, Hardrock Hammond, and Erle Larson check some pannings for color. Here a treasure hunt became a mining operation on a small scale.

takes time but it is interesting. If you can associate with others who already have the know-how, such as lapidarists (gem polishers), mineralogists, or even professional prospectors, your education will be expedited and you will find that you learn fast.

As you slowly emerge as a semi-experienced prospector, you will find that new vistas open up to you. Even a new life. Overnight wealth is not uncommon. If and when you find a rich deposit, it is like money in the bank. Just for example, on the California desert five of us in a little group located and developed a gold mine in a sedimentary deposit. When we worked down to $40 dirt (this means $40 worth of gold per ton of dirt), we closed the mine up and have for years maintained the property, but we have not taken out any more of the mineral than the law required. Now, essentially, if any one or all of us went completely broke, we could go down to a store and buy a shovel and wheelbarrow and start working the deposit. With a little work, it would not be difficult to recover $100 worth of gold each day for each two men and that isn't bad pickings for anybody. As it is, none of us are hard up or in need of money, so the property remains as it was and we are not taxed for the raw gold that lies there.

So, I recommend to you that you learn something about minerals and prospecting to augment the apportunities and success of treasure hunting. Learn about gem materials and file claims on potential deposits. Fifty-cents isn't an unreasonable price for rough gem material, in fact it is cheap, yet that means $1,000 per ton. Some domestic (American) gem materials such as jade are priced at $35 to $100 per POUND; and this means that you can realize as much as $200,000 per ton for this material. Of course, the odds are extremely great that you will not find this kind of a deposit, BUT IT HAS BEEN DONE — and by completely inexperienced people.

RARE EARTHS

The rare earths are the rage now and if you find a good deposit, your worries are over. Any one of a thousand of the industrial and mining giants will take over your properties with rare earths and pay you royalties or other settlements for many of the so-called rare earths.

FRINGE ACTIVITIES

Then, if you are left cold by the very thought of prospecting, you can give some thought to any of the hundreds of activities that are in some way or another associated with treasure hunting. Maybe you would like to operate an antique shop along one of the highways or byways. Or open an old gunshop and deal in old guns. Or establish a coin dealership and deal in old (and new) money. Or, if you have a flair for writing, maybe you would like to write true stories about your experiences while treasure hunting or prospecting as I do. I no longer write adventure articles, but I still receive more requests for articles than I could possibly write in the time allowed. There are many opportunities and all you have to do is recognize them and then get going. For many people, it takes a lot of nerve, or plain guts, to embark on any new activity. This is not unusual. Go ahead!!! But, before you embark, study the situation, make sensible plans, and then don't get discouraged but be ready for disappointment. Play a heads-up game all of the time, and play it fair.

I have had a good many people tell me that they would not go out on some of the ridiculous trips that I do — No, not at any cost. I know that some of these trips have been considered asinine; but I always came back alive. Some people think that I have been unusually brave. This is not the case at all. I have never embarked on a trip or project without carefully planning every phase of it and knowing BEFOREHAND exactly what I should do in case of trouble or an emergency. If it is in the back country, I get quadrangle maps and topography maps of the entire area and memorize them. I plot my coarse and I'm not a bit bashful about using a compass to know for sure which way I am going.

Since I am associated with several prospecting and mining groups, it is often necessary for me to determine just how far we will go in pursuit of a project. In 9 out of 10 projects, I can tell you precisely and exactly how far we will go, how much money we will spend, and at what point we will give up a project as a failure. I am not a pessimist, nor am I in any way pessimistic, but I use common sense to tell me and my associates when we have reached the end of the line.

PLAN

So, before you embark on a treasure project or a business activity, do some doggoned good research and know which way you are going. Determine just how far you can go before you start hurting your pocketbook or your pride. If you want to go into some associated business, let me tell you that it takes capital to start a business, so unless you are loaded with $$$, why not start out as a part-time businessman? Be an evening and weekend merchant! If you locate a good gemstone deposit, you can sell most of the stuff by mail-order by advertising in the gem and mineral magazines such as the *Mineralogist, Gems and Minerals, Earth Science Digest, Lapidary Journal,* and *Rocks and Minerals.* You can handle mail orders in your spare time and at your leisure.

Anyway, plan ahead and don't go overboard in anticipation of immediate success because it just won't happen that way. It will be a long pull for you.

PROSPECTING

Prospecting and treasure hunting go hand in hand throughout the Rocky Mountain Empire and on west to the Pacific. In these areas, you can make your treasure hunting projects double-barrelled affairs when you can prospect along the way. You may find a bonanza, and never locate a dimes worth of treasure, and this is essentially what you were looking for to begin with.

In fact, a fellow, that I hardly know and yet we have been carrying on a correspondence for several years, got the treasure bug something awful a few years back and he actually haunted the mountains behind Colorado Springs for a long time on his weekends and vacations. In a letter to me dated July 22, 1960 he informed me that he'd at last made the grade. He had ACCIDENTALLY struck a mineral deposit while digging for a treasure cache and from this deposit he had already sold enough ore to exceed a years earnings on his regular job. So, if this fellow pursues his mining project frugally and sensibly, he will amass a good deal of wealth and then start enjoying a Cadillac, big house, servants, and all the trimmings. If he spends it as fast as he gets it, he'll be back looking for a job one of these days because it takes money to expand a mining operation and if you don't have money, you either share your mine with investors or fold up.

SAVE

The following remarks will fall on deaf ears, but I will make them anyway. When you do make a strike. GET OUT OF DEBT!! Then, make the most important part of your plans in all cases that part where you lay back (or save) a certain percentage or amount of all gain for that rainy day. *Money attracts money* and don't you ever forget it!!! You will find that almost invariably when you start 'hitting', one success will pile up on top of others. It is like turning the 'money faucet' on and not being able to turn it off. If the lightning of luck should so strike

Looking for a Drift. von Mueller, Hammond, and Larson check the face of a tunnel driven 400 feet beyond a high-graders' cache in search of a rich drift. Note jackhammer, electric lights, and ventilating duct which are necessary for tunnelling.

you, give a little thought to the less fortunate and the underdog. Give as much as you can to charity!

SALVATION ARMY

I want to tell you something. I am not a member of the Salvation Army and I do not know if I am qualified to be a member, but I'll tell you that I'd be doggoned proud to be a member. I have no axe to grind with any other charitable organizations, although it seems to me that some of them spend more money hiring talent, TV time, and beggars than they take in. But, I am partial to the Salvation Army.

I'll tell you why. I have heard so many off-center stories about different service organizations durings World War I. Same for World War II, and the Korean crises. I've read so much in the newspapers about all of them, but I have seen with my own eyes that it is ALWAYS the Salvation Army that is first to the disaster areas with their proverbial coffee and donuts — and every possible other service that really counts at the moment. In one instance, during one of the horrible Malibu fires I saw a fireman break down and weep when he told of the wonderful service and kindness of the Salvation Army.

So, if your sympathies are in accord with mine, should fate deal you a winning hand, share some of it with the Salvation Army first and then if there is some left over to give, spread it around to other organizations. As they say, the fickle finger of fate is funny, and it is a lot easier to go down the ladder of success than up, so if you get to the top and then backslide, the Salvation Army will reach out a helping hand when you need it and you won't have to sign any mortgages on your soul or your few remaining possessions to get this well-meant and sincere help.

FINALLY

I have tried to invest every facit of know-how and information needed to successfully seek and find buried treasure. Most of this information is just simple, plain, everyday reading. Some of it is conceailled in the text and context of these pages. It is neither impossible nor difficult for any rational person to glean the entire 'message' in this book. It will take some study and the more you study these chapters the more you will gain from them. Without any study at all, you will still have the basic fundamentals of successful treasure hunting, but the rereading and contemplation of statements I have made herein will train you to seek facts, clues, and figures, and this you will need to do to become a really successful fulltime treasure hunter.

WELCOME

If our trails ever cross, step over to my camp and introduce yourself. Whether you're a millionaire or a bum, the latchstring at my camp is always out to every squareshooter who isn't running away from his conscience. If I have written something herein that rubs you the wrong way, forgive me! I have merely exercised the liberty of highgrading the float as I saw it. Many of my ideas and philosophies have been expressed or implied herein, and I subscribe to them.

Good Luck to You!! With all of these billions of dollars worth of treasure waiting for the alert, the adventurous, the ambitious, and the deserving, I hope that each of you readers will find more than I have and Lord only knows that I have carted home my share over these years.

Keep your hocks clean, and enjoy life. It's a short, miserable one, at best.

Examino,

KvonM

Appendix A

State Historical Societies

This is a complete list of the main historical societies for each state. Where more than one organization is listed, I have placed an asterisk (*) before the name of the principal society or the public-supported society. Many counties, cities, professional groups, and fraternal groups have their individual and independent societies in practically all states and some of these are large organizations. For example, the Daughters of the Utah Pioneers is a large organization and they maintain a large and beautiful museum and archives at the head of Main Street in Salt Lake City, Utah. Another good example is the Sons of the Golden West in San Francisco.

Not all of these societies are membership affairs since a few of them are operated and maintained by the respective state. In this case, the help you can get is usually limited and the personnel are sometimes mighty independent. My 'beat' has always been the 22 states west of the Mississippi River and I have belonged to almost all of these societies under one or another of my pen-names. The most cooperative, by far, have been the Nebraska and Utah societies and a bare shade behind them has been the Kansas and Missouri societies. From my point of view, the Arizona Department of Archives and Library (or vice versa) has been the least cooperative and this is difficult to understand as the people of Arizona are really big and friendly and the ARIZONA HIGHWAYS Magazine, to me, is the most informative and helpful magazine of its kind anywhere.

If you are interested in treasure hunting in your own state or any other state, I urge you to join the state historical society and become active in its activities and read its publications religiously. Membership usually costs from $2 to $5 per year (which is deductible as an expense) and for this you get the various publications of the society.

Practically all of the state societies publish quarterly magazines which are easily filed and often helpful. The Montana society publishes a magazine which is outstanding and this magazine is included in the membership fee. In fact, just for the publications you receive, I urge anybody interested in treasure hunting to join the Montana, Nebraska, and Utah societies just for the publications, if for nothing else. The publications of all three societies often cover other areas and you get leads regularly from these historical articles. Publications are listed for each society.

ALABAMA Historical Assn., 3121 Carlisle Rd., Birmingham 35213.
Alabama Review
ALASKA State Museum, 10 Whittier St., Pouch FM, Juneau 99801.
ARIZONA State Dept. of Library, Archives & Public Records, 3rd Floor, State Capitol, Phoenix 85007.
ARKANSAS Historical Assn., Dept. of History, Univ. of Ark., Fayetteville 72701.
Arkansas Historical Quarterly
CALIFORNIA Historical Society, 2090 Jackson St., San Francisco 94109.
California Historical Quarterly
COLORADO State Historical Society, 200 - 14th Ave., Denver 80203.
Colorado Magazine (The)
CONNECTICUT Historical Society, 1 Elizabeth St., Hartford 06105.
DELAWARE Historical Society, 505 Market St., Wilmington 19801.
Delaware History
FLORIDA Historical Society, Univ. of So. Florida Library, Tampa 33620.
Florida Historical Quarterly
GEORGIA Historical Society, 501 Whitaker St., Savannah 31401.
Georgia Historical Quarterly
HAWAII Historical Society, 560 Kawaiahao St., Honolulu 96813.
IDAHO State Historical Society, 610 N. Julia Davis Dr., Boise 83706.
Idaho Yesterdays
ILLINOIS State Historical Society, Old State Capitol, Springfield 62706.
Journal of the Illinois State Historical Society

INDIANA Historical Society, 140 N. Senate Ave., Indianapolis 46204.
> *Indiana Magazine of History*

IOWA State Historical Society, 402 Iowa Ave., Iowa City 52240.
> *The Palimpsest*

KANSAS State Historical Society, Memorial Bldg., 120 W. 10th, Topeka 66612.
> *Kansas Historical Quarterly*

KENTUCKY Historical Society, Broadway, Frankfort 40601.
> *The Register; Kentucky Ancestors*

LOUISIANA Historical Assn., 1515 Choctaw, Baton Rouge 70804.
> *Louisiana History*

MAINE Historical Society, 485 Congress St., Portland 04111.
> *Maine Historical Society Quarterly*

MARYLAND Historical Society, 201 W. Monument St., Baltimore 21201.
> *Maryland Historical Magazine*

MASSACHUSETTS Historical Society, 1154 Boylston St., Boston 02215.
> *Proceedings of the Massachusetts Historical Society*

MICHIGAN Historical Society, 2117 Washtenaw Ave., Ann Arbor 48104.
> *Chronicle*

MINNESOTA Historical Society, 690 Cedar St., St. Paul 55101.
> *Minnesota History*

MISSISSIPPI Historical Society, Box 571, Jackson 39205.
> *Journal of Mississippi History*

MISSOURI State Historical Society of Missouri, Hitt & Lowry Sts., Columbia 65201.
> *Missouri Historical Review*

NEBRASKA State Historical Society, 1500 R St., Lincoln 68508.
> *Nebraska History*

NEVADA State Historical Society, 1650 N. Virginia St., Reno 89503.
> *Nevada State Historical Society Quarterly*

NEW HAMPSHIRE Historical Society, 30 Park St., Concord 03301.
> *Historical New Hampshire*

NEW JERSEY Historical Society, 230 Broadway, Newark 07104.
New Jersey History
NEW MEXICO Historical Services Division, State Records Center Archives, 404 Montezuma St., Santa Fe 87501.
NEW YORK State Historical Assn., Lake Road, Cooperstown 13326.
New York History Quarterly
NORTH CAROLINA Literary & Historical Assn., 109 E. Jones St., Raleigh 27611.
NORTH DAKOTA State Historical Society, Liberty Memorial Bldg., Bismarck 58501.
North Dakota History
OHIO Historical Society, 1 71 and 17th Ave., Columbus 43211.
Ohio History
OKLAHOMA Historical Society, 2100 N. Lincoln Blvd., Historical Bldg., Oklahoma City 73105.
Chronicles of Oklahoma (The)
OREGON Historical Society, 1230 SW Park Ave., Portland 97205.
Oregon Historical Quarterly
PENNSYLVANIA Historical Assn., 806 New Liberal Arts Bldg., University Park 16802.
Pennsylvania History
RHODE ISLAND Historical Society, 52 Power St., Providence 02906.
Rhode Island History
SOUTH CAROLINA Historical Society, 100 Meeting St., Fireproof Bldg., Charleston 29401.
South Carolina Historical Magazine (The)
SOUTH DAKOTA State Historical Society, Memorial Bldg., E. Capitol Avenue, Pierre 57501.
South Dakota History
TENNESSEE Historical Commission, 403 — 7th Ave. N., Nashville 37219.
TEXAS State Historical Assn., Sid Richarson Hall 2/306, Univ. Sta., Austin 78712.
Southwestern Historical Quarterly
UTAH State Historical Society, 603 E. South Temple, Salt Lake City 84102.
Utah Historical Quarterly
VERMONT Historical Society, State St., Montpelier 05602.
Vermont History

VIRGINIA Historical Society, 428 North Blvd., Richmond 23220.
: *Virginia Magazine of History & Biography*
WASHINGTON State Historical Society, 315 N. Stadium Way, Tacoma 98403.
: *Pacific Northwest Quarterly*
WEST VIRGINA Historical Society, 400 E. Wing, State Capitol, Charleston 25305.
WISCONSIN State Historical Society, 816 State St., Madison 53706.
: *Wisconsin Magazine of History*
WYOMING State Archives & History Dept., State Office Bldg., Cheyenne 82001.
: *Annals of Wyoming*

A DIRECTORY OF HISTORICAL SOCIETIES & AGENCIES IN THE UNITED STATES AND CANADA is available from the American Association for State and Local history, 1400 - 8th Avenue, South, Nashville, Tennessee 37203. The DIRECTORY is revised and up-dated periodically and has been a standard reference for over 25 years.

Appendix B

Slumbering Cities and Ghost Burgs

When you really get the treasure hunting fever, you'll devote more time and effort to the activity and you'll find that your efficiency will constantly improve. Sooner or later, you'll follow a lead to a town that is not on the map or one that is in ruins.

If your reaction is the customary one, you'll probably have a feeling of idling in a cemetery and, after a quick curiosity gander, will be on your way and glad of it. However, the more of these old towns you visit, the more they will grow on you and you'll find that eventually it will be difficult to tear yourself away. So should it be!

Be kind to these old towns!!! Don't tear them up, deface the buildings, or otherwise destroy or damage them. Don't start fires in the buildings, or near them. Leave them as you found them. Contrary to all the baloney that has appeared in so many stories, very little treasure is found in the old buildings or even within the limits of the town. The big depositories were in gullys, valleys, caves, and other man-made or natural structures away from the town. REMEMBER THIS!!! Regardless of what anybody tells you, the real old professionals who spend all of their working time looking for buried or lost wealth will support me when I say that very little treasure is found in old ghost towns.

The following list of ghost towns covers those located in the twenty-two states west of the Mississippi River, and this list contains *Only A Few Of The Many, Many Towns In These States.* There are thousands more of them, but it is impossible to list them all and give directions to them in the space allocated for this list. Too, I have tried to list only those towns which I have visited or which I have definite knowledge. In almost every instance, if it is listed, I can say I've been there. Some of the directions may be obsolete due to new roads and destruction of the old roads by storms or the elements. Otherwise, the directions are 'on the money'.

ARIZONA

Arizona is literally 'lousy' with ghost towns. In fact, it is almost impossible to cross the state in any direction without passing near several of them. Most of these old towns and sites have exciting histories. Some of them are inhabited part of the year by sheepherders, cowboys, or prospectors. If you meet any natives, you'll find them charming and wonderful.

AUSTERLITZ, Arizona: Located about 7 miles south of Arivaca, or 30 miles west of Nogales. Once a booming, wild border mining camp; now in ruins.

BLUEBELL, Arizona: Located 4 miles off of Hiway 69 south of Prescott. Ruins of the old Bluebell Mine and tramway are visible. Nearby copper and silver smeltery is in ruins. A few residents remain.

BRADSHAW CITY, Arizona: Located south of Prescott on the side of Mt. Wasson in the Bradshaw Mountains. Once a city of 5,000; now a ghost. Ruins of the Crown King mine are nearby.

CALABASAS, Arizona: Located off Hiway 89 and just 6 miles from Nogales. A town with a truly fabulous history. Deposits were discovered and worked as early as 1770s by Spaniards, then Mexicans and Indians. During Civil War it blossomed into a riotous town. Ruins throughout the area and old Fort Mason ruins are nearby.

CERRO COLORADO, Arizona: Located about 60 miles southwest of Tucson, or 30 miles northwest of Nogales. This internationally famous town was headquarters for the equally famous Heintzelman Mine interests and was once known by that name.

CHARLESTON, Arizona: Located 8 miles southwest of Tombstone, or 4 miles south of Fairbank, on the bank of the San Pedro river. Ruins remain of buildings and the famous old Tombstone Mining and Milling Company stamp mills.

CHLORIDE, Arizona: Located 20 miles northwest of Kingman on Hiway 93-466, and then about 4 miles northeast on Hiway 62. Buildings remain, old mines, and diggings.

CONGRESS, Arizona: Located a short distance from the junction of Hiways 71 & 89, 16 miles north of Wickenburg. Ruins of the old Congress Mine, the camp, and lots of diggings remain.

CONTENTION CITY, Arizona: Located about 2 miles north of Hiway 82 and about 5 miles from Tombstone. A few diggings remain and the ruins of the Contention Mine mill. Inquire at Tombstone or Fairbanks.

DOS CABEZAS, Arizona: Located near State Hiway 186 about 10 miles southeast of Willcox. A mountain slope sprinkled with old ruins.

DUSQUESNE, Arizona: Located about 19 miles east of Nogales on the Bisbee-Nogales border road. Once a riotous city of sin with more than 1,000 permanent citizens. Now ruins and shells of buildings remain.

EHRENBERG, Arizona: Located just south of Hiway 60-70 on the Colorado river. Once a supply center and river port; now adobe ruins.

GALEYVILLE, Arizona: Located about 5 miles south of Paradise and often called Rustler's Park and shown as such on some maps. Several unsuccessful mining operations established the town and it later became the headquarters for rustling activities for such outlaws as Ringo, Snow, and Brocius. Many historic ruins in the immediate area.

GILA CITY, Arizona: Located about 25 miles east of Yuma on the Gila river. Once a booming town of over 1,000 people who worked the rich placer deposits. Now a few footings and traces of the placers remain.

HEINTZELMAN MINE, Arizona: See CERRO, COLORADO.

JEROME, Arizona: Located on Hiway 89 between Flagstaff and Prescott. Perched precariously on the side of a mountain. Less than 100 residents remain to keep alive this former boom city of 15,000 souls. Homes, stores, hospital, and other facilities stand idle and falling into ruins.

JOHNSON, Arizona: Located north of Hiway 666 between Benson and Willcox. Ask for directions in either city. Lots of ruins.

KOFA, Arizona: Located about 17 miles east of Hiway 95. Turn off Hiway 95 is about 25 miles south of Quartzite. Camp is in ruins. Buildings and tramways of famous King of Arizona mine are well preserved.

LA PAZ, Arizona: Located on the Colorado river 10 miles north of Ehrenberg. Once had a population of over 5,000 and was considered as site for capitol of the West. Now in ruins.

LOS GUIJAS, Arizona: Located about 65 miles southwest of Tucson, or 7 miles west of Cerro Colorado on old road. Famous Feernstrom Mill ruins are visible. Once a booming border mining town; now reduced to ruins.

MAMMOTH, Arizona: Located on Hiway 77 about 44 miles northeast of Tucson. Town was named after famous Mammoth mine. Town is still populated, but many adobe ruins are evident and other ghost camps are nearby.

McMillanville, Arizona: Located 15 miles northeast of Globe on Hiway 60-77 and 1 mile northwest of hiway. A wild, rich silver camp. Ruins of many buildings and the mill remain.

Mowry, Arizona: Located about 18 miles south of Patagonia on the old trail road. A rich silver and lead mining center. Many ruins remain. WASHINGTON CAMP is 4 miles south of here.

Oatman, Arizona: Located about 17 miles north of Topock (Hiway 66 on the Colorado river) on old Hiway 66 road. Mines closed 1942. A few residents and many ruins.

Paradise, Arizona: Located about 35 miles south of the San Simon-Hiway 86 junction, or 15 miles northwest of Rodeo, New Mexico (Hiway 80). Town was established to supply unsuccessful mining operations and was taken over by outlaws and rustlers. Several dilapidated buildings and a few residents remain to keep the town alive.

Pearce, Arizona: Located off Hiways 181-666 about 50 miles northwest of Douglas. During the 1880's and 90's a booming gold and silver town that produced upward of $30,000,000 in gold alone. Headquarters of the Alvord-Stiles and other gangs.

Planet, Arizona: Located about 15 miles northeast Parker on the Bill Williams River. Location of Arizona's first copper mine. It boomed briefly, then died. A few ruins remain.

Rich Hills, Arizona: Located about 12 miles north of Wickenberg on an old mountain road. A rip-roaring gold camp in the 1860's. A few buildings remain in addition to ruins and an unusual cemetery.

Tubac, Arizona: Located on Hiway 89 only 22 miles south of Tucson. The first Spanish presidio was established here in 1752. De Anza assembled the colonists who established San Francisco here in 1775. About 100 residents remain, but numerous spectacular ruins remain, some dating back to 1752.

Washington, Arizona: Located a few miles east of Nogales on the Mexican border and Santa Cruz River. Mining activity dates back to prehistoric times and diggings, foundations, and ruins of famous Westinghouse tramway may be seen.

White Hills, Arizona: Located 7 miles east of Hiway 93 near Squaw Peak. Old road from Hiway 93-466 ends at the town. Several abandoned buildings remain. Silver camp in N. W. corner of state.

ARKANSAS

Arkansas has a number of ghost towns which date back to the French and Spanish exploration and settlement during the 1700s and early 1800s. Northwest Arkansas has a few old, almost completely abandoned towns which are steeped in outlaw and settler history. The Arkansas and Mississippi river valleys harbor numerous old townsites that date back 150 years or more.

ARKANSAS POST, Arkansas: Located on Arkansas River 24 miles south of DeWitt (Hiway 1-11) and 9 miles east. Founded 1686. Oldest white settlement and first territorial capitol. A few residents remain.

BUTTERFIELD, Arkansas: Located 5 miles west of Malvern near Hiway 270. Named for D. A. Butterfield, builder of the 'Diamond Jo' railroad from Malvern to Hot Springs.

CADRON, Arkansas: Located on Arkansas river about 4 miles west and 1¼ miles south of Conway (Hiway 64-65). Founded 1814. Once a rival of Little Rock; now just a few ruins in a grove of cedar trees.

CAMP, Arkansas: Located 14 miles west of Mammoth Springs near Hiway 9. Founded 1870 as Indian Camp. Original log store is now part of present store.

CANE HILL, Arkansas: Located 16½ miles west of Fayetteville on Hiway 62, then 3½ miles south on Hiway 45. Founded 1827. Once a thriving church and college town; now a ghost.

CHALK BLUFF, Arkansas: Located on St. Francis river about 1 mile from St. Francis (Hiway 62). Founded 1842. Ruins of Confederate fort remain nearby.

CHAMPAGNOLLE LANDING, Arkansas: Located 3 miles east of Calion (Hiway 167) on Ouachita river. Founded 1818 as Scarborough Landing. Changed to Union Courthouse 1840. Assumed present name 1844. Was thriving river port until railroad passed it by.

DAVIDSONVILLE, Arkansas: Located 2½ miles north of Powhatan (Hiway 63) on Hiway 117 to Black Rock, then 6 miles east. Founded 1815. Abandoned during yellow fever epidemic; never resettled. Many ruins .

DWIGHT, Arkansas: Located on west bank of Illinois Bayou near Russellville (Hiway 7-64). Established as Dwight Mission 1822. Ruins.

GOLDEN CITY, Arkansas: Located 3½ miles south of Booneville (Hiway 10-23) on Hiway 116 to Arkansas Tuberculosis Hospital, then 4 miles west. Founded 1886 as a booming gold camp. The mines were salted.

HOPEFIELD, Arkansas: Located about 2 miles up the Mississippi river from Hiway 63-70 bridge on Arkansas side of the river. Founded 1797 across the river from Chicksaw Bluffs (now Memphis) by Benjamin Fox. Now a few pilings and a cabin remain to mark the site.

JACKSONPORT, Arkansas: Located 4 miles west of Newport (Hiway 14-67) along White river levee. Founded 1822. Once a booming, rollicking river town; now only a brick courthouse and a few ruins remain.

KIRBY, Arkansas: Located on Hiway 27-70 about 90 miles west of Little Rock. Once a blow-off town for the mercury miners.

NAPOLEON, Arkansas: Located near junction of Mississippi and Arkansas rivers. Founded 1820. Once an important river shipping town; but abandoned after the flood of 1874.

NORFOLD, Arkansas: Located 13½ miles south of Mountain Home near Hiway 5 at junction of North Fork and White rivers. Once a booming river shipping town; now a small settlement.

OLD AUSTIN, Arkansas: Located 1 mile east of Austin (27 miles N.E. of Little Rock on Hiway 27). Founded 1821. Site is in a grove of trees.

RAVENDEN SPRINGS, Arkansas: Located 6 miles east of Imboden (Hiway 62-63) and 6½ miles north. A booming health resort till 1910; now a deserted cluster of hotels.

RONDO, Arkansas: Located 3 miles east and 2 miles north of Texarkana. A point on the old Southwest Trail. Nothing remains but a church and nearby (2½ miles) is a Confederate cemetery.

WITTSBURG, Arkansas: Located on St. Francis river south of Levesque (Hiway 64) about 2 miles. Founded 1739 as a French fort by Bienville. Later was a river port known as Strong's Point. County seat during 1860s and 1870s. Now, few buildings remain.

CALIFORNIA

California has hundreds of ghost towns. In Northern California, treacherous mountain roads lead you to mining and lumbering ghost towns with few, if any, residents. In Central California, Hiway 49 goes right through and near many old ghosts. In Southern California, the worthwhile ghosts are in out-of-the-way desert or mountain areas. Yes, California has everything including some fine, well-preserved historic ghost towns.

BALLARAT, California: Located 48 miles northeast of Ridgecrest on desert road leading to Death Valley. Ask any cafe or service station in Trona. A few ruins and buildings remain of this fabulous old ghost.

BEND CITY, California: Located 4 miles east of Independence near Owens river. A few stone buildings remain.

BENNETVILLE, California: See TIOGA, California.

BETTYSBURG, California: Located near present town of Quincy. Ruins is its landmark. Also known as Elizabethtown. Many other ghosts in the area.

BIDWELL BAR, California: Located 9 miles east of Oroville on old road. Once a booming mining camp and county seat; now one building and lots of ruins remain.

BODIE, California: Located about 20 miles east of Hiway 395. This was one of the roughest, toughest boomingest towns in the West. It has been memorialized in hundreds of western stories.

BODFISH, California: Located 36 miles northeast of Bakersfield on Hiway 178. A gold camp during the 1880's.

CALICO, California: Located in the Calico mountains about 4 miles northwest of Yermo. Once a prosperous silver town of almost 4,000, now being restored as a historical site.

CERRO GORDO MINE, California: Located about 3 miles northwest of Keeler. This historic mine produced over $25,000,000 in silver, gold, lead, and zinc. Ruins of the mine and foundations of the camp building are visible.

CLARAVILLE, California: Located about 23 miles southeast of Bodfish in Sequoia National Forest. Was a rip-roaring boomtown in the 1860's, now in ruins.

COARSE GOLD, California: Located on Hiway 41 about 36 miles northwest of Fresno. Only a few foundations along with odds and ends of machinery remain.

COLUMBIA, California: Located about 8 miles north of Sonora. Once a thriving city of over 20,000 people, it was typical of the towns of the Mother Lode country.

DALE, California: Located about 15 miles east of 29 Palms on the north side of Joshua Tree National Monument. Many of the old buildings are in a remarkable state of preservation; vandals are doing more harm than the elements.

Elizabethtown, California: See Bettysburg, California.

Havilah, California: Located about 7 miles south of Bodfish near Breckenridge mountain. Was once a thriving town and county seat of Kern County.

Hawkinsville, California: Located near Hiway 99 about 2 miles north of Yreka. Once a mining town with a main street 3 miles long on Yreka Creek.

Hiway 49, California: Hiway 49 from Sattley (about 45 miles northwest of Lake Tahoe) to Mariposa (about 30 miles southwest of Yosemite Park) is literally a continuous string of deserted mining towns. The Division of Mines, Ferry Building, San Francisco, California published a book showing pictures and listing hundreds of these towns. Write to attention of Mrs. Eigenhoff for price of this book if available.

Iowa Hill, California: Located about 15 miles east of Colfax. In its time, the mines around this town were among the richest producers in California. The town was reduced to ruins due to hydraulic operations and little if anything remains. Numerous old mining camps are in the area, however.

Jacumba, California: Located 70 miles east of San Diego near Hiway 80 and Mexican border. Founded 1852 by James McCoy. Now a tumbled-down, deserted health resort.

Kearsage, California: Located at base of Kearsage Peak on the south side. Only evidence of town are a few footings.

Kernville, California: Originally named Whiskey Flat. Located on the Kern River 10 miles north of Isabella. Ruins, and parts of equipment are visible.

Keysville, California: Located about 4 miles west of Isabella in the Greenhorn mountains. Ruins of a few buildings and an old fort remain.

Kingston, California: Located near Hardwick on south bank of the Lower Kings River. Ruins and foundations are all that remain.

Laport, California: Northwest of Downieville, California. There are a few inhabitants remaining and a number of the old buildings.

Lundy, California: Located on the shores of Lundy Lake. The town is most inundated by the lake but some old buildings and workings may still be seen.

Ogilby, California: Located 15 miles west and 4 miles north of Winterhaven (Hiway 80). From 1879 to 1918 a mining boom town; now just a railroad station remains. Up the track 6½ miles is site of TUMCO, another boomtown that had 4 wide-open saloons for 3000 residents.

OLEMA, California: Located about 30 miles north of San Francisco on Hiway 1. Few old buildings still used. Ruins include limestone kilns south of town.

ONION VALLEY, California: About 12 miles north of Downisville, California. Town was once a thriving town of 1500, few remains visible today.

PANAMINT, California: Located about 52 miles northeast of Ridgecrest, 4 miles beyond Ballarat on desert road. This was one of California's most notorious mining camps. Ruins of tranway, old smelter and some buildings remain.

PICACHO, California: Located on the west bank of the Colorado river about 25 miles north of Yuma, Arizona, and Winterhaven, California. Ruins are visible. The Picacho mine is located on the desert road about 6 miles before the town. Ruins of the mill, old buildings, and diggings remain. A caretaker lives at the mine. At one time the mine employed nearly 2,000 men. A small cemetery with white picket fence is along the road.

PURISIMA, California: Located 4 miles south of Half Moon Bay on Hiway 1. Deserted buildings may be found among the cypress trees.

QUARTZBURG, California: Located 9 miles north of Isabella on the Kern River near lake. A few ruins of walls and stone chimneys remain.

RICH BAR, California: On Hiway 24 between Oroville and Quincy. Only foundations and cemetery remain. A boom town in the 1850's.

ROUGH AND READY, California: A rootin-tootin mining camp in the 1850's. On Hiway 20 about 5 miles west of Grass Valley.

SCOTT BAR, California: East of Yreka and 3 miles south of Hiway 96. Many of the old buildings are still standing and a few of the mines are being worked.

SKIDOO, California: Located on the western edge of Death Valley near Telescope Peak. Building ruins and old workings are visible.

TAILHOLT, California: See WHITE RIVER.

TIOGA, California: Initially named Bernetville. Located a few miles south of the old town of Lundy. An active town in the late 70's and early 80's. Many ruins and parts of machinery remain.

TRAVER, California: Located along Hiway 99 approximately 18 miles north of Tulare. Before the turn of the century this was a prosperous agricultural city of over 1000. Today the remains of dilapidated buildings and a windmill are all there is to be seen.

TUMCO, California: See OGILBY, California.

WHISKEY FLAT, California: See KERNVILLE.

WHITE RIVER, California: Originally named TAILHOLT. Located about 22 miles southeast of PORTERVILLE on the Balance Rock or Glennville Road. A very active and well-known placer camp in the late 1850's. A few people remain in the community.

COLORADO

Colorado is littered with old town sites from which the buildings have been moved, or torn down. This is especially true on the plains as they approach the Rockies. Once, in the Rockies, old mining camps still abound, but it is necessary to get off of the highways and onto the cruder mountain roads to find them.

ALTONA, Colorado: Located 9 miles north of Boulder. A planned metropolis that boomed and failed.

ASHCROFT, Colorado: Follow Hiway 82 for 9 miles west of Aspen, turn left and follow old road to site. A well preserved ghost complete with old equipment and trash (called antiques in the city). Silver Dollar Tabor built a home here and declared a holiday, with drinks on him, every time 'Baby Doe' Tabor came to visit the town.

CALIFORNIA GULCH, Colorado: Founded in early Spring of 1860 as a gold camp. First known as Boughtown, then as Oro City, and then California Gulch. At the end of the first year it had a population of 5,000. By 1870, the gulch was worked out after the removal of $5,000,000 in gold. Today ruins are in evidence and the few good homes remaining are used by workers in the smelter. Located 2 miles south of Leadville.

COLUMBINE, Colorado: Located 32 miles northwest of Steamboat Springs in Rout National Forest. A former mining camp.

CRIPPLE CREEK, Colorado: At the height of the mining activity in the 1890's there were 11 mining camps in the Cripple Creek vicinity, all connected by electric tramways. These were: Cripple Creek, Victor, Goldfield, Independence, Anaconda, Gillett, Elkton, Altman, Lawrence, Arequa, and Mound City. Today, only Cripple Creek and Victor are active. Ruins of the rest with a few scattered buildings are in evidence.

CRYSTAL, Colorado: Located 6 miles from Marble (Hiway 133) on a treacherous road suitable only for hiking, horseback, or jeep. Nearby are the Sheep Mountain mines and mill. Deserted in winter; a few prospectors live here in summer.

ELDORA, Colorado: Located about ½ mile south and 3 miles west of Nederland. An old gold camp.

GILLETT, Colorado: Located about 6 miles northeast of Cripple Creek a few miles east of Hiway 67. Once the site of a large reduction mill and racetrack. It became most famous as a resort town for the gold fields, and bullfights were staged by 'Arizona Charlie' Wolf on 8-24-95. The town is now abandoned.

GOLD HILL, Colorado: Located west of Boulder on Hiway 19. In the area between Boulder and Nederland are SALINA, SUNSHINE, CRISMAN, and GOLD HILL; all towns whose glory is far behind them.

GOLD PARK, Colorado: Located about 10 miles from Mount of Holy Cross marker on Hiway 24, on the road to Camp Tigiwon from north of Pando.

GOTHIC, Colorado: Located 8 miles from Crested Butte (Hiway 135). A scattering of well-preserved buildings and some ruins. Here is the summer school of the Rocky Mountain Biological School. The dirt road is usually impassable until midsummer.

GRANITE, Colorado: Founded 1859 as a rip-roaring mining camp for the gold activity on Cache Creek and Kelly's Bay. Ruins of a few buildings remain and evidence of the early activity is to be seen. Located on Hiway 24 about 16 miles north of Buena Vista.

HAMILTON, Colorado: Established in 1859 as a rival gold camp to Tarryall, across Tarryall Creek. Most mining operations were sluicing and panning, but a number of glory holes remain to be seen.

HANCOCK, Colorado: Located just west of the ghost town of ROMLEY at the end of a spur from Hiway 162. Several spectacular ruins and parts of old buildings remain.

INDEPENDENCE, Colorado: Located near Hiway 82 on the west side of Independence Pass. At one time had a population of 2,000, the diggings pooped out and the town dwindled to one man who held all of the city offices. He finally left and a deserted town remains with the buildings slowly falling to ruins.

ISLE, Colorado: Located 23 miles south of Cannon City.

JULESBURG, Colorado: Sites of OLD JULESBURG and SECOND JULESBURG are located within a few miles of fourth and present, Julesburg. Third town is now known as WEIR. Several robbers loots have been found in locality.

KOKOMA, Colorado: Located 19 miles north of Leadville on Hiway 91, it is a deserted mining camp.

LIVERMORE, Colorado; Located 3 miles west of The Forks (Hiway 287).

MARBLE, Colorado: Located 12 miles south of Redstone on Hiway 133. Only a section of the town is a ghost. Part was destroyed in flood 1941. From here went marble for Lincoln Memorial and Tomb of the Unknown Soldier. Stone was cut to blueprint ready for erection at destination.

MURPHY'S SWITCH, Colorado: See ROMLEY.

NEWETT, Colorado: Located about 1 mile southwest of Trout Creek Pass on Hiway 24-285, about 13 miles east of Buena Vista. Old concrete and stone foundations and abutments are all that remain. Some buried treasure has been recovered in the vicinity.

OHIO, Colorado; Located 9 miles northeast of Parlin. Another town on the same road is QUARTZ (14 miles north) and TINCUP (24 miles north).

OLD OPHIR, Colorado: Located 2 miles east of Ophir Station and Hiway 145.

PORTLAND, Colorado: Located 33 miles south of Montrose near Hiway 550. Established 1883 as future railroad town. The railroad never came.

PRIMERO, Colorado: Located 1 mile north of Segundo. Few walls and foundations remain.

QUIDERA, Colorado: Located 8 miles east of Silver Cliff. ROSITA is 3 miles south. An abandoned mining camp.

ROMLEY, Colorado: Located near Hiway 162 and St. Elmo. Just before reaching St. Elmo, take left fork of road to Romlay and Hancock. Ruins of many buildings and mill remain. Town was first known as MURPHY'S SWITCH.

ROSITA, Colorado: About 9 miles east of Westcliffe (Hiways 69-96) on Hiway 96, then 2 miles south. Several old buildings remain of a boomtown which included 3 churches, a brewery, creamery and cheese factory. A mile or so south of town is an old cemetary complete with old tombstones.

SPANISH FORT, Colorado: Located 7 miles south of Badito; 10 miles north of LaVeta. The fort was built in 1819. Now in ruins.

TARRYALL, Colorado: Established in 1859 when gold rush started to the area. Across Tarryall Creek is site rival town of Hamilton. John Parson started mint here in 1861 and minted $2.50 and $5.00 gold coins. Site is located 14 miles northwest of Lake George on Hiway 77.

TELLER, Colorado: Located 20 miles east of RAND and accessible only by packhorse. Founded in 1879 due to rich silver strike; by 1880 had a population of 2,000. Town died due to difficulty of getting in supplies. Ruins remain to mark the site.

TINCUP, Colorado: Located 11 miles north of Gunnison to Almont on Hiway 135, then northeast on Hiway 306 to site. One of the wildest towns in the west; the outlaws elected the Marshall. The nearby cemetary has four independent hills; Catholic, Protestant, Jewish, and 'Boot'. Several old buildings remain in good condition.

WARD, Colorado: About 29 miles north of Central City on Hiway 160. Gold town.

WHITEPINE, Colorado: Located 34 miles east and 11 miles north of Gunnison. Once a city of 3,000. Nearby are sites of NORTH STAR and TOMICHI, old silver towns.

WHITE RIVER, Colorado: Located 19 miles west of Meeker and 2 miles south of Hiway 64. An old cow town.

IDAHO

Idaho has a great multitude of old ghosts with a few, if any, inhabitants. One thing about this state, vandals haven't had the urge to enter and destroy the old towns and it is not unusual to find a town with the assay office almost intact and a little of the merchandise left on the shelves of the deserted stores.

ALBION, Idaho: Located 9 miles east and 9 miles south of Burley. Once a county seat and on the main road to Utah, the town was completely abandoned while on its outskirts one of the two Idaho normal schools was continuing to prepare educators for Idaho schools.

BONANZA, Idaho: Located 8 miles north of Hiway 93 in the Yankee Fork district of Custer County. Established in 1877 as a gold mining town. In 1879 it had 5 lawyers and 9 saloons.

CLAYTON, Idaho: Located 224 miles west of Missoula on Hiway 93. Several ghost towns including CRYSTAL, CUSTER, BONANZA, and BAY HORSE (Aetna) are in the area.

CUPRUM, Idaho: Located 39 miles northwest of Council and Hiway 95. Ghost hotel and ruins.

GALENA, Idaho: Located near Galena Peak on Hiway 93 about 36 miles northwest of Hailey. Old boom town.

GEM, Idaho: 4 miles northeast of Wallace and Hiway 10. Several ghost towns nearby.

IDAHO CITY, Idaho: Located 40 miles northeast of Boise on Hiway 21. Once a metropolis. Other ghost towns in nearby area include PIONEERVILLE, OLD and NEW CENTERVILLE, PLACERVILLE, and QUARTZBURG.

KINGSTON, Idaho: Located on Hiway 10 about 7 miles west of KELLOGG. Several ghost towns in this area.

LEESBURG, Idaho: Located about 6 miles west of Salmon. Old shacks and ruins.

MOUNT IDAHO, Idaho: Located 3 miles east of Grangeville. Once a boomtown seeking territorial capitol.

SILVER CITY, Idaho: Located 24 miles east of Jordan Valley, Oregon and Hiway 95, or 22 miles southwest of Murphy, Idaho. Many buildings remain including saloons, courthouse and hotel. Nearby are DELMAR (9 miles and DEWEY (5 miles with pianos still in parlors and equipment still in assay offices. Bill Hawes is the sole yearround resident of the city and in addition to being a full-fledged deputy sheriff, he is self-appointed mayor, police chief, fire chief, postmaster, street commissioner, saloon keeper, and merchant.

SPALDING, Idaho: Located 11 miles east of Lewiston. Settled in 1836 by Rev. Henry Spalding.

SPRINGTOWN, Idaho: Located on the rim of Snake River Gorge just west of Hansen Bridge. Some ruins remain.

IOWA

Iowa ghost towns are restricted almost entirely to the Mississippi River bottoms; that is, if you want to find buildings standing and mills or equipment still somewhat like it was. In the north, a few good towns remain.

BURRIS CITY, Iowa: Site located on the north bank of the Iowa River at its junction with Missouri River; 1½ miles north of Toolesboro (Hiway 99). A deserted river boom town.

GALLAND, (Nashville), Iowa: Site located 3 miles east of Montrose; about 12 miles north of Keokuk on Lake Shore Drive. Town founded in 1830.

HAUNTOWN, Iowa: Located 5 miles south of Sabula (Hiway 67). Old mill and distillery town. Old mill and millrace between the hiway and the river. ELK RIVER (now Almont) is another ghost town nearby and was an outlaw hangout after the Civil War.

ICARIAN COMMUNITY, Iowa: Located 4½ miles northeast of Corning. Founded in 1858. Several old buildings remain.

IOWA PHALANX, Iowa: Located along Des Moines River 16 miles northwest of Oskaloosa. Social settlement which was abandoned in 1845.

KOSSUTH, Iowa: Located 2 miles east of Mediapolis (Hiway 61). Once an educational center, now a ghost.

PREPARATION, Iowa: Located in Preparation Canyon State Park 19 miles north of junction of Hiways 75 and 183 near Mondamin. Two houses remain in the town. A Mormon colony.

RIVER SIOUX, Iowa: Located 24 miles north of Missouri Valley on Hiway 75. Across Sioux River was the town of MALTA. Neither town prospered.

SANDUSKY, Iowa: Located 5 miles north of Keokuk on Lake Shore Drive. Established as a trading post in 1820.

TALMAGE, Iowa: Located near Hiway 169 about 13 miles east of Creston. Mormon log tabernacle was here.

VANDALIA, Iowa: Located 17½ miles east of Des Moines on Hiway 163, then 4½ miles south. Daniel Pulver home, built in 1854, remains in good repair.

KANSAS

Kansas has a few good towns left, but in so many cases the buildings were torn down to reduce property taxes, or they were carted away and used for other purposes.

ABRAM, Kansas: Site located 2 miles east and 2 miles south of Lincoln. Barley County seat. Now only a monument and basements remain.

ALBANY, Kansas: Located 2 miles east of Sabetha. An important station on the Underground Railroad.

ALTON, Kansas: Site located about 1 mile south of Drury.

AURELLVILLE, Kansas: See CHICKASKIA.

BIG TIMBER, Kansas: Located about 5 miles northeast of Randolph. Very little remains, but in early days it was a popular supply center. Across the Blue River are sites of Spring Lake and Bellegarde.

CENTRAL CITY, Kansas: Located 8 miles southwest Garnett. Church, parsonage, farmhouse rebuilt from old hotel, and ruins are all that remain of this early booming trading post.

CHIKASKIA, Kansas: Site located on Chikaskia River about 6 miles north of Caldwell. Other ghost towns in immediate vicinity are Hessell, Aurellville, and Alton.

FREDERICKSBURG, Kansas: Located almost directly south of Alma, Nebraska 7 miles from state line. About 3 miles west of Prairie Dog Creek is the village of Woodruff, Kansas which is now just a ghost of its former self.

HESSELL, Kansas: See CHIKASKIA.

HOLLIDAYSBURG, Kansas: Located about 3 miles west of Syracuse on the Arkansas River. A booming stage station and camp ground before the coming of the railroads.

IOWA POINT, Kansas: Located on Hiway 7 about 6 miles north of Highland. Once a booming town of 3,000 people.

LIMESTONE, Kansas: Located about midway between Hanover and Hollenberg on the Little Blue River.

QUEEN CITY, Kansas: Located on the north side of the Arkansas River about 4 miles north of Haven.

RAVANNA, Kansas: Located 8 miles west and 6 miles north of Kalvesta (Hiway 156). Few ruins remain. Just east is site of Beersheba,, an unsuccessful Jewish farm of the 1880's.

RICHFIELD, Kansas: Located near junction of Hiways 27 and 51 in southwest Kansas. A boomtown of 1500 permanent residents in its heyday; now reduced to a few dugouts and old buildings.

SILVER CITY, Kansas: Located 5 miles southwest of Yates Center (Hiway 54 and 75). Mine shafts remain from a false silver boom of the 1850's.

WALLACE, Kansas: Located 9 miles east of Sharon Springs on Hiway 40. Boomtown of 1500 people in 1870's. Fort Wallace was nearby.

WOODRUFF, Kansas: See FREDERICKSBURGH, Kansas.

LOUISIANA

Louisiana has many old, deserted, abandoned towns; but in so many instances the well preserved ghost towns are difficult to explore because of inaccessibility and lack of good roads to their sites. Inquiry to local chambers of commerce or historical societies in any of the small cities of the state will usually result in directions to one or more nearby ghost towns. Not only are many of these towns well preserved but so many of them have interesting historical backgrounds.

ALTO, Louisiana: See PORT HUDSON.

BELLWOOD, Louisiana: Located 14 miles south of Hagewood, on Hiway 39 in Kisatchie National Forest. Once a booming lumber town; now a few people keep the town alive. Several other ghosts are in the area but they require hiking.

BRAITHWAITE, Louisiana: Locatd 19 miles southeast of New Orleans on Hiway 1. A prosperous industrial town until 1930.

FAIRFAX, Louisiana: Site located 4 miles east of Centerville near Hiway 90. An old townsite dating back to the 1700's. It has been long abandoned and a Negro village in on part of the old site.

GALVEZ TOWN, Louisiana: Located 2½ miles south of Oak Grove; then 6 miles east; or, 2½ miles west of Port Vincent. A town that was inhabited only 15 years (1775-1789), but a few traces remain. Now a picnic ground. According to local legend some of Jean LaFitte's pirate gold lies on the opposite side of the Amite River; some say it is in or near the picnic grounds. Nevertheless, some treasure has been found in the area as late as 1956.

GRAND ECORE, Louisiana: Located almost midway between Natchitoches and Clarence on bluffs overlooking the Red River. By 1850, the town was a shipping center for all east Texas. In 1853, yellow fever decimated the population and Federal troops sacked the town in 1863. About 75 people remain. Nearby is old Fort Selden and other historic sites.

ISLE DERNIERE, Louisiana: Located across Terrebonnie Bay directly south of Mouma (Hiway 90). Boat must be used to get to the island. Once a fashionable resort, most of the buildings were destroyed by hurricane 8-10-1856. A few camps are located on the island and treasure hunters regularly visit the place with various degrees of success.

JEFFERSON ISLAND, Louisiana: Not an island, but a salt dome located about 9 miles west of New Iberia on Hiway 25. Known first as Cate Carlin, and then Miller's Island, and later as Orange Island. Numerous camps and small settlements were in the area until it was purchased in 1870 by the actor, Joseph Jefferson. Legend has it that this was one of LaFitte's treasure storehouses and in 1923 a Negro, named Daynite, unearthed a fortune in Mexican and Spanish coins here while digging a culvert.

NIBLETT'S BLUFF, Louisiana: Located 4 miles west of Vinton on Hiway 90, then 2½ miles north on Hiway 121, then 2½ miles west. Once a prosperous river port, then a Confererate stronghold during the Civil War. An epidemic in May 1863 decimated the Confederate troops camped here. Ruins of the old town and Confederate breastworks remain near the church.

KERNAN, Louisiana: Located 10 miles north of Gillis on Hiway 171 to junction with Hiway 190; then 2 miles west on Hiway 7. Only a schoolhouse and church mark the site of this lumber boomtown.

LAFITTE VILLAGE, Louisiana: Located at southern end of Hiway 30 about 21 miles south of MARRERO. Not a real ghost town, but the 6-mile area between LaFitte Postoffice and LaFitte Village is the site of several old ghost towns. LaFitte Village is the original pirate settlement and has been the scene of much treasure hunting. Local tradition says Napoleon Bonaparte, John Paul Jones, and Jean LaFitte are buried side by side in the cemetary 2 miles north of town.

LINCECUM, Louisiana: Located 4 miles south of Selma on Hiway 165, then 1½ miles east. Once an important lumber town now reduced to little more than a railroad siding. A local treasure legend deals with a party of eastbound California miners being killed near here by Indians. They had a fabulous amount of gold prior to the attack, so the story goes.

LONGVILLE, Louisiana: Located 19 miles south of DeRidder on Hiway 171. One of many ghost towns in the southwest part of the state resulting from the lumber industry. Founded 1906; by 1910 it had over 2,000 residents. Today less than 100 people inhabit the town.

LOS ADAIS, Louisiana: Site located 14½ miles west of Natchitoches on Hiway 6, then ½ mile north on top of the hill. Founded 1721 as Presidio de Nuestra del Pilar de Los Adais, a Spanish fort. Abandoned February 1806 when the Spanish were evacuated. On opposite hill is site of Mission of San Miguel de los Adois.

OLD ATHENS, Louisiana: Located 2½ miles west of present town of Athens at the highest point (415' altitude) in Louisiana. Founded 1833. The town declined after a disastrous fire 1849. Several old buildings, a church, and two cemetaries mark the site.

POINT PLEASANT, Louisiana: Located near Hiway 165 about 2 miles south of Bastrop. A booming steamboat landing on Bayou Bartholemew during the early boat era. Now, all that remains is the name and a few ruins.

PORT HICKEY, Louisiana: See PORT HUDSON.

PORT HUDSON, Louisiana: Located 5 miles west and ½ mile north of Plains (Hiway 61-65) at junction of Thompson Creek and Mississippi River. One of the most interesting ghost areas in the West. It is still possible to find old guns, bullets, trenches and trophies of the Civil War. Town was a river-trading post in the early 1800's. During the Civil War, it was a Confederate outpost until 1863. Ruins of many old buildings remain. Also, in the immediate area remain ruins of the ghost towns of Port Hickey, Alto, and Thompson's Creek. Town was moved several times due to floods so there are 3 distinct sites, at least.

QUEBEC, Louisiana: Located on Hiway 80 about 6 miles west of Tallulah on Tonsas River. Now reduced to 35 residents, it once was a busy steamboat landing.

RAMSEY, Louisiana: Located 4 miles north of Covington on Hiway 34. A vacant house, a store, and a skeleton of a mill are all that remain of the hustling lumber town. One mile east of the townsite is the St. Joseph Seminary with about 100 students.

ST. MAURICE LANDING, Louisiana: Located 6 miles west of city of New Roads near Hiway 30. A booming river town in the early days; now a few ruins mark the townsite and in the landing, at low water, can be seen the iron prow of the passenger ship J. M. White. It burned in January 1886 with loss of more than 80 lives.

SOUTHPORT, Louisiana: Located 5 miles west of New Orleans on Hiway 90 on west side of levee, than ½ mile south. Southport is not a ghost, but the southern limit of the old town of VILLAGE DES CHAPITOLES founded in the late 1600'. Old ruins remain between Southport and Hiway 90.

TCHOUPILOULA VILLAGE, Louisiana: Same as Southport.

THOMPSON'S CREEK, Louisiana: See Port Hudson.
VILLAGE DES CHAPITOLES, Louisiana: See Southport.

MINNESOTA

BUCHANAN, Minnesota: Site located 10 miles south of Two Harbors on Hiway 61, or 3 miles south of Knife River. In 1856, the first Federal land office was established here and the town boomed—and died. A marker is in Hiway 61 near site.

CONCORD, Minnesota: Site is located 3 miles east of West Concord. When the Great Western railroad missed the town, everybody moved 3 miles west and established the new town of West Concord.

FORESTVILLE, Minnesota: Located 1½ miles west of junction of Hiways 16 & 52, then 8½ miles south; or 2 miles east and 8½ miles south of Preston. Founded 1855 around the popular Meighen Store which still stands. Other ruins include the Old District School, Gristmill, dam, and the old stage station. The town was depopulated during the Civil War and later when the railroad missed the town, it folded. See TOM MEIGHEN.

FRONTENAC, Minnesota: Located 1 mile from Frontenac Station (Hiway 61). The land was donated 2 miles inland for a railroad station by Gen. Israel Gerrard and this act isolated the old town. Today, grass grows in its streets.

GRAND PORTAGE, Minnesota: Located 7 miles south of International border on Hiway 61, then 6 miles east on shore of Lake Superior. In operation as a trading post before the Declaration of Independence, but 1793 it had 16 log buildings enclosed by a high stockade. Now a few houses and a general store and postoffice remain and a few Chippewa Indians reside there.

HIGH FOREST, Minnesota: Located 1 mile south and 2 miles west of Stewartville. Once a thriving village, today the site is marked by a flagstaff which was presented to the community by Rear Admiral A. H. Foote after the Civil War.

ITASCA, Minnesota: Located 2½ miles north of Albert Lea on Hiway 13. Once a rival of Albert Lea for county seat, the community lost heavy bets on a horse race and capitulated to Albert Lea. The Itasca School is on the site.

LAPRAIRIE, Minnesota: Located 1 mile from Grand Rapids toward the Mississippi River. No buildings remain but old streets are visible. Some treasure has been found here.

LONDON, Minnesota: Site located on old Hiway 22 miles from Finland, or 44 miles from Schroeder. This was a booming logging camp, now deserted. Other camps may be found on the old logging roads in the vicinity.

LOTHROP, Minnesota: Site located near Ten Mile Lake and Hackensack. In 1895, a railroad terminus with 2,000 people. When the Minnesota and International Railroad was routed to the north, the townsite was abandoned.

MANTORVILLE, Minnesota: Located 3 miles north of Kasson on Hiway 57. A still inhabited town dating back over 100 years. In the 1880's the Great Western Railroad by-passed the town and most residents moved to Kasson. Many century-old buildings remain.

METROPOLISVILLE, Minnesota: Located near Cannon River and Dundas south of Northfield. This is one of a string of several ghost towns which boomed and fell during the 'Cannon River Land Boom of 1856.'

NININGER, Minnesota: Located 3 miles west of Hastings on Hiway 55, then 5 miles north. Once a boomtown of over 500 people, the bank failures of 1859 ruined the town.

OTTER TAIL CITY, Minnesota: Site located at extreme northeastern end of Otter Tail Lake near the mouth of the river, south of Perham. An important trading post in the 1850's; later a county seat when the land office moved to Alexandria in 1862 and the county seat to Fergus Falls in 1872, the town declined. Now, it is a field of crops with a small marker indicating the site.

PELAN, Minnesota: Located midway between Greenbush and Karlstad on South Fork of Two Rivers. Only foundations and remains of boardwalks are evident.

RED ROCK, Minnesota: Located 5 miles from St. Paul near Hiway 61 or 11 miles from Hasrings. An early trading center and mission. A Methodist mission was established near Kaposia in 1837 and moved across the Mississippi River in 1840. Now a small settlement remains.

SACRAMENTO, Minnesota: Located near Mantorville. A town that bloomed and fell on a spurious gold strike. The promoter salted the banks of the Zumbro River with gold dust but the boom failed. The tavern he built still stands on its original site one block south of the old Courthouse in Mantorville.

ST. LAWRENCE, Minnesota: Site located on the outskirts of

Jordan toward the river. Samuel Burton Strait built a hotel here in 1857 in anticipation of a land boom which never occurred. The hotel is now used as a barn.

ST. NICHOLAS, Minnesota: Located on a county road which skirts south end of Albert Lea Lake. First town in Freeborn County and once a busy village. Now, only a monument marks the site.

SALOL, Minnesota: Site located 9 miles east of Roseau. Once a thriving lumber town; now everything has been removed except some old sawdust piles.

SWIFT, Minnesota: Located 6½ miles from Baudette on Hiway 11. Named for its rapid growth, it is now a small hamlet with one mill left.

WASIOJA, Minnesota: Located 2 miles from Mantorville. In 1861, Peter Mantor recruited Company C here to fight for the Union cause with Minnesota's second regiment. Nearly all men were killed in action and the widows and orphans abandoned the town. Ruins of a mill and Methodist Seminary remain.

In the northern iron country of Minnesota may be found many well-built, but decaying old ghost towns. Make local inquiry for information on nearby ghost towns.

MISSOURI

Missouri has a remarkable number of standing ghost towns, despite its heavy population. Too, a great number of sites of old ghost towns dating back over 100 years can be found from one end of the state to the other. Old groves on many of the river bottoms hide old, abandoned towns dating back a century or more.

ADAM-ONDI-AHMAN, Missouri: Founded 1837 as a ferry station on the great bend of the Grand River by Lyman Wight, a veteran of the War of 1812 and an Elder of the Morman Church. Located about 4 miles northwest of Gallatin. On 5-19-1838 Prophet Joseph Smith and other Church officials visited the Wight settlement and selected the site for a 'stake.' They named the town 'Adam-ondi-Ahman,' which means Adam's Consecrated Land in the Reformed Egyptian language. By October 1838 over 200 homes had been built, and in November trouble between the Mormons and the Gentiles arose resulting in a military hearing by Brig.-Gen. Robert Wilson. The Mormons were exhonerated, but were ordered to abandon Missouri. The prosperous community fell into ruins and today only the Wight cabin remains.

BIRD'S POINT, Missouri: Located on the Missouri side of the Mississippi river at the foot of the Interstate Bridge on Hiway 60. Established 1800 by Abraham Bird as a trapping post opposite the junction of the Ohio and Mississippi rivers. As emigration west grew, the Bird mercantile activities expanded and his settlement became a center for river freight between New Orleans and Ohio river towns. The Civil War and the railroads ended the settlement's importance and it died. Many old buildings and points of interest remain.

CARTERVILLE, Missouri: Located 9 miles west of Carthage. Once a booming zinc-mining town of over 12,000 people. Now its big broad main street is all but abandoned.

DANVILLE, Missouri: Located on the old Boon's Lick Trail 12½ miles from Jonesburg. Established 1834. On the evening of October 4, 1864 Bill Anderson with 80 guerillas ransacked and burned the town, and it never recovered. Many deserted buildings remain.

FAR WEST, Missouri: Located 9 miles south of Hamilton to Kingston, then 4½ miles east. Founded December 29, 1836 when Caldwell County was established as a Mormon refuge by the Legislature. By 1838, the town had a population of over 4,000. Trouble between the Mormons and their Gentile neighbors resulted in violence in 1838 and State officials declared the Mormons a public menace and sent troops to control them. The Mormons fled to Illinois and their houses were torn down. Today, a farm marks the site.

HICKORY SPRINGS, Missouri: Located near Mountain Grove (Hiway 60). Founded 1851. By 1857, the town had several stores and the Mountain Grove Seminary. When the railroad by-passed the town in 1833, the merchants moved to present Mountain Grove and established the town 3 years later.

KOUNTZ FORT, Missouri: Site located one mile from Cittleville. Established 1812 by John & Nicholas Kountz.

MARLIN CITY, Missouri: Located 4 miles east of Palmyra on bank of Mississippi River. Founded 1835 by Col. William Muldrow. Flooded 1836, 1841, and 1851. By 1850, it was a principal livestock market but the flood of 1851 ended the towns prosperity. A few scant ruins are visible in the swamp at times.

MILLVILLE, Missouri: Site located near Versailles in Morgan County. Trade center and county seat until 1834 when seat was moved to Versailles.

MINE LA MATTE, Missouri: Located on Hiway 61-67 about 5 miles north of Fredericktown. Probably the oldest town in Missouri. Founded 1715 by Sieur Antoine de la Matte Cadillac, Governor-General of Louisiana, as a lead-mining town. Ruins are visible among trees and vines on hill above creek.

OLD FRANKLIN, Missouri: Located 25 miles west of Columbia on Hiway 40 and ½ mile north on Hiway 87. Founded 1816 on Missouri River bank. In 1821, it was the eastern terminus of the Santa Fe Trail . Establishment of boat landings farther up the Missouri River at Lexington, Independence, and Westport led to its depopulation and by 1843 it was a ghost town. From here, William Becknell, in 1821, began the first commercial operations over the Santa Fe Trail and Kit Carson arrived as a 2 year old boy in 1811 (before the founding of the town) and lived till 1826.

NEW SANTA FE, Missouri Founded 1833 on the Santa Fe Trail as Little Santa Fe. Incorporated 1851 as New Santa Fe. It was a booming supply town on the trails to Santa Fe and Mexico, but the Border War of 1855-56, the Civil War, and outlaw raids thereafter reduced the town. When the railroads bypassed it, it died. Located about 20 miles south from Kansas City, or 6 miles southeast of Hickman Mills.

NOUVELLE BOURBON, Missouri: Founded 1793 by Baron de Carondelet, Governor of Louisiana, for a group of French Royalist refugees. The settlement was too near the original town of St. Genevieve to prosper. Site located on Mississippi River bluffs near St. Genevieve.

OLD LEBANON, Missouri: Located on outskirts of present Lebanon. A few old buildings dating back to the 1850's and 1860's remain.

OLD ST. GENEVIEVE, Missouri: Site located about 3 miles below (southeast) of present St. Genevieve on the Mississippi River. Oldest town in Missouri but actual date of founding is unknown. Several buildings in St. Genevieve date back to the mid-1700's.

ORONGO, Missouri: Located 4 miles north of Webb City (near Joplin). A dilapidated village remaining from the rich lead and zinc mines. Over a dozen millionaires have been made here since 1854.

RIVERCENE, Missouri: Located on bank of Missouri River between Rock and Boonville. The 3-story Kinney house remains and is used as a museum. The boatyards of Capt. Joseph Kinney were around the house.

SLIGO, Missouri: Located 1 mile east of Hiway 19, about 15½ miles northeast of Salem. Ruins of a number of buildings remain from the iron mining days which extended from 1875 to 1921. Over 2,000 men worked and lived here; now only a handful remain and they are engaged in farming.

SPARTA, Missouri: A once-booming farm and trade town and county seat (1840-46) of Buchanan County. Now, all that remains is the small white Sparta church about 4 miles south of St. Joseph on the west side of Hiway 71.

SPLITLOG, Missouri Founded 1887 as a mining camp in the salted McDonald County. Located 4 miles northeast of Anderson. The promotion was innocently financed by Mathias Splitlog, an illiterate Wyandotte Indian who made a fortune in Kansas City real estate. When the promotion was discovered and exposed, the promoters fled, leaving behind Splitlog a ruined, broken man. The town all but died with him.

WEAUCANDAH, Missouri: Founded 1794 by Godfrey le Sieur as a trading post on the confluence of the Wyaconda and Mississippi Rivers. Site located on southern outskirts of LaGrange (Hiway 61). It was outgrown by the new community of LaGrange in 1930.

MONTANA

Montana is literally riddled with ghost towns. Hundreds of them boomed and died in the short space of a few months. The mountainous areas have a number of old boom mining towns which are now deserted. The valleys of the Missouri, Musselshell, and Yellowstone rivers are spotted with sites of old ranch and farm-towns.

BANNACK, Montana: Located 25 miles west of Dillon (Hiway 91). Montana's oldest town and first Territorial Capitol. Old remains of the first capitol building, hotel, and jail remain along the single street of the gulch. A few residents live in good dwellings adjacent to the ruins of the old town. Some mining is still being done. Town was founded 1862.

BEARTOWN, Montana: Located 12 miles northwest of Drummond (Hiway 10), then south thru Bearmouth to Beartown, 6 miles. A boomtown during the 1860's, it once was in contention for the state capitol. Home of the notorious 'Beartown Roughs.' Nearby is 'Chinee Grade' with all its buried treasure legends.

CHICO, Montana: Located 25 miles south of Livingston on Hiway 89, then 3 miles southeast. Two miles more is Yellowstone City. Located in Emigrant Gulch where gold was discovered 8-30-1864. The town boomed, then died. A few miners who work the side gulches remain in the vicinity and will give directions to visitors.

COOPEROPOLIS, Montana: Located about 11 miles east of White Sulphur Springs on Hiway 6. Several old deserted shacks and mine shafts mark this old ghost.

GARNET, Montana: Located 12 miles northwest of Drummond, then 11 miles south. A ghost town that booms and dies from time to time. Several good buildings remain.

GARNIELL, Montana: Located 21 miles south of Moore (Hiway 87), or 26 miles north of Harlowtown (Hiway 6). An old trade center now reduced to about 100 residents. When the Central Montana Railroad established its station here in 1903, it named the station UBET. About the same time, the Prohibitionists laid out North Garniell, which remains. The 'Wets' laid out wide-open South Garniell. There were three distinct settlements separated only by railroad tracks, streets, or imaginary lines. Present Garniell at first appears to be a single brick store, but behind this are a church, school, and dwellings. Beyond these are the old deserted collapsing dwellings.

GILTEDGE, Montana: Located 1 mile north of Lewistown, then 20 miles east, near old Ft. McGinnis. During the late 1880's, it was a booming gold town and a blow-off town for soldiers; now it is a decaying ghost with a few inhabitants.

GOLD CREEK, Montana: Located 8½ miles northwest of Garrison (Hiway 10), then ¼ mile south near junction of Clark Fork and Gold Creek. A few inhabitants remain, but the town is dead. A rip-roaring gold camp in the old days.

GREENHORN GULCH, Montana: Located 3½ miles west of Helena (on Hiway 10N), then 11 miles north. A rich, booming town and mining camp in the 1880's. The small railroad town of Austin is located on part of the old townsite.

HASSEL, Montana: Located 5 miles west of Townsend (Hiway 10N). A famous gold camp of the 1890's. A few lessees still work the area intermittently and the town is almost a ghost of the original boomtown.

HELL GATE RONDE, Montana: Located 1½ miles northwest of Missoula on Hiway 10, then 3 miles south to old Hell-Gate Store. This was the first mercantile store in Montana and around it grew the settlement of Hell Gate Ronde. On 1-27-1864, six members of the Henry Plummer gang were rounded up here and hanged by vigilantes. Only the log cabin store remains and it is used as a chicken house.

HIGHLAND CITY, Montana: Located 11 miles southeast of Butte on Hiway 10S, then 4 miles south on Roosevelt Drive at the Foot of Red Mountain. A rip-roaring gold camp that was larger than Butte. When the ore pinched out, the miners moved away. A few buildings remain and basements among the ruins can be found in the sagebrush. A cemetary with graves of well-known frontier characters (including Shotgun Liz) marks the town limits.

INDEPENDENCE, Montana: Located by turning south in Big Timber (Hiway 10) on McLeon Street for 40 miles. A boomtown just before the turn of the century. By 1893, it had 500 residents. Today, old buildings and machinery remain to mark the site. A few trappers occupy some buildings during the winter season. Three miles north is old site of Contact, a stage station.

LANDUSKY, Montana: Located on south edge of Ft. Belknap Indian Reservation about 48 miles southeast of Harlem (Hiway 2). A rip-roaring town founded because of Pike Landusky's famous August Mine. The outlaw Curry Brothers had a ranch 5 miles south of town. A few residents remain in this ghost which is perched on a mountain side.

LOUISVILLE, Montana: Located 16 miles northwest of Superior (Hiway 10) on the Cedar Creek Road. Gold was discovered here 1869 by Barrette and Lanthier, French-Canadians. Over 10,000 people rushed to the camp and as its deposits were worked out, the camp moved. Several ghosts are in the vicinity on Cedar Creek; among them Forest City, Mayville, and Cedar Creek.

LUMP CITY, Montana: Located 2 miles west of Clancey (Hiway 91), about 12 miles south of Helena. A rich silver town in the 1890's. Now, nothing remains but an idle schoolhouse and ruins.

MAIDEN, Montana: Located 18 miles northeast of Lewistown.

A booming gold camp of the 1880's and 1890's. A few old buildings remain.

MARYSVILLE, Montana: Located 14 miles north of Helena on Benton Avenue, then 6½ miles west. It had over 3,000 residents during the late 1880's and early 1890's. Today, less than 100 people remain. Old boardwalks, stores, and saloons remain among the ruins of cabins.

MONARCH, Montana: Located 49 miles southeast of Great Falls on Hiway 89. An old, mostly-deserted gold mining camp.

NEVADA, Montana: Located 1 mile west of Virginia City on Hiway 34. An abandoned, decaying town that was questionably a part of Virginia City in its heyday. Here is where George Ives was tried and hanged; the first of the Plummer Gang to be tried by the Vigilantes.

NEW YEAR, Montana: Located 1 mile north, then 12 miles east of Lewistown. A rich gold camp of the 1880's. The famous Crystal Cave opens off of the main shaft of the New Year Mine.

PARKER, Montana: Located 8 miles west of Totson (Hiway 10N). A few buildings remain to mark the old mining camp. Just 5 miles further west is Radersburg which has been intermittently a boom- and then a ghost-town.

PIONEER, Montana: Located 8½ miles northeast of Garrison (Hiway 10), then 9 miles south. A rich, booming gold town which died because of lack of transportation and the rush to the Bannack gold fields. Cabins built in the early 1860's remain.

RUBY, Montana: Located 8 miles west of Virginia City on Hiway 34. A booming mining camp in the 1860's; now a group of cabins with sod roofs. A store and service station are modern additions to the old town and about 25 residents remain.

SUPERIOR, Montana: Located near present town of Superior on Hiway 10, about 60 miles northwest of Missoula. The old town was founded at the mouth of Bear Creek, 1 mile east of the present town. In 1869, the new town was built and the name taken from the old town. The present town is divided by Clark Fork; the second old town of the 1870's on one bank and the newer town on the opposite bank.

UBET, Montana: Located 3 miles west of the ghost town of GARNIELL. A couple of log cabins remain on the site of the old stage station. When the Central Montana Railroad came through, they named the nearest station UBET in honor of this famous old stage station. See GARNIELL.

YELLOWSTONE CITY, Montana: Located 25 miles south of Livingston on Hiway 89, then 5 miles southeast. Beginning as a tent town in 1864, it boomed. When the gold pinched out and the Crow Indians raided the settlement, it was abandoned 1866 leaving many log cabins. Since then miners periodically occupy some of the cabins, and some have built new ones, but the town is dead and deserted. See CHICO.

ZORTMAN, Montana: Located on south edge of Ft. Belknap Indian Reservation about 50 miles southeast of Harlem (Hiway 2). A 1929 fire wiped out most of the business district but the buildings and a few inhabitants remaining in this town are genuine remnants of the gold era.

NEBRASKA

Nebraska is littered with old ghost towns and sites. It was criss-crossed with emigrant trails, cattle trails, and military freight roads. Many of the old Missouri river landings boomed and grew with the emigrant tide and then died when the railroads spread their lines west. The historic towns of Springranch on the Blue River and Newark on the Oregon Trail and Platte river near Fort Kearny are old towns which lost their railroads and folded in the past quarter-century.

AMBOY, Nebraska: Located about 5 miles east of Red Cloud on Hiway 3. Once a booming mill town and farm center. Now, all but a ghost. Dam, millrace, and mill ruins are evident.

BLOOMINGTON, Nebraska: Located about 5 miles west of Franklin. Onetime trading center of the Republican River and County Seat of Franklin County, and site of Government Land Office. Now reduced to an abandoned city of about 100 buildings with miles of concrete paving and very few inhabitants. Town dates back to the early 1800's.

BROOKLYN, Nebraska: Located about 3 miles west of old town of Bloomington. Remains of old foundations are evident and part of the mill remains.

CENTORIA, Nebraska: Located on south side of Platte River oppose city of Kearney. Nearby is site of early town of Kearney City. Little evidence of either remains, although treasure hunters occasionally resurrect some treasure.

COTTONWOOD SPRINGS, Nebraska: Located about 1 mile east

of Ft. McPherson National Cemetery, or 4 miles south of Maxwell. Monument on site and several treasures have been discovered near this old site.

DEVILS NEST, Nebraska: Located 5 miles north of Lindy. A notorious outlaw and desparado hideout in the early days. Many infamous outlaws rested and hid here to avoid arrest. Ruins and evidence of dugouts remains. Devils Nest is a tract of woodlands and rough meadow along the Missouri River and it was referred to as Bonhomme Island in the Lewis and Clark Journals.

DOBYTOWN, Nebraska: located 1 mile west of Ft. Kearney on Hiway 10. During the 1840's, this was one of the wildest, wickedest towns in the world. Soldiers coming from nearby Ft. Kearney and travellers on the Oregon and Mormon Trails made it one of the few wide-open, 24-hour-a-day celebration towns. The site is being farmed but guns and other reminders of its past are frequently found. One of its outlaw mayors once proclaimed that it had the longest main street in the world; from Westport Landing, Missouri to Astoria, Oregon.

FACTORYVILLE, Nebraska: Located 1 mile south of Union. Nothing remains but depressions where a flour mill, business buildings, and the Factoryville College stood.

KEARNEY CITY, Nebraska: Site is located on south side of Platte River about 4 miles west of Ft. Kearney or 1 mile south of the site of Centoria.

LOWELL, Nebraska: Located 10 miles south of Gibbon. Once a booming cattle shipping center on the Burlington and Missouri Railroad. It was the terminus of many trail drives and at one time had a population of 5,000 people living in frame shacks and tents. In its day, it was a tough cattle town; equally as tough as Wichita or Dodge City.

MARTINVILLE, Nebraska: Site located on Martin Farm 9 miles west of Doniphan. One of the original farm buildings remains. George Martin settled here in 1850 and his trading post served the Oregon and Mormon Trailers.

NEAPOLIS, Nebraska: A paper town which never existed. Selected as site for the state capitol by the legislature of 1858, the area boomed and opportunists buried or cached booze, money, and merchandise in the area to be ready for the big boom. The legislature reversed itself and much of the hidden merchandise was left where it was hidden. Site is located near

Cedar Bluffs on south side of the Platte River and is still known as Capitol Hill.

NEWARK, Nebraska: Located 10 miles north and 1 mile west of Minden. Once a thriving frontier and farm town. The railroad left and so did the population. Now a ghost town hidden among the hundred-year old cottonwoods which stretch north of the old hiway.

OREAPOLIS, Nebraska: Located 2½ miles north of Plattsmouth on the Platte River near the bridge approach. Nearby on the north side of the river is Moses Merrill's Mission site.

RYLANDER, Nebraska: Located about 3 miles northwest of Farnam. A trading post established in the 1860's by John Rylander. When opened to homesteading, he homesteaded the tract he settled on. Nothing remains but depressions of dugouts, the cistern, icehouse, and the well. Still known as the Rylander Homestead.

SPRINGRANCH, Nebraska: Located about 5 miles west of Fairfield on Blue River. Town is still shown on some maps. Old depot, stockyard, and ruins of old business section remain. A mile west of town is the old frontier cemetery. The Pony Express and the stage stations are gone.

STOCKVILLE, Nebraska: Located on Hiway 23S about 28 miles southeast of Wellfleet (Hiway 83). Once a booming frontier town; now, a county seat with less than 200 people.

YANKTON, Nebraska: Located 1 mile south of Rulo on Stephen Cunningham farm. Only holes and depressions in earth mark this old town.

NEVADA

Nevada has ghost towns galore. Almost any sideroad from the main highways will lead you to an old mining camp or deserted town.

AURORA, Nevada: Located almost on the California-Nevada state line, just off of Hiway 30, or 26 miles from Bridgeport, California on the Bridgeport-Brawley Peaks road, or 23 miles from Hawthorne, Nevada. During the Civil War the town had a population of almost 10,000 people; now only a few ruins remain.

AUSTIN, Nevada: Located near Austin Summit on Hiway 50 in center of Nevada. A boom town in the Civil War days.

BELLEVILLE, Nevada: Located 7 miles southwest of Hiway 95 turn-off which is 6 miles south of Mina. Once a prosperous town, it is now waiting for the last of its residents to die or leave. Some buildings still standing and many ruins.

BELMONT, Nevada: Located 47 miles northeast of Tonopah on Hiway 82. A few residents remain to keep this roaring town of the post-Civil War days on the map. Buildings still standing and many ruins.

BETTY O'NEAL, Nevada: Located 14 miles south of Battle Mountain. A deserted mining camp, busy as late as the 1920's. The mill and boarding house remain.

BONNIE CLARE, Nevada: Located 5 miles west of Hiway 95, just off of Hiway 72 which goes to Death Valley Scotty's castle. One building and a few ruins remain.

BRISTOL WELLS, Nevada: Located about 45 miles north of Caliente (Hiway 93), to the south of Fairview Peak. Founded in 1873, it became a prosperous mining town with a smelter. Today, 3 kilns, two cabins, and other ruins remain.

BULLFROG, Nevada: Located near Hiway 58 about 5 miles southwest of Beatty in the Death Valley National Monument. Some ruins of wood and stone buildings may be seen.

CANDELARIA, Nevada: Located 12 miles northwest and 7 miles west of Coaldale. Claimed at one time to be the richest silver producer in the world; now mostly ruins.

CHARLESTON, Nevada: Located 50 miles north of Deeth (Hiway 40). Once the rowdiest town in Nevada; now only 2 old cabins on '76 Creek remain in ruins.

CLAN ALPINE, Nevada: Located 21 miles north of Eastgate (Hiway 50). Ruins of the mill, company buildings, and barracks, and other buildings mark this site in the Clan Alpine Mountains.

CORTEZ, Nevada: Located south of Mt. Tenabo on east side of Hiway 21 about 38 miles south of Hiway 40; or 45 miles southeast of Battle Mountain. A boomtown of 1,000 residents in 1868; today less than 10 residents live among the old ruins of a mill, cabins, and hotel.

GILBART, Nevada: Located 16 miles east and 12 miles north of Coaldale. An active silver camp before the turn of the century, it died and was resurrected after World War I only to fade again. Buildings remain in a well-preserved condition. Correct name for town is GILBERT, but some old-timers insist the faded old town has an A instead of an E in the name.

GOLDFIELD, Nevada: Located 180 miles northwest of Las Vegas on Hiway 95. Fifty-two blocks of burned out ruins plus the old brick hotel, stone courthouse, and a few other buildings are still standing on the plateau.

GOLD POINT, Nevada: Located 14 miles southwest of Hiway 95, or 11 miles southeast of Lida. Many ruins, a few buildings along with a few residents remain.

GOODSPRINGS, Nevada: Located near Hiway 53 about 7 miles northwest of Jean. Many old buildings and ruins remain.

HAMILTON, Nevada: Located 10 miles south of Hiway 50 between Hamilton and Treasure Peaks in the Nevada National Forest. This famous old silver camp produced nearly $75,000,000 in the 1870's. Many ruins are visible over a large area.

HIKO, Nevada: Located 4 miles north of Crystal Springs. Once a booming mining camp and county seat; now in ruins.

HORNSILVER, Nevada: See GOLD POINT.

JEFFERSON, Nevada: Located 6 miles north of Round Mountain (Hiway 70), which is 55 miles north of Tonopah on Hiway 8A-70. Mining began 1866 and by 1876 a town of almost 1,000 people was there. Today, a number of good buildings remain among the ruins of others.

JOHNNIE, Nevada: Located near Hiway 16 about 13 miles south of Hiway 95, or about 15 miles north of Pahrump. Numerous old buildings are standing and ruins of the old mill and other buildings mark the site.

LIDA, Nevada: See PALMETTO.

LUDWIG, Nevada: Located 17 miles north of Wellington. One of the best preserved abandoned towns in Nevada.

MANHATTAN, Nevada: Located 5 miles east of Hiway 8A from turn-off 41 miles north of Tonopah. Years ago it was a boom town; now just a dying town on the boundaries of the Toiyabe National Forest. There are still a few inhabitants, some buildings, and many ruins.

MIDAS, Nevada: Located 63 miles east of Winnemucca on Hiway 18. A boom town in the early 1900's; it now has only a few old residents.

MINA, Nevada: Located about 28 miles north of Coaldale on

Hiway 95. In a great mining district of the past, Mina still is a little city but just a shadow of its former self. Many other ghost camps and towns are in the area.

ORIENTAL, Nevada: Located 9 miles south of Gold Point in the Grapevine Mountains. This camp and another on Gold Mountain just to the north started a gold and silver rush that soon petered out. Now only foundations and stone walls remain of the two camps.

OSCEOLA, Nevada: Located 40 miles southeast of Ely on the old hiway road; 4 miles off of Hiway 50. Ruins of several buildings remain.

PALISADE, Nevada: Located 10 miles west of Carlin on Hiway 40, then 6 miles south. Three railroads formed a junction here; the Southern Pacific, Western Pacific, and the Eureka and Palisade. Townspeople visualized a railroad center with tracks radiating to every point of the compass. Something went wrong because today a few railroad employees live among the old houses, business buildings, and ruins of others.

PALMETTO, Nevada: Located near Palmetto Mountain and Hiway 3 about 22 miles east of Oasis, California; or 35 miles southwest of Goldfield, Nevada. It's mile-long main street still is lined with ruins of cabins, stores, and the stage station. About 4 miles east is LIDA, another ghost with old buildings and mementos.

PINE GROVE, Nevada: Located in the Toiyabe National Forest south of Mount Etna. A crude mountain road leaves Hiway 3 below the East Walker River and leads thru a pass between Moun Etna and Sugarloaf Mountain to the site.

RAWHIDE, Nevada: Located 40 miles northeast of LUNING (Hiway 95). The ghost of a rip-roaring town of almost 5,000 population; now only in ruins.

RHYOLITE, Nevada: Located 2 miles west and 2 miles north of Beatty. Once a rip-roaring mining town with more than 6,000 residents; now falling into ruins. The railroad depot, some business buildings, are in fair condition. There are many ruins. The world-famous 'Bottle House,' built from discarded bottles from saloons, may still be seen.

ROCKLAND, Nevada: Located in the Toiyabe National Forest near Sugarloaf Mountain. A crude mountain road leaves Hiway 3 below the East Walker River and leads to Rockland and PINE

GROVE. Area has been worked in recent years but many ruins remain untouched.

SEARCHLIGHT, Nevada: Located 55 miles south of Las Vegas on Hiway 95. This famous town is now a water and gasoline stop, with a few residents and several good buildings standing.

SEVEN TROUGHS, Nevada: Located about 3 miles north of Vernon. One of several booming mine camps within walking distance of each other; all of them ghosts.

SILVER PEAK, Nevada: Located near the southern terminus of Hiway 47. A few ruins and footings remain of this abandoned mining camp.

SODAVILLE, Nevada: Located a short distance to the east of Hiway 95 about 3 miles south of Mina. A once famous boomtown now reduced to rubble.

TUSCARORA, Nevada: Located 50 miles northwest of Elko on Hiway 18 near Mt. Blitzen at the 6400-foot level. A booming mining town before the turn of the century, it is now a skeleton of the original with a few buildings remaining.

VERNON, Nevada: Located 25 miles northwest of Lovelock. An active mining town of the past; now just a dying hamlet.

VIRGINIA CITY, Nevada: Located on Hiway 17-45-51-80 between Dayton and Reno. Not a ghost, but many old historic buildings remain in good repair. Well worth seeing if you are ever in the area.

NEW MEXICO

New Mexico is littered with old ghost towns and sites . In so many places, only a fence post, an old adobe building in ruins, or piles of rubble mark the site of an old, once-rambunctious settlement. Some towns just moved over a couple miles to get near the railroad and didn't even bother to change their names.

BINGHAM, New Mexico: Located 29 miles east of San Antonio on Hiway 380. A ghost of the nearby Carthage coal mines.

BONANZA, New Mexico: Located about 15½ miles southwest of Santa Fe near Hiway 10. Ruins remain. Was mining town and then became an outlaw hideout.

BUCKMAN, New Mexico: Located near Otowi on old D&RGW railroad. Ruins of old stock pens remain.

CANONCITO, New Mexico: Located 6 miles southwest of

FLORIETA on Hiway 84-85. An active settlement during Civil War and an important stage station. Ruins remain.

CERRILLOS, New Mexico: Located 9 miles southwest of Santa Fe on Hiway 85, and 14 miles south on Hiway 10. Once a thriving mining town with 21 saloons; now a quiet mining-ranching settlement. It once was called the turquoise capitol of the world.

CHICO, New Mexico: Located 22 miles east of Maxwell (Hiway 85) on old road. Was headquarters for Ingersoll Ranch till Ingersoll's health failed 1892.

CHLORIDE, New Mexico: Located 7 miles north and 29 miles west of Hot Springs on Hiway 52 to Winston, then 2½ miles southwest. Founded 1879. A rich silver town in its time.

COLFAX, New Mexico: Located 29 miles southwest of Raton on Hiway 64. Tourists keep it barely alive.

COLMON, New Mexico: Located near Hiway 85 on Ocate Creek 11 miles south of Springer. An early settlement that faded. A few inhabitants remain. South a few miles are the towns of LEVY and NOLAN.

CUCHILLO, New Mexico: Located 7 miles north and six miles west of Hot Springs on Hiway 52. A non-descript village is all that remains.

DAYTON, New Mexico: Located 9 miles south of Artesia. First a cowtown, then an oil boomtown in the late 1920's; and now a ghost town.

ELIZABETHTOWN, New Mexico: Located 5 miles north of Eagle Nest on Hiway 38. Old mining town.

ENDEE, New Mexico: Located 5 miles west of the Texas state line on Hiway 66. A wild cowboy blowoff town in the early days; now a ruin of shacks.

FRENCH, New Mexico: Located at junction of Southern Pacific and AT&SF railroads 5 miles below Maxwell. A willful, wild, booming cowboy blowoff town in its day; now reduced to a few shacks with grass in the streets.

GOLDEN, New Mexico: Located 9 miles southwest of Santa Fe on Hiway 85, and 30 miles south on Hiway 10. A booming copper town until 1918. Now all but forgotten.

HOLMAN, New Mexico: Located 35 miles northwest of Las Vegas on Hiway 3. A ghost of the booming town on the Santa Fe Trail.

KINGSTON, New Mexico: Located about 20 miles west of

Caballo on Hiway 180. The old town and buildings are hidden behind a grove of trees, but it's there, yet.

Las Palomas, New Mexico: Located 1 mile north of the junction of Hiway 85 with Hiway 180; about 14 miles south of Hot Springs near the Rio Grande River. A primitive village near the ruins of a pueblo.

Levy, New Mexico: Located 5 miles north of Wagon Mound (Hiway 85). A trade center once; now almost abandoned. A few miles north are COLMON and NOLAN.

Madison, New Mexico: Site is located a short distance from village of Folsom on Hiway 32. A shack and a few mounds mark this once wild cowtown.

Madrid, New Mexico: Located 9 miles southwest of Santa Fe on Hiway 85, and 17 miles south on Hiway 10. An abandoned coal-mining town, only about 15 of the 700 boom-time families remain. Abandoned company buildings cover the townsite.

Mogollon, New Mexico: Located 8 miles east of Alma on Hiway 78. An old gold-silver camp. Nearby are several abandoned ghost camps.

No Agua, New Mexico: Located 25 miles south of Colorado state line on Hiway 235. Once a railroad station; now deserted.

Nolan, New Mexico: Located on Hiway 85 about 15 miles south of Springer. An early settlement that is all but gone. COLMON is four miles north.

Pearl, New Mexico: Located 30 miles west and 7 miles south of Hobbs. Nothing remains but a few foundations.

Quarai, New Mexico: Located near Hiway 10 about 1 mile north of Mountainair. Mission settlement which was abandoned about 1674.

San Pedro, New Mexico: Located 16 miles east of Albuquerque on Hiway 66, 15 miles north on Hiway 10, then 1 mile east. A copper boomtown that died in 1918. Golden, Madrid, and Cerrillos are other ghost towns a few miles to the north.

Torrance, New Mexico: Located 8 miles north of Corona. Formerly a railroad boom town.

Turley's Mill, New Mexico: Located 2 miles west of Arroyo Hondo (Hiway3). Settled 1830 by Simeon Turley. Ruins of mill and distillery remain.

White Oaks, New Mexico: Located 15 miles east of Ancho. It is an old mining town that has been abandoned.

YANKEE, New Mexico: Located 8 miles northeast of Raton on Hiway 72. A coal-mining town that was deserted when the projected railroad failed.

NORTH DAKOTA

North Dakota was the focal point for many agricultural developments that failed. The Missouri River is lined with sites of old towns and a few well-preserved towns remain on the plains. Some of these old ghosts are no longer on or near travelled roads.

ANTELOPE, North Dakota: Located 31 miles east of Dickinson near Hiway 10. Custer's troops passed by there on their way to the Little Big Horn and eternity, and a military road is along the same route. Ruts remain to be seen.

ARVILLA, North Dakota: Located 22 miles west and 1 mile south of Grand Forks near Hiway 2. A booming college town in the 1880's. Fire destroyed the academy in 1893 and the town never recovered.

ASHTABULA, North Dakota: Located 19 miles north of Valley City (Hiways 1-10-52) on Sheyenne River. Ruts of several famous trails are evident here and in the vicinity. Nothing remains of the settlement.

AUBURN, North Dakota: Located 7 miles north of Grafton on Hiway 81. A larger town than its neighbor, Grafton, was until the railroad passed it by.

BARTLETT, North Dakota: Located near Hiway 2 about 4 miles west of Lakota. Once a booming railroad town with 21 saloons. Now, only a scant few people live here.

BELMONT, North Dakota: Located on Red River about 14 miles south of Grand Forks on Hiway 81, then 11½ miles east. A booming river port in the 1870's. The flood of 1897 ruined most of the buildings and the inhabitants departed.

BOWESMONT, North Dakota: Located 24 miles south of Pembina near Hiway 44. Old town site is on valley floor between present town and the Red River.

BUFFORD, North Dakota: Located 8 miles south of Hiway 2 near Montana state line. Remains of American Fur Company settlement established 1828 are here. Nearby is old Fort Bufford and the National Cemetery.

COMFORT, North Dakota: Located 3 miles east of Hallson

near Hiway 5. Now known as Camp Comfort, and it has picnic facilities. Settlement established at junction of old Hunters Trail with Tongue River. Nothing remains of old buildings.

DEAPOLIS, North Dakota: Located on Missouri River a few miles below Stanton (Hiway 25). A single grain elevator remains to mark this ghost of the river boat trade.

FORT CLARK, North Dakota: Located 1 mile east of Hiway 25 on south bank of Missouri River, about 50 miles upstream from Bismark. Founded 1829 as a trading post by the American Fur Company. A few excavations remain.

FORT RANSOM, North Dakota: Located 27 miles north of Oakes on Hiway 1, and then 7 miles east. Founded 1818 near military post of the same name. A few people remain in the settlement. Old fort is nearby on top of hill and is being restored.

FORT RICE, North Dakota: Located directly upstream on the Missouri River from Fort Yates. Established 1864 and abandoned 1877. When Fort Yates was established Ft. Rice was abandoned.

GRANDIN, North Dakota: Located 33 miles north of Fargo on Hiway 81. One of four boomtowns under the Grandin Brothers bonanza system. Nearby Mayville is another. Original Grandin site is a few miles east but nothing remains at the site.

GRAND RAPIDS, North Dakota: Located on James River and Hiway 63 about 40 miles southeast of Jamestown. County seat until 1886; then it declined.

GRIFFIN, North Dakota: Located 6 miles west and 3 miles north of Bowman (Hiway 12-85). Known originally as Atkinson, it lost a bitter fight with Bowman and dwindled.

HUNGRY GULCH, North Dakota: Located 5 miles south and 3 miles east of Wheelock (Hiway 2). A false gold rush to Tabacco Garden Creek in 1902 on land owned by James Moorman started the settlement.

LE ROY, North Dakota: Located 3 miles north and 4 miles east of Walhalla then 3, miles south (of Hiway 55) on south side of Pembina River. Remains of Hudson's Bay Company settlement. Log cabins scattered through the timber.

LITTLE MISSOURI, North Dakota: Located ½ mile west of present Medora. Site is marked by a few cellar pits. Town preceded Medora.

MANHAVEN, North Dakota: Located on east bank of Missouri River about 15 miles north of Stanton. Founded 1809 as Ft.

Manuel Lisa or Fort Lewis. Abandoned 1812. Occupied 1822 as Fort Vanderburgh. Later, the town of Mannhaven was resurrected nearby.

MEDORA, North Dakota: Located on Hiway 10 about 24 miles east of Beach. Once a booming cowtown. Across the Little Missouri River on the west bank was LITTLE MISSOURI CANTONMENT, established 1879 to protect railroad workers.

OAKDALE, North Dakota: Located about 10 miles northwest of Killdeer (Hiway 22-25) on eastern slope of South Killdeer Mountain. Once a prosperous frontier town; now a ghost town with few buildings.

OJATA, North Dakota: Located 9 miles west of Grand Forks and 1 mile south. Once was a thriving town and railroad terminal called Stickney. Swamp land and extension of railroad spelled its doom.

OLD BOTTINEAU, North Dakota: Located about 1 mile from present Bottineau (Hiway 5) on Oak Creek. Nothing remains; not even a monument. A few treasure hunters, however, have struck it rich here.

OLD LUDDEN, North Dakota: Located on Hiway 1-11 near South Dakota line. Founded 1833 by Frank Randall. Town was moved in 1886 to present site.

PLEASANT LAKE, North Dakota: Located 45 miles west of Devils Lake near Hiway 2. Settlement between lake and railroad station is gone.

ROCK HAVEN, North Dakota: Located 2 miles north of Bismark on banks of Missouri River. Once a dry-dock and boat yard for river boat traffic. Few structures remain.

ST. JOE, North Dakota: Located near summit of Pembina Mountains near Lookout Point west of Walhalla. Nearby is Protestant Cemetery. Established 1851 as a trading post. Nothing remains.

ST. JOSEPH, North Dakota: Located on north bank of Pembina River about 15 miles west of Walhalla.

VERENDRYE, North Dakota: Located 11 miles northeast of Velva (Hiway 41-52) on Mouse River. Founded as Falsen, a trading post. Few people remain.

WAMDUSKA, North Dakota: Located near Lake Wamduska about 10 miles south of Lakota (Hiway 1-2). Founded during 1880's as a Great Northern railroad town. The railroad ran 10 miles north of townsite and the town declined. A 75 room hotel remains and is used as a storehouse.

WINONA, North Dakota: Located across Missouri River from Fort Yates (Hiway 24) near South Dakota line. Once a wild, rip-roaring army and, later, ranch town. Nothing remains but a group of trees and cellars. No river crossing from Fort Yates.

OKLAHOMA

Oklahoma has a number of old towns which were abandoned during the dust storms of the 1930's. Often, a lone building in the center of a large wheat field marks the site of a once baudy, lusty boom town. Along the valleys of the Arkansas and Canadian rivers are the sites of many old towns.

ARMSTRONG ACADEMY, Oklahoma: See CHOCTAW TOWN.

BIGHEART, Oklahoma: Located on Hiway 99 about 10 miles south of the Kansas state line. Once a thriving trading center for the Indians. Named for Osage Chief James Bigheart. Now only four houses and a store remain.

BOGGY DEPOT, Oklahoma: Located about 13 miles northwest of Atoka (Hiway 69-75) near (1 mi.) Clear Boggy Creek. Founded 1837, postoffice established 1849. Was confederate outpost for 4 years during Civil War. When the M-K-T railroad bypassed the town, it died. Ruins of buildings and traces of old streets are visible and evidence of the cemetery remains.

BURNETT, Oklahoma: Located near Bishop on the Little Robe Creek. Established by W. F. Burnett. In 1899, he built the Burnett Gristmill which operated until 1925 when it was abandoned. Ruins remain.

CAMP MASON, Oklahoma: Located on the east bank of the Canadian River in the vicinity of Lexington. Here in 1835 was held the great peace council between the Five Civilized Tribes and the Plains Indians. After the council, the Chouteaus of St. Louis established a trading post on the site. Nothing remains.

CHATA TAMAHA, Oklahoma: See CHOCTAW TOWN.

CHOCTAW TOWN, Oklahoma: Located 2½ miles north of Bokchito (Hiway 70). Known also as ARMSTRONG ACADEMY and CHATA TAMAHA. Founded 1844 as a school for Choctaw Indians. School building burned 1921, but ruins of some old buildings remain.

CORNISH, Oklahoma: Located 1 mile south of Ringling (Hiway

70). Nothing remains but the diggings of some treasure hunters.

DOAKSVILLE, Oklahoma: Located 1 mile north of the town of Ft. Towson (Hiway 70). Founded by the Doaks Brothers, traders, in 1821. Until the Civil War, a thriving trading settlement, now a few ruins remain.

FRED, Oklahoma: Located 4 miles south and 1 mile east of Chickasha near Hiway 19. At this point, the Boggy Depot-Fort Sill Road crossed the Chisholm Trail. A trading post, stage station, and small settlement was located here. The trading post was moved here from the Washita River crossing of the Chisholm Trail.

GIBSON, Oklahoma: Located 3 miles north of OKAY (Hiway 69). For a few months in 1871, Gibson was the terminus of the M-K-T Railroad while the Arkansas River to the southwest was being bridged. During this time, the town boomed and continued until 1886 when the Arkansas Valley and Kansas Railroad formed a junction with the M-K-T at Wagoner to the north. After that, the wild town tamed and died. Few residents remain today.

GRAND, Oklahoma: Located 12 miles south of Arnett on Hiway 283, then 1½ miles west. A boom town during first World War. Dust storms of the early 1930's drove the settlers out. Vacant buildings and old foundations are drifted with dirt and sand.

INGALLS, Oklahoma: Located 3½ miles east of Ripley. Ripley is 9½ miles west of Cushing (Hiway 33) and 2½ miles north. The few remaining buildings are falling to ruins. The infamous TRILBY SALOON, interior of which is bullet scarred, was the hangout of the Doolin and Dalton gangs and it remains as the most prominent ruins. Hereabouts, too, a patent medicine king from New York built a now-gone railroad, irrigation project, and a mill. The streets have now reverted to grass and weeds.

KREBS, Oklahoma: Located 3 miles east of McAlester. A mining town (coal) until the 1930's; now a farm community. Nearby are ruins of mines and small settlements.

MAYHEW COURTHOUSE, Oklahoma: Located 4 miles north of Boswell. Seat of the tribal court of the Choctaws. Nothing remains except ruins.

NORTH FORK TOWN, Oklahoma: Located 2 miles east of Eufaula (Hiway 69) on North Fork of the Canadian River.

Founded 1836 as a Creek Indian Town, name was changed to MICCO when the post office was established 1853. The Texas Road and a branch of the California Trail crossed the river here. When Eufaula was platted on the railroad in 1872, North Fork Town was deserted by residents who moved to be near the railroad. Few ruins remain.

NUNIH WAYAH, Oklahoma: Located 1½ miles west of Tuskahoma (Hiway 271). Old capitol of the Choctaw Nation. A pile of rocks from the capitol chimney marks the site. Other similar sites are within a 5 mile radius.

OKAY, Oklahoma: Located 13 miles north of Muskogee. A town too tough to die; too unlucky to thrive. Known successively as CORETTA SWITCH, NORTH MUSKOGEE, REX, and finally as OKAY. Stove, plow, truck, and airplane factories became bankrupt; storms, fire, and floods have ravaged the town. One of the oldest white settlements in Oklahoma, a few people keep it on the map. A half-mile south of town is famous Three Forks, confluence of the Arkansas, Grand (Neosho), and Verdigris Rivers, where the traders Brand & Barbour, established a trading post which was sold in 1822 to the Chouteau interests and again sold 1828 to the Government for use as a Creek Agency.

PERRYVILLE, Oklahoma: Located 8½ miles south of McAlester, then ½ mile west on side road. Founded 1838 by James Perry. Postoffice established 1841. Town was used as Confederate outpost and supply depot during the Civil War. After Battle of Honey Springs, Federal army pursued Confederate forces here where the reinforced Confederates were again beaten. The Federals fired the town and it was never rebuilt. Ruins remain and a replica of the old stage station is on site of original station.

SALT WORKS, Oklahoma: Located 7 miles north of Gore on Saline Creek. Founded by Bean and Sanders 1820. Nothing remains of over 100 salt kettles, warehouses, and homes.

SCULLYVILLE, Oklahoma: Located near Hiway 271 about 11½ miles southwest of Fort Smith, Arkansas. Founded 1822. Demolished by Confederate troops at end of Civil War; the town never recovered. A few buildings and ruins remain.

SEWELL'S STOCKADE, Oklahoma: Located about ¾ mile south of Jefferson and then ¾ mile east. Built by a settler named Sewell for protection from Indian mourning and war parties.

It became a rest stop for trail drivers. Built in the early 1870's, nothing remains but a monument.

SILVER CITY, Oklahoma: Located about 2 miles north of Tuttle near the south bank of the Canadian River. An important watering place for trail herds and trade center for cattlemen. On the eastern outskirts of Tuttle (Hiway 37) is a 12-ton boulder marking the Chisholm Trail and site of SILVER CITY TRADING POST.

SOUTH COFFEEVILLE, Oklahoma: Located on the Verdigre River across the state line from Coffeeville, Kansas. In the early days when both Indian Territory and Kansas were dry, saloons and palaces of pleasure ran wide-open. When U.S. Marshalls arrived, liquor stocks were moved into Kansas temporarilly. When Kansas officers arrived, the stocks were moved a few feet back into Indian Territory. Enraged Kansans frequently ignored the line of demarcation and destroyed or burned the saloons. Remnants and mementos of the wide-open town will be found along the river and on the outskirts of town, yet.

TULLAHASSE SCHOOL, Oklahoma: Located 6 miles from Muskogee. Established 1850 by Rev. R. M. Loughridge as a Presbyterian Mission to the Creek Indians. Damaged in Civil War and burned 1880, it was rebuilt and used for years by Creeks in educating Negro freedmen.

UNION MISSION, Oklahoma: Located about 10 miles southeast of Chouteau (Hiway 33-69). Founded 1819 as a Presbyterian Mission to the Osage Indians. A settlement grew around the mission. Foundation stones and a few ruins remain. Nearby in field is Union Mission Cemetery and in nearby locust grove is French Cemetery with toppled and broken headstones of early French traders.

OREGON

Oregon is littered with abandoned or almost-abandoned towns. Almost every river is marked frequently with sites of old towns. Any old building in the mountains can mark the site of an old ghost town.

ALTHOUSE, Oregon: Located 2½ miles east of Hiway 199 on Hiway 46, which runs from Cave Junction to Oregon Caves National Monument. Several ghost towns are on or near this Hiway 46, including BROWNTON, GRAYBACK CAMP, and HOLLAND.

AUBURN, Oregon: Located 7 miles south of Baker (Hiway 7-30) on Hiway 7, then 2.6 miles west, and 3½ miles south. Founded 1861 as gold camp. Named county seat 1862. In 1864, it was the second largest town in Oregon with 5,000 residents. Gold in Idaho attracted the miners and by 1868 the county seat was moved to Baker. Two cemeteries remain; one for Chinese, one for the white people.

AURORA, Oregon: Old town site is situated across the creek from present town, about 33 miles south of Portland on Hiway 99E. Many old buildings still remain in the area.

BOSTON, Oregon: Located 12 miles south and 2 miles east of Albany (Hiway 99). Once a booming mill and trade center with a popular annual fair and festival. The railroad missed the town by 2 miles in 1871 and the residents moved away. Everybody moved to SHEDD, 2 miles away on the railroad. The old Thompson Flour Mill, built in 1856, remains.

BROWNTON, Oregon: See ALTHOUSE.

CARSON, Oregon: See CORNUCOPIA.

CECIL, Oregon: Located on Hiway 74 about 15 miles south of Heppner Junction (Hiway 30). An early settlement at the Oregon Trail crossing of Willow Creek, and a busy stage station. The famous Oregon Trail well remains in the center of main street.

COPPERFIELD, Oregon: Located 20 miles north of ROBINETTE (Hiway 86) on the Snake River. Founded 1908 as a construction town for a power plant and the railroad. Because of lawlessness, the National Guard invaded the town on 1-1-1914 and inaugerated maritial law. A few months later fire razed the town. Few buildings remained and the town never recovered. HOMESTEAD, a few miles north, absorbed many of the people after the fire, but now it, too, is a ghost.

CORNUCOPIA, Oregon: Located about 21 miles northwest of Robinette (Hiway 86). This and nearby CARSON were booming gold and silver camps during the 1880's. Now, both are ghosts.

DENIO, Oregon: Located on Oregon-Nevada state line about 175 miles southeast of Burns. Once a wool and borax center with a population of nearly 1,000. Now less than 100 people remain. The 50-year old adobe hotel is standing.

DIXIE, Oregon: Site is located just north of PRAIRIE CITY. Founded 1862 as a gold boomtown. In ten years, the gold petered out and the residents moved down to the new farm town PRAIRIE CITY, or to other gold fields. A few ruins remain.

ELDORADO, Oregon: See MALHEUR CITY.

ELK CITY, Oregon: Located about 6 miles east of TOLEDO (Hiway 20-229). Founded 1866 as a terminal on the Wagon Road. Platted 1868. A ghost town frequently resurrected by hunting and fishing parties.

ELKTON, Oregon: Located 13 miles west of DRAIN on Hiway 38. Founded 1832 as a Hudson's Bay Company trading post. Abandoned 1851 by HBC and resettled 1854. Once it was a stage station.

ELLENDALE, Oregon: Located 2½ miles south of Dallas (Hiway 22-223). Founded 1844 by James O'Neal. Known as O'Neal Mills and later as NESMITH'S MILLS. South on nearby Hiway 223 are several deserted towns.

FORT HAYS, Oregon: Located 2½ miles north of Selma on bank of Clear Creek. Founded 1852 as a stage station and tavern. A battle of Rogue River Indian Wars was fought here 3-24-1856. Site is also known as ANDERSON STAGE STATION. Original buildings remain. 1½ miles south at second crossing of Clear Creek is pioneer cemetery.

FORT ROCK, Oregon: Located 3 miles south of Horse Ranch near Hiway 31, then 7 miles east. Just a mile south of the basalt rock formation 'Fort Rock.' Founded 1908. The town once had 3 stores, 2 saloons, a creamery and cheese factory, newspaper, and school, now a deserted cluster of old frame buildings remain.

FRANKFORT, Oregon: Located near Hiway 101 about 44 miles south of Bandon. A former ocean shipping town. Docks were on Sister Rocks and connected to town by bridge and a wooden railway.

FRENCHGLEN, Oregon: Located 64 miles south of Burns (Hiway 20-78-205-395) near Blitzen River. A colorful cowtown founded by Peter French in 1875. One mile south and 1 mile west is the old P Ranch headquarters among a stand of tall poplars.

GALICE, Oregon: Located 21 miles northwest of Grants Pass, 14 miles past old MERLIN. Ruins of Rogue River Indian War powder house and arsenal, built 1854, are here beside the gold diggings.

GRANITE, Oregon: Located on Granite Creek about 41 miles

west of Baker (Hiway 30). Founded 7-4-1862 as INDEPENDENCE. Ruins of 3-story Grand Hotel and other buildings remain of this mining supply metropolis of yesteryear.

GRAYBACK CAMP, Oregon: See ALTHOUSE.

HARDMAN, Oregon: Located on Hiway 207 about 20 miles southwest of Heppner (Hiway 74-207). Known originally as RAWDOG, name was changed to DAIRYVILLE, and then to HARDMAN. Once a stage station and prosperous settlement.

HARNEY, Oregon: Located 12 miles east of BURNS on Hiway 20, then 2 miles north, on Rattlesnake Creek. Once the social center of Harney Valley; now it is abandoned. A few years ago, the fixtures were still in the deserted general store. Two miles north is site of FORT HARNEY.

HOMESTEAD, Oregon: See COPPERFIELD.

JACKSONVILLE, Oregon: Located 4 to 5 miles west of Medford on Hiway 238. Not a ghost town . . . yet, but significant because many century old buildings remain in use.

KERBY, Oregon: Located 28 miles southwest of Grants Pass on Hiway 199. Founded 1856 as KERBYVILLE. In 1858, it became county seat with 500 residents. When the placer deposits were worked out, the miners left. The old stage station, with balcony and columnades, and the stagebarn remain among the ruins of other old buildings.

LOWER TOWN, Oregon: See SCOTTSBURG.

MALHEUR CITY, Oregon: Now known as MALHEUR. Located 20 miles northwest of Brogan (Hiway26). Founded 1872. Up the gulch are sites of MARYSVILLE and ELDORADO.

MARYSVILLE, Oregon: See MALHEUR CITY.

MERLIN, Oregon: Located 7 miles northwest of Grants Pass. A few years ago the old assay office remained intact. Site of prehistoric pit houses is nearby.

MITCHELL, Oregon: Located 45 miles east of Prineville on Hiway 26. Founded 1867 as a stage station on the Dalles-Canyon City route. Not yet a ghost, it has been beset by fire, flood, and outlaws repeatedly. Now, it is just a shadow of the town of the 1870's.

OAK POINT, Oregon: Located 4 miles north of Clatskanie (Hiway 30-47) on Fanny's Bottom. Founded 5-26-1810 by Capt. Nathan Winship as a river port and trading post. Nothing remains but rubble and a few questionable graves.

PARKERSBURG, Oregon: Located about 4 miles east of Bandon on Hiway 101. Before 1900, lumber mills, shipyards, and a salmon cannery were located here. The cannery burned, the lumber business dwindled, and the town folded.

SANTIAM CITY, Oregon: See SYRACUSE.

SCOTTSBURG, Oregon: Located 11 miles east of Reedsport on Hiway 38. Founded 1850; floundered 1861 due to closing of mines and a flood. LOWER TOWN was lost in 1861 flood of the Umqua River and the site is a lone waste of sand and sagebrush below Scottsburg.

SPARTA, Oregon: Located 21 miles east of Baker (Hiway 30) on Hiway 86, then 12 miles north. Founded 1863 as a gold camp; now ruins of a few buildings remain.

SUMPTER, Oregon: Located 25 miles west of Baker on Hiway 7-220. Founded 1862 as a farm settlement. Discovery of gold boomed the town. By 1900, 3,000 residents lived here. After 1915, the town declined. Today it is in ruins.

SYRACUSE, Oregon: Located on south side of Santiam River about 1 mile west of Jefferson (6 miles north, 3 miles east of Albany). Founded 1848. Milton Male, the founder, established a ferry that filled the town with immigrants. North across the river was SANTIAM CITY which prospered and then died with Syracuse. Nothing remains of either except the cemetery.

TAKILMA, Oregon: Located 5 miles east and 1 mile south of O'Brien (Hiway 199). A ghost of the gold rush, then copper operations. WALDO is 1 mile north.

WALDO, Oregon: Located 5 miles east of O'Brien (Hiway 199). TAKIMA is 1 mile south.

WELLS SPRING, Oregon: Located 15 miles south and 1 mile east of Boardman (Hiway 30). The town has been gone a half-century but the cemetery remains enclosed in a tight fence. Col. Cornelius Gilliam, who was killed 3-24-1849 in a gun accident, is buried here.

SOUTH DAKOTA

South Dakota has become well settled, but a number of towns remain. The Missouri River valley is marked by old town sites throughout the state, but there are some good ghosts in other areas, particularly in the northeast section of the state.

ASHTON, South Dakota: Located near present city of Ashton.

First county seat of Spink County, it was involved with Redfield over change of the county seat. Now gone, a few signs of the town remain. Site is known locally as 'Old Ashton.'

BLOOMINGDALE, South Dakota: Located on east side of creek about 5 miles north of Vermillion.

BUGTOWN, South Dakota: Located 3 miles north of Custer on Hiway 85, then 4 miles west on old road. Once a rooting, tooting mining camp, now just a cluster of rotting cabins.

CAMP GORMAN, South Dakota: See SILVER CITY.

CROOK CITY, South Dakota: Located on Hiway 14A about 7 miles from, and over the hill west of, Whitewood. Once a city of over 3,000 residents, when the railroad missed the town in 1888 the town of Whitewood was platted on the other side of the hill and Crook City slowly died. A log cabin and cemetery remain.

FOSYER CITY, South Dakota: Located 22 miles south of Aberdeen, then 5 miles east near entrance to Armadale Park. In 1879 when CMSTP&P railroad surveyed a line through town, it boomed. When the railroad didn't build, the town declined. Nothing remains but a few signs of a town.

LE BEAU, South Dakota: Located 15 miles south of Selby, then 17 miles west. A lone building remains to mark a town which was complete with ferry, stockyards, railroad, and a trading post. Even the railroad is gone.

LEROY, South Dakota: Located on west bank of Big Sioux River about 4 miles north of Richland.

MACY, South Dakota: Located 10½ miles south of Redig near Hiway 85. Only the abandoned postoffice remains. The settlement dates back to the earliest days of the area's settlement and people travelled long distances to pick up their mail here.

MAXWELL, South Dakota: Located on the James River about 2 miles south of Oliver.

MEDARY, South Dakota: Site located immediately south of present Brookings. Founded in 1857 as the first townsite in Dakota Territory. When Brookings was platted in 1879, it absorbed the village of MEDARY. A couple old buildings remain.

MINNESELA, South Dakota: Located 3½ miles east from Belle Fourche on the St. Onge road, then 4 miles north from the east approach to the Redwater bridge. It once had a number of business places, including a drug store, harness shop, blacksmith, hardware store, hotel, and several saloons. Nothing remains today but the hotel which was cut in size and used for a farmhouse until 1936.

NELSON ROADHOUSE, South Dakota: Located near Pukwana (Hiway 16) and now called the Custer Farm. A busy settlement grew here during the gold rush days of the late 1870's and Gen. Custer stopped here on his expedition to the Black Hills in 1875. Prior to this, it had been a military supply base. Now only the main building remains.

OAKWOOD, South Dakota: Site located in Oakwood Lakes State Park. At one time the town had a hotel, flour mill, drugstore, and hardware store, along with a blacksmith shop. Now, nothing remains standing.

OLD SIEM, South Dakota: Located near Hiway 73 bridge across the Grand River. Once a postoffice and trading post in range days. Nothing remains but a marker.

ORDWAY, South Dakota: Located southwest of the Hamlin Garland Homestead site which is 9 miles north and 5 miles east of Aberdeen. Once a booming town and prospective state capitol; when Bismark became capitol the town declined.

ROCHFORD, South Dakota: Located 20 miles south of Pluma, then 12 miles west and south. Founded 1877 by M. D. Rochford who discovered gold while hunting. By 1879, the Standby Mine was operating full blast, but a series of events closed the mine. A number of buildings remain and a few residents live here yet.

ROCKERVILLE, South Dakota: Located near Hiway 16 at foot of Storm Mountain in Black Hills. Founded 1876; by 1882 it was one of the most active towns in the west. Now only a few buildings remain, and nearby are more ghost towns.

SHERIDAN, South Dakota: Founded as GOLDEN CITY 1875 when prospectors found rich placer deposits along Spring Creek and in nearby meadows. In 1876, the camp was organized and the name changed to Sheridan. It then became county seat of Pennington County and the first Federal Court west of the Missouri River was established. In 1878 the county seat was moved to Rapid City and with mines playing out and the railroads building elsewhere, the town declined. It is located on Hiway 85 about 6 miles northeast of Hill City.

SILVER CITY, South Dakota: Located 26 miles south of Pluma on Hiway 85A, then 4 miles west. Founded 1876 by the German

Brothers as Camp German; but seven miners organized, platted, and patented the town as Silver City. A general store and white Catholic Church contrast with the old junk and ruins in the area.

TERRY, South Dakota: Located about 1½ miles south of Lead on Hiway 85, then southwest on the old mining road for 2 miles. Once a city of 1,000 residents, now only a few people live among the ruins.

TIGERVILLE, South Dakota: Located about 5 miles northwest of Hill City. Named for the Bengal Tiger mine which closed 1887. Once a town of 500, now a few chimneys mark the site.

TEXAS

Texas has ghost towns galore, but many of them are on ranches, out of sight and out of reach. Every river in the state has actual deserted towns or old town-sites along its banks.

ADOBE WALLS, Texas: Site located 25 miles north of Borger (Hiway 112) and 13 miles east. Follow the signs. Scene of the famous Battle of Adobe Walls.

BELCHERVILLE, Texas: Located 37 miles east of Wichita Falls on Hiway 82. Once a prosperous cattle and cotton shipping town.

BUFFALO GAP, Texas: Located 15 miles south of Abilene. Ruins of courthouse and jail remain. Few residents remain.

CAMP SAN SABA, Texas: Located 11 miles south of Brady near Hiway 87-183-283. The remains of a settlement which grew on the site of an old Texas Ranger fort.

CENTER CITY, Texas: Located on Hiway 84 about 9 miles east of Goldthwaite. Once believed to be the exact geographical center of Texas.

DOAN'S CROSSING, Texas: Located on the Texas-Oklahoma state line (Red River), 3 miles east of Hiway 283. Shown as DOAN'S on most road maps. A supply center during trail herd days; now an adobe house and ruins.

EL COPONO, Texas: Located about 10 miles south along Copono Bay from Bayside. Founded 1749. Ruins remain.

ENGLISH, Texas: Located 6 miles northwest of Avery (Hiway 82). Founded 1840. A few ruins remain.

GAIL, Texas: Located on Hiway 180 about 35 miles west of Snyder. One of the few remaining cowtowns.

IDIANOLA, Texas: Located at end of Hiway 316 near Port Lavaca. Once the most important part in Texas with over 7,000 residents; now in ruins.

HELENA, Texas: Located on Hiway 80 between Nixon and Karns City. Name changed 1852 from ALAMITA to HELENA. An old Chihuahua Trail town. Now just a few houses remain.

KENNEY'S FORT, Texas: Located 2 miles east, ½ mile south, of Round Rock (Hiway 79). A settlement of 4 log cabins in a log stockade on Brushy Creek. Ruins remain.

MOUNT STERLING, Texas: Located 8½ miles downstream (southeast) from Goodman Crossing (Angelina River). Site is across river from Wells (Hiway 69). Founded in 1840's as a booming shipping and trade center.

MYRTLE SPRINGS, Texas: Located 3 miles north of Hiway 82. See road map. A few 100-year-old buildings remain.

NASHVILLE, Texas: Located on west bank of Brazos River 6 miles southwest of Hearne (Hiway 79). Cemetery marks site.

OAKVILLE, Texas: Located on Hiway 9 about 7 miles east of Three Rivers (Hiway 281). An outlaw hangout until cleaned up by Texas Rangers in 1876.

OCHILTREE, Texas: Site located 15 miles south of Perryton near Hiway 83 bridge across Wolf Creek. Nothing remains but a few mounds and some rubble.

OLD PRESTON, Texas: Located 15 miles west of Denison. Founded in the 1830's. In 1840, Texas Republic established Fort Preston nearby. Coffe home (1845) remains in good repair.

OLD SPANISH FORT, Texas: Discovered 1859. Mentioned in reports of 1759. Located 17 miles north of Nocona (Hiway 82). During the 1860's a settlement grew near here, but it disappeared and only mounds of the old fort and town remain.

OLD STONE FORT, Texas: Located ½ mile from San Ygnacio. An unusual rock fort remains in good condition and nearby is evidence of a settlement by the same name.

OLD TASCOSA, Texas: Located 22 miles north of Vega (Hiway 66) on bank of Canadian River. Giant Cottonwoods shelter the rock courthouse and adobe ruins. Boys Ranch uses the courthouse as headquarters. Boothill with 28 visible graves is nearby.

OLD ZAVALLA, Texas: Located between Zavalla and Jasper

on Hiway 63, 18 miles from Zavalla. Famous settlement on the old Beef Trail to Louisiana.

ORIENT, Texas: Located near Aspermont (Hiway 83-380). A boomtown of several thousand persons due to a 'salted' silver mine. Only a caved-in mine shaft remains at the site.

PINERY, Texas: Located near Hiway 62-180, 1½ mile from Pine Springs; about 112 miles east of El Paso. An old stage station and supply settlement now in ruins.

RATH CITY, Texas: Located southeast of Aspermont (Hiway 83-380) on Double Mountain Fork. A thriving dugout town and supply center for buffalo hunters. Faint evidence remains.

SAINT MARY'S, Texas: Located near Bayside (Hiway 136). Founded 1840 on Copona Bay. Once an important port; now a few homes and cemetery.

SAN FELIPE, Texas: Located a few miles east of Sealy (Hiway 36-90). Established by Stephen Austin 1823. Now a state park.

SANTA RITA, Texas: Located 4 miles northeast of Brownville on Hiway 281. Home of Juan Cortinas, Mexican Robinhood.

SCOTTSVILLE, Texas: Located 8 miles east of Marshall near Louisiana state line. Religious camp meetings have been held here since 1840.

SUTHERLAND SPRINGS, Texas: Located ½ mile from Hiway 87 and 32 miles southeast of San Antonio. Old building remains.

TEE PEE CITY, Texas: Located near Hiway 62-70 at crossing of South Pease River between Paducah and Matador. Frontier supply center with old ruins still in evidence.

TOWER HILL, Texas: Located 8 miles southeast of Sterling City near Hiway 87. On hill are ruins of old fort. Many artifacts, skeletons, and some treasure has been found here.

UTAH

Utah has a number of old abandoned Mormon settlements, complete with church, and they can be found all of the way from the Idaho state line to the north to the Arizona state line to the south. Drouth and climate drove out pioneering settlers after a few years, and they departed leaving buildings as they were with the possible hope of someday returning. Old mining camps in the eastern part of the state remain, some of them are well-preserved.

BONANZA CITY, Utah: See SILVER REEF.

CAINESVILLE, Utah: Located on Hiway 24 about 20 miles west of Hanksville; or 15 miles east of Capitol Reef National Monument. A Mormon farm colony founded in 1879. Drouth discouraged the settlers during the depression of the 1930's. Many old buildings remain.

EUREKA, Utah: Not a ghost town, but a town of about 1500. Around Eureka are many ghost towns and sites. In the desert area to the west as far as the Nevada state line will be found such ghosts as CALLAO, GANDY, IBOPAH, GOLD HILL, DUNLAP, and several others.

FRISCO, Utah: Located 16 miles west of Milford near Hiway 21. One of the wildest mining towns in history during the heyday of the Horn Silver Mine. A store, old kilns, a few buildings going to ruins, and many walls and foundations mark this boisterous mining camp which at one time during the 1880's had 26 saloons. Founded 1875, a mine disaster on 2-12-1885 brought an overnight end to the town.

GRAFTON, Utah: Located on the south edge of Zion National Park near Hiway 15 about 7 miles from Springdale. Founded 1859 by Mormon people about one mile down the Virgin River from the present site. After years of trouble with floods and irrigation problems, the settlers, one by one, abandoned the site. A motion picture company bought the site, restored it, and uses it as a movie set.

HARRISBURG, Utah: Located 15 miles northeast of St. George near Hiway 91. Founded 1861 as a Mormon farm colony. By 1895, drouth had driven the settlers away. Many ruins of rock buildings and considerable stone fences remain with remnants of old orchards and vineyards.

HATTON, Utah: Located 2 miles west of Hiway 91 and 3 miles north of Kanosh. Founded 1854 as a Mormon farm settlement and stage station on the Pioche, Nevada Route. A few residents keep the town hardly alive.

HEBRON, Utah: Located about 5 miles west of Enterprise near Hiway 120. Founded 1862 as a Mormon agricultural colony. When the mines failed, the markets faded and the town declined. By 1910, all residents had gone. Now cellars, foundations, remanents of an old orchard, grass-littered streets, and the cemetery mark the site.

KNIGHTSVILLE, Utah: Located 2 miles south of Eureka. Established by Jess Knight 1897, the town grew to 250 population. A rush caused by the rich silver pocket in one of Knight's mines boomed the town to more than 1,000 people and a smelter. The pocket fizzled out and so did the town. Its principal claim to immortality is the record that 'it was a mining camp without a saloon.' Nothing remains but the schoolhouse foundations and a few other footings.

LA PLATA, Utah: Located 60 miles northeast of Ogden near the road leading to Hiway 39 from Laketown. Also known as SUNSET. Founded 1893 on site of Sunset Mine. When the mine played out, the miners left. Ruins and mill remain.

LEWISTON, Utah: See MERCUR.

MERCUR, Utah: Located 10 miles west of Cedar Valley near Hiway 202. Founded as LEWISTON 1869, it died 1880 after a silver boom. Revived as a gold camp 1883, it enjoyed its greatest prosperity. Since then it has boomed and busted periodically . . . and now it is a ghost.

NEWHOUSE, Utah: Located 23 miles west of Milford on Hiway 21, then 2 miles northeast. The famous Cactus Mine financed many buildings and improvements in Salt Lake City. Today, a single building and numerous footings and ruins marked the once-prosperous old townsite.

PARIA, Utah: Located on the Paria River about 38 miles northeast of Kanab, or 15 miles south of Henriesville. Established 1868 as a Mormon farm community, repeated floods doomed the town. During the depression of the 1930's, a gold mining company failed here. Now, not a soul lives here to tend the cabins, assay office, mill, or cemetery.

PINE VALLEY, Utah: Located about 15 miles north of St. George on Hiway 18 to Central, then 4 miles east. Once a thriving Mormon colony, now deserted in winter and only a half-dozen summer residents. The 90-year old Mormon church remains in good condition.

SILVER CITY, Utah: Located near Hiway 6-50 about 4 miles south of Eureka. Founded 1870 as a silver camp and soon had 750 residents. The mines flooded and the town faded to its present few people.

SILVER CITY, Utah: A mining town on paper that existed only for a day and was absorbed by Silver Reef. Not to be confused with the actual Silver City.

SILVER REEF, Utah: Located near Hiway 91 about 20 miles northeast of St. George. Companion camp to Silver City and Bonanza City . . . all ghosts near Tecumseh Hill. Born of a silver boom and high land prices in the adjoining town of Bonanza City in 1875; it died due to reduced values and labor trouble in 1888. Resurrected by a mild boom from time to time, it has today only 2 buildings—one of them a well-preserved Wells Fargo Office.

SUNSET, Utah: See LA PLATA.

WIDTSOE, Utah: Located near Hiway 22 near junction of East Fork Sevier River and Sweetwater Creek. Founded as WINDER, name was changed 1915 to Widtsoe. Drouth and depression of 1930's and 1940's caused evacuation of residents. A few buildings remain along with the cemetery on the outskirts of town.

WINDER, Utah: See WIDTSOE.

WASHINGTON

Washington has a great number of good ghost towns and probably an equal or greater number of rotting, mossy old ruins. The shores of Puget Sound are littered with settlements which were abandoned years ago and which were not removed to make room for modern improvements. Eastern Washington has a number of well-preserved towns and mining camps, but vandals and tourists have carried away so much of the more accessible towns. In the Puget Sound area, a few housing tracts have built over some splendid old ghost towns.

ASOTIN, Washington: Located 6 miles south of Clarkston on Hiway 3, near the Idaho state Line. The old town near the flour mill has fallen into ruin.

ATTALIA, Washington: Located 14 miles south of Pasco near Hiway 395. A former railroad boomtown; now dead among a few trees. Nearby is Wallula and Fort Walla Walla.

BEVERLY, Wahington: Located on west bank of Columbia River 10 miles south of Vantage (Hiway 7-10). Once a thriving river shipping point.

BLEWETT, Washington: Located 8½ miles south of Peshastin on Hiway 97. Once an active gold town; now a few cabins remain on the site.

BRADY, Washington: Located about 14 miles east of Aberdeen

on Satsop River, opposite town of Satsop. A reminder of earlier prosperity; now almost a forgotten spot along the road.

BURNETT, Washington: Located 3 miles south of Buckley on Hiway 5-5E. When the coal mines closed 30 years ago, this thriving town went into decline.

CASHUP, Washington: Located 4 miles north of Steptoe near Hiway 195. Once an important trading post of Jim Davis; now it is not even on the map.

COLBERT, Washington: Located near Hiway 6-10-195 about 13 miles north of Spokane. Fifty years ago this town had 5 sawmills, 3 saloons, 3 livery barns, 2 blacksmith shops, 2 whorehouses and 5 stores. The mills closed down and a few residents live among the ruins.

COLLINS, Washington: Located on the outskirts of Uniontown (Hiway 3-195) about 18 miles south of Pullman. Known as 'Old Collins Roadhouse,' it was a small settlement catering to the stage and freight lines in the early days.

CONCONULLY, Washington: Located 17 miles northwest of Okanogan (Hiway 10-97). Founded 1886. County seat 1888. Burned out 1892. Rebuilt 1893. Died 1915. The cluster of old mining and logging buildings are protected in a cup of the mountain.

DALKENA, Washington: Located on Hiway 6 about 11 miles northwest of Newport. Founded 1902. Fire destroyed the big sawmill in 1935 and the town died.

DODGE, Washington: Located 45 miles west of Clarkston at junction of Hiways 3-295-410. Once a rip-roaring stage connection for Idaho.

EAGLE CLIFF, Washington: Located near Hiway 830 about 9 miles east of Cathlamet. A shed stands beside the hiway; below the cliff is remains of worlds first salmon cannery built in 1865.

FORT RAINS, Washington: Located ½ mile east of North Bonneville near Hiway 830. Old blockhouse was built 1856 and has been restored.

GOLD BASIN, Washington: Located 31 miles east of Marysville (Hiway 99). A once booming mining town; now a camp. Nearby Silverton is a ghost of a copper town.

GOLDEN, Washington: Site located on south end of Waunacut Lake (about 10 miles southwest of Oroville). Once a booming mining town. Not a trace remains but a mound or two.

GRANGE CITY, Washington: Located at junction of Tucannon and Snake Rivers about 12½ miles west of Delaney (Hiway 295-410). Once a river port for the Grange. Now a ghost.

JERRY, Washington: Located 6 miles south and 3 miles west of Clarkston near the Idaho state line. Once a booming horse town in stage coach days; now a nondescript village.

McCORMICK, Washington: Located 26 miles west of Chehalis (Hiway 99) on Hiway 12. The 53 mile stretch of Hiway 12 between Chehalis and Raymond has a dozen ghost towns or sites remaining from logging days.

MILAN, Washington: Located 1 mile west of Hiway 6-10-195 on west bank of Little Spokane River, about 24 miles north of Spokane. A relatively recent ghost town clustered about the old dismantled sawmill.

NEWCASTLE, Washington: Located near Hiway 5 north of Renton. This is one of several abandoned coal towns in the area.

NORTH DALLES, Washington: Located on the Columbia River opposite the Dalles, Oregon. Settled in 1880 by Rev. Orson Taylor, it was promoted in eastern cities as a boomtown. Taylor was arrested in 1895 and later freed, but the town died.

PATHA, Washington: Located 30 miles west of Clarkston on Hiway 3-410. Founded 1861 by Jim Bowers. Later known as WATERSTOWN and FAVORSBURG. What is left of the settlement is a short distance from the old flour mills.

PINKNEY CITY, Washington: Site located on Mill Creek near site of American Fort Colville about 3 miles east of present town of Colville. Was first county seat of Stevens County.

REPUBLIC, Washington: Located at junction of hiways 4 and 4A in northern Washington. Not a ghost town, but a skeleton of its former self. In 1900 it was 5th among eastern Washington towns in population. It had 28 saloons, 2 dance halls, and an opera house. Still looks much the same although most of the population has departed.

ROGERSBURG, Washington: Located at junction of Grande Ronde with Snake Rivers, below Clarkston. A river boomtown stimulated by gold discovery. Now a town of less than 25 residents.

SALKUM, Washington: Located on Hiway 5 about 10 miles east of Mary's Corner (Hiway 99). A dilapidated town remaining from the lumber industry. On farther east on Hiway 5 are the ghost towns of MAYFIELD and RIFEE.

SILCOTT, Washington: Located 9 miles west of Clarkston on Hiway 3-410, beside Snake River. A booming river town which burned out in 1885. Was rebuilt but never prospered again.

SPOKANE BRIDGE, Washington: Located on Hiway 10 about 1 mile west of Idaho state line. A boomtown of the 1860's; now a store, depot, and a few buildings.

WALLULA, Washington: Located on Hiway 395-410 about 30 miles west of Walla Walla near junction of Walla Walla and Columbia Rivers. Once a rip-roaring river town for miners and cattlemen. Now a quiet railroad town. Nearby are ruins of old FORT WALLA WALLA.

WILLAPACIFIC, Washington: Located midway across bay from Bay Center (Hiway 12-101) about 54 miles south of Aberdeen on Hiway 101. A town the size of a city block was to be built in 1900 on pilings in Willapa Bay. The piles remain jutting out of the water but the platform and buildings are gone.

WYOMING

Wyoming has a considerable number of ghost towns which are in better than usual condition and some of them are easily accessible. Atlantic City and South Pass City each have at least 15 buildings remaining and can easily be reached by automobile a few miles off of State Hiway 28. Other towns in equally good condition are accessible throughout Wyoming.

ALMY, Wyoming: Site located 6 miles north of Evanston in Bear River Valley. A booming coal town in the 1870's and 1880's. A mine disaster in 1895 took 67 lives. The miners thereafter hesitated to enter the mines and the town slowly died.

ATLANTIC CITY, Wyoming: Located 4 miles south from Hiway 28 and about 40 miles from Farson. A historic old town with many buildings still standing and in good condition. A store, restaurant, and saloon are still open for business, as is the jail although only 2 people live in the town. It had a population of 2,000 in 1870.

REARTOWN, Wyoming: Site located 15 miles south of Evanston. Once a tough construction camp on the Union Pacific railroad. Now little remains of the camp.

BENTON, Wyoming: Site located 3 miles south of Parco

(Hiway 30) near the 20-mile post. Old railroad construction camp and later a trade center.

BLAIR'S STOCKADE, Wyoming: Site located 1 mile northwest of Rock Springs. Established 1866 by Archie & Duncan Blair as a trading post. A few rock ruins remain. About 200 yards south of the site is a crevice marking No. 6 powder house. On 7-17-1891, two drunken men fired into the powderhouse, setting off 700 pounds of dynamite and 1200 kegs of powder. Four men were killed.

BONANZA, Wyoming: Located 13 miles east of Manderson at the junction of Paintrock and Norwood Creeks. A mistaken oil discovery in 1887 started the boomtown. Only one building remains.

BOTHWELL, Wyoming: Located 15 miles west of Alcova on Hiway 220, and 2 miles north, near Horse Creek. Nothing remains of the town but the graves of Jim Averill and his wife, Ella. She was the infamous 'Cattle Kate' Maxwell who was hanged with Averill as rustlers in Spring Creek Gulch. In 1889, the town had a store, blacksmith, newspaper, postoffice, and Averill's saloon. Some buried treasure has been found here.

BROWN'S HOTEL, Wyoming: Located across the Laramie River from old Fort Laramie. During the 1860's, Brown's Hotel and other buildings were situated here and it was a celebration point for soldiers and civilian emigrants. The army stopped the whiskey traffic and the town folded.

BRYAN, Wyoming: Site located 13 miles west of Green River on Hiway 30, then ¼ mile north. Established 1868 as a Union Pacific railroad overhaul depot. In 1869 it became a freighting center. When the railroad moved its tracks the town died. Cemetery remains.

CAMBRIA, Wyoming: Site located 12 miles from Prairie Store (Hiway 85) near Flying V Ranch. A coal mining town which was abandoned 1928.

CARBON, Wyoming: Site located 6½ miles west and 2 miles south of Hanna (Hiway 30). Old coal mining town, abandoned 1902.

CUMMINS CITY, Wyoming: Located about 40 miles southwest of Laramie near Hiway 230. Named for John Cummins who 'salted' the area with gold and founded a boomtown overnight. He sold out to a Denver company for $10,000 and left. Town of JELM (another ghost) is adjacent to the site.

DILLON, Wyoming: Located on Encampment-Boggs Road, south of Rawlins. A mining town with ruins of many buildings remaining. Nearby is ghost town of RUDEFEHA with its mill in ruins.

ENCAMPMENT, Wyoming: Located 20 miles south of Saratoga on Encampment river. Town is on site of Grand Encampment of 1851, the famous trapper rendezvous. The town, although a ghost, is shown on most highway road maps.

FAIRBANKS, Wyoming: Site located 2 miles northwest of Guernsey. Now known as Kelly's Park, a picnic grounds. It was a booming copper town in the 1880's. Now only one original cabin remains.

JELM, Wyoming: See CUMMINS CITY.

MARBLETON, Wyoming: Located ½ mile north of Big Piney on Hiway 189. Founded 1912 by Charles P. Budd to overshadow Big Piney which was founded by his father, D. B. Budd, in 1888. When his plans failed, he abandoned the town and moved to Big Piney.

ORIN, Wyoming: Located 13 miles southwest of Douglas near the present town of Orin. Its deserted buildings still stand near the railroad station.

PORTUGUESE HOUSES, Wyoming: Site located 11 miles east of Kaycee. Established 1828 by Antonio Mateo. A few mounds and ruins remain. Sixteen miles farther along the road is old Ft. Connor and another mile along is old Ft. Reno.

RAMBLER, Wyoming: Located on the Encampment-Boggs Road, south of Rawlins. Ruins of mines and buildings along the shores of Battle Lake. This is in the center of a very interesting area with the sites and ruins of many old trappers, traders, and miners camps scattered around the area.

RUDEFEHA, Wyoming: See DILLON, Wyoming.

SOUTH PASS CITY, Wyoming: Located about 4 miles south of Hiway 28 about 40 miles northwest of Farson. A historic old mining camp which has many of the old buildings still standing and in good condition. It is about 4 miles from Atlantic City, another ghost town; and 4 miles from the site of old Fort Stambaugh. Founded 1867. In 1868 it had 2 hotels, 13 saloons, 2 meat markets, 2 bakeries, a gun shop, and 2 doctors. By 1870 it had a population of 4,000. The town died in December 1873, but the high, dry air has preserved it wonderfully.

TUBB TOWN, Wyoming: Located 2 miles southeast of Newcastle. Established in May 1888 by Deloss Tubbs as a store. F. R. Curran set up a saloon and the town boomed. On 9-10-1889 the first lots were sold in Newcastle and Tubb Town was a ghost in 2 days.

Numerous roads to the Pacific Ocean traversed Wyoming in the early days, and there were a number of popular routes to the Montana mining areas. The Oregon and Mormon Trails followed in the North Platte River to South Pass and shortly thereafter divided to go their separate ways. The stage and Pony Express routes ran further to the south along the Colorado-Wyoming state line. The Bozeman Trail ran north across the state with numerous variations. All of these old trails and routes left behind them a series of ghost camps and towns. This applies to most of the states of the west, so if you are familiar with frontier history, you will have little trouble finding hundreds of old towns and townsites which have not been listed herein.

Treasure Literature

Most of the really valuable and helpful treasure books do not have the world "treasure" in their titles and some of the poorest books simply reek with implied treasure in the title. Most, but not all, treasure articles in periodicals are, essentially, fictionized versions of age-old stories or they are expansions of published material with the authors personal opinions and beliefs thrown in for the further confusion of the reader.

Article writing in the treasure field is just about the lowest paying of all categories and in the publishing of books, publishers of any stature consider only the works of recognized authorities or the material written by or for famous people. The beginning treasure author can be sure of getting a rejection slip for his manuscript unless he is well-known outside of, as well as in, the treasure field.

Far too much of modern treasure literature is not new, at all, but merely compilations and rewrites of what has already been published. Some of these rewrites are valuable to the treasure enthusiast since they bring to his attention material that he might have otherwise missed. However, in most treasure books today, the book is neither annotated nor are the references listed in the bibliography. In some instances, the authors do list their references and then have them deleted by the small publisher who handles his book on a royalty basis that is favorable to the publisher. For example, I have in my files a long letter from a first-book author who lived in California and co-authored a book that was published by a new and inexperienced publisher. The author pled my understanding in the fact that he had duly and truly listed references to the Treasure Hunter's Manuals, which he had copied freely, and from which the references had been deleted by the publisher.

Another letter in my files relates to an instance where an author had copied the inaccurate material from a history book, and then carefully annotated the book. When the book was published, well-informed readers were quick to lambast the author when, actually, it was the publisher who was at fault for deleting the references even though they added immeasurably to the value and stature of the book and author.

Some authors, on the other hand, are quick to copy without researching or giving credit until they find that material is incorrect and then they are quick to point a critical finger at the author they copied.

It is not a discredit to cite sources of material, and for every author there has to be a source for different segments of his work. Citations are given in all of the professions (medicine, engineering, history, etc.) and the top authors in treasure literature, such as Batholomew and Nesmith, have always given credit to their sources. As a result, reputable publishers are always willing, and ready, to publish anything these two authors prepare for publications. Bartholomew's and Rascoe's material is published by Frontier Book Company, but, much of it is rewritten and republished by authors who do not provide just and due credit to these sources.

Nesmith's books are widely read and frequently used by authors who do not give credit. His "Treasure—How and Where to Find it" is probably the most informative and helpful book ever written for the beginner and, of course, Nesmith gave lavish credit to the sources of his material. His "Dig for Pirate Treasure" was a landmark in treasure literature.

J. Frank Dobie prepared several books dealing with legends of the Southwest and he, honestly and conscientiously, inserted a notice in each of these books that the stores therein were legends he had heard, and nothing more. Anybody who has lived in the Southwest and mingled with the people is aware of the fact that treasure yarns come by the dozen in every town and hamlet. Anybody who has pursued any of these yarns is also aware that probably no more than one in one-hundred has any substance. Nevertheless, some of Dobie's stories have been expanded into full-fledged treasure stories and all of this, usually, without the slightest bit of research by the second-hand author. One of my treasure author acquaintances has never set foot on land west of the Mississippi river except in California, Arizona, and Nevada—and then only to enjoy himself at resorts and casinos. Depite this absence of personal exploration and experience, he has managed to generate hundreds of treasure tales of the west that have been sold to publisers at the going rate. Two of his stories were buried in books that flopped and they related to Forts Kearny and Laramie where he completely changed the geography in his versions. Thankfully, just a few people read these yarns and investigated, and found the stories to be entirely untrue.

ARE YOU INTERESTED...

In treasure and coin hunting, relic collecting, ghost-towning, prospecting and/or nugget hunting? For free information on how to get outfitted properly and be successful in the great outdoor hobby of metal detecting visit your local equipment supplier. The new, correctly calibrated VLF/TR Ground Canceling Detectors are being used successfully all over the world. You can easily enter this profitable and exciting field.

ALABAMA: Birmingham, P&S Business Machines, 4511 5th Avenue So., 35222, (205-595-8322, 672-9310); **Fairhope,** Bradley Enterprises, Route 3, Box 19, 36532, (205-928-2167); **Florence,** John G. Link, 310 Colonial (ZIP 35630), P.O. Box 682 (ZIP 35631) (205-766-0087); **Gadsden,** Owens Construction Co., 1806 MacArthur St. 35901, (205-546-6561); **Huntsville,** Alabama Treasure Hunter, 909 Chatterson Road, 35802, (205-881-7772); **Lanett,** Belcher's Coins, 19 South 16th Street, 36863, (205-644-1881); **Mobile,** Confederate Ordnance, 2202 Government Street, P.O. Box 66075, 36606, (205-473-3731); **Semmes,** Tommy Burns, 30 Downing St. 36575, (205-649-5996).

ALASKA: Kodiak, Nelson Enterprises, P.O. Box 814, 99615, (907-486-3672); **Wasilla,** Sluice Box, P.O. Box 382, 99687, (907-376-2365).

ARIZONA: Mesa, A&B Prospecting, 3929 E. Main St. Godfrey Square #32, 85206, (602-832-4524); **Phoenix,** Lucky Treasure World, 6005-D West Thomas, 85033, (602-247-4506); **Scottsdale,** The National Treasure Hunters League, 7350 East Jenan Drive, 85254, (602-948-0327); **Tucson,** Desert Trails, 230 West Ajo Way, 85713, (602-624-3804); Morey Detector Sales, 3825 E. Hardy Drive, 85716, (602-323-0071).

ARKANSAS: Camden, W. W. Mosley, P.O. Box 7, 768 Crestwood Drive, 71701 (501-836-5314); **Forrest City,** Beck Electronics, Radio Shack Dealer, 122 E. Broadway, 72335, (501-633-8144); **Fort Smith,** Treasure Cove, 1127 N. "S" Street, 72904, (501-785-2467); **Harrison,** Ozark Treasure Hunters League, P.O. Box 1601, Industrial Park Road, 72601, (501-741-4122); **Lamar,** J. C. Wheeler, Rt. 2, Box 299, (501-754-3507); **Little Rock,** Bill's Detectors, 5623 R Street, P.O. Box 7347, 72217, (501-666-6355); **Mountain Home,** Trammell's, 619 Baker Street, 72653, (501-425-3615); **Prescott,** Otasco, 121 West Main St., 71857 (501-887-3971); **Rogers,** L. L. Lincoln, Route 1, 158 Pyramid Drive, 72756, (501-636-6867).

CALIFORNIA: Auburn, Pioneer Mining Supplies, Keene Engineering, Inc., 943 Lincoln Way 95603, (916-885-1801); **Bakersfield,** Griff's Mining Supplies, 317 Kentucky St., 93305, (805-325-0300); **Bellflower,** G. C. De Fabrizio & Assoc., 16238 Lakewood Blvd., 90706, (213-925-2271); **Bloomington,** Prospector's Supply, 868 Ironwood Avenue, 92316, (714-823-6165); **Brea,** Brea Bike & Sporting Goods, 141 S. Brea Blvd., 92621 (714-529-3353); **Buena Park,** Aurora Prospecting Supply, 6286 Beach Blvd., 90621, (714-521-6321); **Canyon County,** Gentle Buzzard Mining Co., 16715 Gazeley St., 91351, (805-252-1640); **Carlsbad,** Carlsbad Coins, 2975 State Street, 92008, (714-434-4119); **Carmel,** Carmel Bay Mining Co. — Treasure Finders, 27383 Schulte Road, 93923, (408-375-1934); **Chowchilla,** Rencher Welding & Machine Works, 312 Calusa Avenue, 93610, (209-665-4219); **Chula Vista,** Axiom Coin Exchange, 314 "E" St., 92010 (714-425-1333); **Coulterville,** Carmel Bay Mining Co., 5047 Main Street.

95311, (209-878-3707); **El Dorado,** Thomas Murry, P.O. Box 406, 6001 Pleasant Valley Road, 95623, (916-622-5245); **Fair Oaks,** Sacramento Coin Exchange, 8528 Madison Avenue, 95628 (916-961-0455); **Forest Ranch,** Roy Gene Rolls, Hwy. 32 at Sugar Pine, 95942, (916-342-4829); **Fresno,** Fresno Hobby & Crafts, 3026 N. Cedar, 93703, (209-226-4880); **Goleta,** Futronics, P.O. Box 1400, 93116 (805-967-7936); **Lafayette,** Fumble Fingers, 1027 Brown Avenue, 94549, (415-284-7406); **Lakeside,** Gem & Treasure, Store #2, 13334 F. Old Hwy 80 at Los Coches Rd., 92040 (714-561-9445); **Lancaster,** Antelope Acres Market, Ron Farrell, 48011 90th St. West, 93534, (805-948-4190, 942n7165); **Lodi,** Pay Dir Mining Supply, 225 North California Street, 95240, (209-334-6565); **Modesto,** Gold Nugget Miner's Supply, 1302-9th Street, 95354, (209-529-5277); **Northridge,** Keene Engineering, Inc., 9330 Corbin, 91324, (213-993-0411); **Orange,** Allied Services, 966 No. Main Street, 92667, (714-637-8824); **Pasadena,** Cal-Gold, 2400 East Foothill Blvd., 91107, (213-792-6161); **Pleasant Hill,** Landing's Electronics, R. S. Landing, 182 Cortsen Road, 94523, (415-935-3737); **Redding,** Chesty's Dredges, 2930 So. Market St., 96001 (916-244-2119); **Riverside,** Pioneer Recoveries, 3510 Audubon Pl., 92501, (714-682-4302); **Rosemead,** Bill & Melba Dibble, 8851 E. Lansford Street, 91770, (213-287-7996); **Sacramento,** Mother Lode Dive Shop, Keene Engineering, Inc., 2020 H St., 95814, (916-446-4041); **Salinas,** B. C. Douglass, 1537 Placer Way, 93906, (408-449-1131); **San Bruno,** D. E. Witkowski, Coins & Supplies, 2281-Valleywood Drive, 94066 (415-589-8179); **San Diego,** Gem & Treasure Hunting Association, 2493 San Diego Avenue, 92110, (714-297-2672); (Open Seven Days a Week); **San Francisco,** Mining & Lapidary, 131 10th Street, 94103, (415-626-6016); **San Jose,** Castello's Guns & Sporting Goods, 2279 Lincoln Ave., 95125, (408-264-6212); **San Luis Obispo,** Ed's Sports Center, 729 Higuera Street, 93401, (805-544-2323); **Santa Maria,** Johnny's Metal Detectors, 209 N. Broadway, 93454, (805-922-8703); **Santa Rosa,** Cloutier's, 258 Dutton Ave., 95401, (707-545-1328); **Shandon,** Price's Treasures, P.O. Box 201, 93461, (805-238-6487); **Signal Hill,** Hidden Rod Shop, 2623 Gardenia Avenue, 90806, (213-427-8060); **Simi Valley,** Gemstone Equipment Mfg. Co., Inc, 480 E. Easy Street Bldg. 1, 93065, (805-527-6990); **Sunnyvale,** R&B Enterprises, 926 Carson Drive, 94086 (408-736-6321); **Sylmar,** Treasure Emporium, 12823 Foothill Blvd., 91342 (213-361-7126); **Thermal,** Roadrunner Recovery & Supply, 83-731 Avenue 55, 92274, (714-398-7114); **Torrance,** Rockteria Lapidary & Mining, 1664 Cravens Ave., 90501, (213-328-2500); **Vacaville,** Stan & Pats Gold Pan, 247 N. Orchard, 95688, (707-448-7571).

COLORADO: Colorado Springs, Terry's Treasure Hut, 1217 N. Circle Drive, Circle East Shopping Mall, 80909, (303-597-4709); **Denver,** C & D Detection Enterprises, Inc., 5885 W. 38th Ave. 80212, (303-424-7780); **Englewood,** The Prospectors Cache, 25 W. Girard,

80110, (303-781-8787),**Ft. Collins**, Dave's Detectors & Dredges, 208 S. Mason, 80524, (303-482-6050/221-5397); **La Junta**, The Fun Hut, 2018 Carson Avenue, 81050 (303-384-5567); **Poncha Springs**, Doc's Holiday Sales, Hwy. 50 & 285, 81242, (303-539-3577).

CONNECTICUT: Cheshire, Prospector Al, 252C Robin Lane, 06410 (203-272-2128); **Middletown**, Beachcomber's Detector Sales, 2330 South Main Street, Ext., 06457, (203-347-2392); **Stratford**, Edward Perchaluk, 304 Circle Drive, 06497, (203-378-1660); **Suffield**, J & E Enterprises, 1242 South Street — Route 75, 06078, (203-668-0029); **Wethersfield**, A & R Electronics, 9 Yale Street, 06109, (203-563-3913).

DELAWARE: Rehoboth Beach, Old Inlet Dive Shop, 143 Hwy. 1, 19971, (302-227-9988).

FLORIDA: Boca Raton, Bob's Metal Detector's, 1522 N.W. 9th, 33432, (305-368-0734); **Fort Lauderdale**, Josh Wilson's Detector Sales, 4704 NE 17th Avenue, 33334, (305-776-1076); Lawson LaTourrette Studio, Inc., 1503 E. Las Olas Blvd., 33301, (305-463-5311); **Fort Pierce**, The Treasure Cache, Old Dixie Hwy/N. County Line, 33450 (305-465-1994); **Fort Walton Beach**, Collins Treasure Cove, 524 N. Elgin Parkway, 32548, (904-862-5656); **Hallandale**, Silver & Gold Metal Detectors, 24 N.W. First Street, 33009, (305-457-9999); **Jacksonville**, Old Kings Road Treasure Inn, 6946 Old Kings Road So., 32217, (904-733-1928); **Lakeland**, John M. Pease, 3806 Timberlake Road North, 33805, (813-858-1325); **Maitland**, Kellyco Detector Distributors, 1443 S. Orlando Avenue (Hwy. 17-92), 32751, (305-645-1332, 628-5152); **Melbourne**, Zephyr Treasures, 2898 Zephyr Lane, 32935, (305-254-2796); **Merritt Island**, Mail Order Electronics, 200 Mustang Way, 13-B, P.O. Box 1133, 32952, (305-452-8236); **Miami**, American International, 0810 NW 133 St., 33167, (305-688-8360); Seatech Metal Locators, 985 N.W. 95th Street,33150, (305-693-1431); **Naples**, Homer C. Neely, Sr., 2923 Terrace Ave., 33942 (813-774-1066); **North Palm Beach**, Treasure Trove Metal Detectors, 636 U.S. 1, 33408 (305-842-5222, after 6 P.M. 305-622-2165); **Ocheechobee**, Trash & Treasure, 250 Hwy. 441 South, 33472 (813-763-9537); **Panama City**, Comet Treasures, 944 South Comet Avenue, 32401, (904-871-3427); **Pensacola**, Fiesta Treasure, Dr. Roy Clipper, Forte Estates, 7342 Templeton Rd., 32506 (904-453-6057); **Sarasota**, Ideal Metal Detectors, 2121 Dodge Ave., 33580, (813-953-6082); **Sebring**, Lloyd's Electronic Sales, Garrett Metal Detectors, 4717 Howard St., 33870 (813-385-6080); **Tampa**, Carl Anderson, Box 270270, 33688; Treasure Shack, 3934 Britton Plaza, 33611, (813-833-9841); **West Palm Beach**, Treasure Trove Metal Detectors, 1609 S. Dixie Hwy., 33401, (305-833-4057; after 6 P.M. 622-2165).

GEORGIA: Albany, Bob Branecky, 1713 Jones Drive, 31707, (912-435-6889); **Atlanta**, (Lithonia), Southern Metal Detector Sales & Service, P.O. Box 452, 2307 Parc Chateau Dr., 30058 (404-482-9228); **Carnesville**, W. T. Mize Detector Sales, Box 266, 30521 (404-384-4638); **Dahlonega**, Bucks Marine & Gold, Town Square, 30533, (404-864-7733); **Decatur**, Finders Company, 225 Upland Road, 30030, (404-377-0974, Call Evenings); **East Point**, Ernest M. Andrews, Atlanta Tri-City Area, 2755 Sylvan Rd., 30344, (404-766-8141); **Lafayette**, Bob's Detectors & Gold Dredges, Route 1, Box 1736, 30728 (404-638-3629); **Mableton**, C.A.R. & Detector Sales, 6579 Factory Shoals Road (Near Six Flags), 30059, (404-948-1181); **Marietta**, Ashe Marble & Granite, 1872 Canton Hwy., 30066, (404-427-2635; Evenings—479-3059); **Norcross**, North Georgia Detector Sales, 622 Glochester Place, 30071, (404-449-9042); **Stone Mountain**, Malone Electronics, 5385 Five Forks Rd., 30087 (404-921-1891); **Sycamore**, Boardman Enterprises, Hiway 41 South, Box 228, 31790, (912-567-2545, 386-2678); **Warner Robins**, Hobby Shack, Zayre Plaza, 834 N. Houston Rd., 31093, (912-923-6159); **Waycross**, J. C. Ballentine, P.O. Box 761, Hatcher Point Mall, 31501, (912-285-3250).

HAWAII: Honolulu, Metal Detection Hawaii, 1718 Anapuni, Suite #203, 96822, (808-955-4385).

IDAHO: Boise, Boise Basin Mining, 6060 Morres Lane, 83709 (208-377-3477); Q's Trophy Cabin, 3940 Overland Road. 83705, (1-800-632-5137 in Idaho; 1-800-635-5150 other states); **Burley**, Len Fuhr Enterprises, 2616 Brentwood Ave., 83318, (208-678-3942); **Coeur d'Alene**, Sign Mart, 5815 N. Colfax, 83814 (208-772-3093); **Lewiston**, Tommie T. & Sue Long Outdoor Hobby Supply, 2416½ E. Main, 83501, (208-743-1768); **Mountain Home**, The Rock Shop, 490 N. 2nd E., 83647, (208-587-4874); **Pocatello**, Powers Home Games & Hobbies, Powers Candy Co. Inc., 602 So. 1st Avenue, P.O. Box 4338, 83201, (208-232-1693).

ILLINOIS: Bethany, F. H. Bland & Sons, Inc., Box 249, Hwy. 121, 61914, (217-665-3394/665-3619); **Bloomington**, Rene's Treasure Trove, 214 East Front Street, 61701, (309-829-4538, 828-9986); **Chebanse**, Jerry's Treasure Hunter's Supply, RR #1, Meents Lane, 60922, (815-939-3815); **Chicago**, The Book Mark, 1515 W. Foster, Ave., 60640, (312-275-4022); **Decatur**, Russell's Hobby Corner, 5501 North Fork Road, 62521, (217-429-2253); **Galesburg**, Detectors Unlimited, 1671 Summit Street, 61401, (309-342-4032); **Joliet**, Robert Martis, 806 Winthrop Ave., 60435, (815-725-6519); **Lombard**, Electronic Exploration, 575 W. Harrison Rd., 60148, (312-620-0618); **Moline**, Hidden Treasure, Rev. John J. Costas, 3116 11th Avenue "A", 61265, (309-797-3098); **Omaha**, Paul "Joe" Edwards, P.O. Box 137, R.R. #2, 62871, (618-962-3367); **Pekin**, D & D Metal Detector Sales, 206 Reservoir Rd., 61554, (309-346-4377); **Quincy**, Mid-West Treasure Detectors, 507 So. 8th Street, 62301, (217-223-4723); **Salem**, Southern Illinois Treasure Sports, Rt. 37 N., Box 42, 62881, (618-548-5892); **Schaumburg**, F. C. C. Electronics, 31 E. Golf Rd., 60195 (312-882-4448); **Tama**, McGrew Oil Co., 120 West 4th Street, 52339, (515-484-2946); **Wedron**, Memory House, 1 N. Chestnut St., 60557, (815-434-3568).

INDIANA: Anderson, Pat's Metal Detectors, RR. #7 Box 145, 46011, (317-378-0475); **Bloomington**, B&M Metal Detectors, 4513 So. Hwy 37, 47401 (812-824-9722); **Decatur**, O-D Western Store, Robert A. Everett, RR #5, 46733, (219-724-2097); **Fort Wayne**, A-Z Coins & Stamps, Glenbrook Center,4201 Coldwater Rd., 46805, (219-483-3743); **Gas City**, Phil's Enterprises, 915 E. N.H.Street,46933,(317-674-5803);**Griffith**, Blythe Sport Shop, 138 North Broad, 46319 (219-924-4403); **Hammond**, J & J Coins, 7019 Calumet Avenue, 46324, (219-932-5818); **Indianapolis**, L & M Sales, 7310 Hazelwood Avenue, 46260, (317-255-4236); The Prospectors Pouch, Indiana Treasure Hunting Headquarters, 246 S. Butler Avenue, 46219, (317-356-7343); **Oaklandon**, Pioneer Metal Detector, 11901 E. 65th Street, 46236, (317-823-4202 or 898-4510); **Portland**, Silver Dollar Metal Detectors/Allen Towell, Rural Route #5, Box 81, 47371, (219-726- 2455); **Seymour**, Wray's Treasure

Shop, RR #5, 47274, (812-497-2537); **South Bend,** Keller Electronics, 2218 Mishawaka Avenue, 46615, (219-289-8485).

IOWA: Baxter, Richard Cross, 314 South Main, 50028, (515-227-3391); **Bettendorf,** Ralph Barnett, 2918 Summit Hill Ct., 52722, (319-355-6366); **Cedar Rapids,** Cedar Rapids Lock & Key Service, 3217 1st Avenue SE, 52402, (319-365-5162); **Des Moines,** Mid-Iowa Metal Detectors, 3911 E. 40th St., 50317, (515-265-8988); **Waverly,** Trading Post, 403 West Bremer, Box 251, 50677, (319-352-9874 or 352-2942).

KANSAS: Belleville, Kesl Jewelry & Sporting Goods, 1800 M Street, 66935, (913-527-5193); **Colby,** Maurice Rasmussen, 265 W. 6th, 67701, (913-462-2576); **Dodge City,** Carl Clare, 911 3rd Avenue, 67801, (316-225-5005 or 225-4701); **Manhattan,** Radio Shack Associate Store, 2609 Anderson Avenue, 66502, (913-539-6151); **Phillipsburg,** Central Plains Recoveries, 605 C. Street, 67661, (913-543-6707); **Pratt,** Epp's Coin Shop, 112 S. Main Street, 67124, (316-672-6181, 672-6277); **Sedan,** El Dorado Detectors, 407 North Hooper, 67361, (316-725-3784); **South Hutchinson,** Armstrong Detectors, 117 Forest, 67505, (316-665-8693) **Wichita,** Coins, Etc., 519 S. Woodlawn, 67218 (316-682-3511); Mid-Western Research & Supply, 1427 W. 69th St. N., 67204 (316-744-0668).

KENTUCKY: Ashland, Gambill Lock & Electronic, 1004 Comanche, 41101, (606-325-7931); **Louisville,** Charlie's Metal Detectors, 6809 Fernview Road, 40291, (502-239-9449); **Nicholasville,** Paul Phillips, 109 Lake Street, 40356, (606-885-3648).

LOUISIANA: Alexandria, Larry Parker Coin Exchange, Inc., 1804 McArthur Drive, 71301, (318-443-2236); **Baker,** J&F Enterprises, 12027 Whispering Oaks Drive, 70714 (504-774-0955); **Baton Rouge,** Confederate States Metal Detector Sales, 2905 Government Street, 70806, (504-387-5044); **Bossier City,** A-Able Treasure Electronics, 2705 Valkyrie Dr., 71111 (318-747-2954); **Delhi,** Roy Hammett, Jr., Route 1, Box 90, 71232, (318-878-9992 Bus., 878-2105 Hm.); **Lafayette,** John's Printing Shop, 109 E. Main Street, 70501, (318-235-3147); **Lake Charles,** O. Gregg Moore, 2344 Lake St., 70601 (318-439-6073); **Madisonville,** Steve's Precious Metal's, P.O. Box 201, 70447, (504-845-3753, 892-3334); **Many,** The Sabine Index, 850 San Antonio Ave., 71449, (318-256-3495); **Metairie,** Southern Treasures, 3032 Ridgelake Drive, 70002, (504-831-0567); **Natchitoches,** Carl P. Lofton, P.O. Box 2144, Rt. 4, Box 436, 71457 (318-352-8944); **Slidell,** St. Tammany Detector Sales, 625 Dale Drive, 70458, (504-641-0687, 504-649-1315).

MAINE: Dexter, Bob's Tackle Co., Route 2, Box 800, 04930, (207-924-6843).

MARYLAND: Arnold, Bay Country Metal Detectors, 1058 Ulmstead Circle, 21021, (301-974-7799); **Baltimore,** Codi Treasure Outfitters, 408 South High Street, 21202 (301-837-9387); Treasure Detectors of Maryland, 4069 Beach Road, 21222, (301-477-8827); **Cassville,** Brocks Home Appliance, West Side of Square, 65625, (417-847-4796); **Edgewater,** Finders Keepers, John Reichenberg, Route 4, 3316 Oak Drive, 21037, (301-798-1833); **Glenburnie,** Franks Detectors, 408 Arbor Drive, 21061, (301-768-3157).

MASSACHUSETTS: Agawam, E & D Electronic Sales & Service, 83 Parker Street, 01001, (413-786-7190); **Ashby,** Prospectors Haven, West Main Street, 01431, (617-386-2251); **Auburn,** Found Enterprises, 65 Auburn Street, 01501, (617-832-3721); **Bedford,** Middlesex Metal Detectors, 5 Washington St., 01730 (617-275-8588); **Buzzards Bay,** Ace TV and Radio, 8361 Cranberry Highway, Rt. 6&28, 02532, (617-759-4889); **Haverhill,** Gold Key Detector, 62 Crystal Street, 01830, (617-373-0004); **Hyde Park,** J&L Metal Detectors, 11 Walter St., 02136, (617-364-5876); **Rehoboth,** Larry Violette, Box 74, 02769, (617-252-4497); **West Springfield,** Dumais Electronics Corp., 37 Spring Street, 01089 (413-733-9548); **Whitman,** Coach Road Shoppe, 44 Old Mansion Lane, 02382, (617-583-7106).

MICHIGAN: Bay City, Buzzard's Metal Detector Sales, 1724 E. Salzburg Rd., 48706, (517-684-4765); **Burton,** Great Lakes Detector Sales, 1407 Gram St., 48529, (313-743-2380); **Dearborn,** International Salvers, Inc., 1537 Monroe Ave., 48124 (313-278-1940); **East Tawas,** Nordic Sports, 218 W. Bay St., 48730, (517-362-2001); **Grand Rapids,** Grant's Book Store, 601 Bridge Street NW, 49504, (616-458-6580); **Lansing,** Finders Keepers Metal Detectors, 2112 Cumberland Road, 48906, (517-321-6594, 323-4250); **Plainwell,** Curtis Trailer Center, Detector Div., 1227 W. M. 89, 49080 (616-685-5841); **Temperance,** Treasure Depot, 3591 M-151, 48182, (313-856-1162); **Trenton,** D&S Treasure Sales, 3132 Grange, 48183 (313-676-5517); **Union Lake,** The Prospector's, 7124 Cooley Lake Road, 48085, (313-363-7328); **Walhalla,** Schillings, 136 Fair Oaks, 49458, (616-757-2912); **Wyoming,** Treasure Hunter's Supply, 3930 Burlingame SW, 49509, (616-538-1957).

MINNESOTA: Bloomington, Mid-West Metal Detectors, 8338 Pillsburg Avenue So., 55420, (612-881-5254); **Minneapolis,** Garrett Metal Detector Specialists, 3249 Nicollet Avenue So., 55408, (612-827-3113); **Rochester,** Mid West Metal Detectors of Rochester, 808 12th Avenue NE, 55901, (507-288-7100); **St. Paul,** N. H. Mason III, 902 Goodrich Avenue, 55105, (612-226-5118).

MISSISSIPPI: Gautier, Treasure Island, 1439 Hallmark Plaza, 39553, (601-497-5651); **Jackson,** The Talk Shop of Mississippi, Inc., 4966 Hwy. 80 W., 39209, (601-922-8424).

MISSOURI: California, Twin City Gun & CB, 500 Cooper Street, 65018, (314-796-2166); **Desloge,** Smitty's Metal Detectors Sales & Accessories, 805 E. Chestnut, 63601, (314-431-0642); **DeSoto,** Doug's Detectors, Rt. 5, Box 337, 63020 (314-586-4263, 314-586-2436); **Edina,** L. Richard Parton, 602 East Front Street, 63537, (816-397-2430); **Florissant,** The Prospector's Shack, 975 Grenoble Lane, 63033, (314-837-4703); **Fredericktown,** Allen's Hobby Shop, 123 East Main, 63645, (314-783-5500); **Hillsboro,** E & R Detector Sales, Box 213, 63050, (314-789-2078); **Joplin,** Frank's Sales & Service, Rt. 3, Box 834, 64801, (417-781-6597); **Kansas City,** Clevenger Metal Detector Sales, 8206 North Oak Tfwy., 64118, (816-436-0697); **Lebanon,** Lost and Found Detector Sales, 523 South Adams, 65536, (417-532-9725); **Overland,** Gerald H. Smith, 10540 Homestead, 63114, (314-427-5569); **Poplar Bluff,** The Treasure Hut, 1315 North Main, 63901, (314-785-1164); **Springfield,** Radford Jewelers, 1864 South Glenstone, 65804, (417-881-7308); **St. Joseph,** Stanley Johnson Co., 2607 So. 14th, 64503, (816-232-5163); **St. Louis,** Plateau Detector Center, 9837 Kimker, 63127, (314-842-0413); **Trenton,** Bruce Bartlett-The Galvanized Confederate, 2600 Oklahoma Ave., 64683 (816-359-4273).

MONTANA: Great Falls, Treasure Seekers, 1513 9th Ave. So., 59405 (406-761-5934); **Helena,** Big Sky

Recreation, 3386 Highway 12 East, 59601, (406-442-3666); **Missoula,** Electronic Parts, 1030 S. Ave. West, 59801 (406-543-3119); **Ronan,** Western Seed & Supply, Inc., P.O. Box 67, Round Butte Rd., 59864, (406-676-4100) **Terry,** Gackle's Locksmithing & Garrett Metal Detectors, Box 567, 313 Adams St., 59349 (406-637-5554).

NEBRASKA: Ames, Exanimo Establishment, Main Street, 68621, (402-727-9833, 721-9438); **Lexington,** L&N Detectors, 209 E. 11th, 68850, (308-324-3420); **Sprague,** L. P. Enterprises, Box 46, 1420 W. 3rd Street, 68438, (402-794-5730).

NEVADA: Carson City, Gold Prospector's Supply, 1441 Rand Avenue, 89701, (702-883-8444); **Fallon,** Scott Goodpasture, 9525 Pioneer Way, 89406, (702-867-2015); **Reno,** Sierra Detectors, P.O. Box 60037, 89506, (702-323-2712); **Winnemucca,** Great Basin Detector Sales, 5815 So. Grass Valley Road, 89445, (702-623-2643).

NEW HAMPSHIRE: Concord, Don Wilson Sales, 93 So. State Street, 03301, (603-224-5909); **Keene,** George Streeter, Streeter Electronics, 14 Vernon St., 03431; **Seabrook,** The Village Trader, U. S. Route 1, 03874, (603-474-2836), **West Swanzey,** ANL Floor Covering, Winchester St., 03469, (603-352-7799).

NEW JERSEY: Park Ridge, Cliff Snyder, 36 South Fifth Street, 07656, (201-391-8218); **Pennsauken,** Ted's Engine House, 6307 Westfield Ave., 08110, (609-662-0222); **Trenton,** Treasure Cove, 1055 S. Clinton Avenue, 08611, (609-393-3631, 989-7382); **Vineland,** Al's Detector Sales, 55 S. Mill Rd, 08360 (609-696-1853); **Wayne,** Mt. View Electric Co. (The Treasure Chest, 866 Rt. 23 Mountain View, P.O. Box 177, 07470, (201-694-0177).

NEW MEXICO: Albuquerque, Kohl's Rock Shop, 928 Eubank NE, 87112, (505-298-6536); **Aztec,** Wooley's Trailer Sales, 635 Aztec Boulevard, 87410, (505-334-2871); **Roswell,** Roswell Treasure Center, #12 Monterey Shopping Center, 1400 West Second Street, 88201, (505-623-2242).

NEW YORK: Bronx, CT-Detectors, 4443 Murdock Avenue, 10466, (212-325-9582); **Cheektowaga,** P. Bernhard Enterprises, 70 Beach Rd., 14225 (716-631-3858); **Fairport,** Lost Coins Enterprise, Darrell C. Kilburn, 721 Mosley Rd., 14450, (716-223-2139); **Garnerville,** Magnum Detector Sales, 40 High St., 10923, (914-429-8708); **Geneva,** J. Panna's Electronic Sales, P.O. Box 167, 14456, (315-789-0809); **Glen Cove,** Bond Electric, #2 Leech Circle S., 11542, (516-676-1310); **Grand Island,** Roy Sexton, Hobbies Unlimited, 1550 Allenton 14072, (716-773-4969); **Kenmore,** Trade Mart Enterprises, 94 Keller Ave., 14217, (716-875-0951); **Manhattan,** Louis Calamia, 54 East 8th Street, 10003, (212-254-1763); **Poughkeepsie,** Storm Enterprises, P.O. Box 668, 12601 (914-471-5556); **Syracuse,** Jerry's Treasure Den, 527 Charles Ave., Geddes Plaza, 13209, (315-468-3615); **Walton,** Doc Dave's Treasure Finders, 54 Stockton Avenue, Route 206, 13856, (607-865-5188).

NORTH CAROLINA: Charlotte, Ernie "Carolina" Curlee, Detector Sales Co., Division of Chemation, 3201 Cullman Avenue, 28206, (704-375-8468, 537-5115); **Durham,** Anderson & Roghelia Classic Coins, 817 Ninth St., 27705 (919-286-4007); **Glen Raven,** Barbee Detector Sales, c/o Barbee Fabrics, Inc., P. O. Box 4235, 27215, (919-584-7781, 584-7873); **Statesville,** Carson's Coin & Stamp, 112 N. Center St., 28677, (704-873-9671);

Wilmington, Stanley's Metal Detector Sales, 5-7 N. Front St., 28401, (919-763-7329); Russ Simmons, 414 Biscayne Drive, 28405, (919-686-7009); **Yadkinville,** Courtney Treasure Quest, Rt. 4, Box 514, 27055, (919-463-2682).

NORTH DAKOTA: Fargo, Treasure Island, West Acres Shopping Center, 58103, (701-282-4747).

OHIO: Akron, Bennett's Metal Detectors & Treasure Hunting Supplies, 203 E. Market St., 44308, (216-376-9694); **Chillicothe,** The Treasure Isle, 308 Plyleys Lane, 45601, (614-772-2767); **Cincinnati,** Treasure Hunters Supplies, 7416 Hamilton Avenue, 45231, (513-729-2084 or 521-0678); **Columbus,** Davis Crafts, Inc., 86 W. Old Wilson Br. Road, 43085, (614-846-3764); **Elyria,** T & K Cycles, 36668 Butternut Ridge Rd., 44035, (216-327-3783); **Lewisburg,** Fox Metal Detectors, 8193 Shields Road, 45338, (513-962-2937); **Marion,** Marion Electronics Dist., 698-708 North Main Street, 43302, (614-382-0913); **Millersport,** The Penny Place, P.O. Box 578, 3163 North Street, 43046, (614-467-2864); **Newark,** Spike's Metal Detectors, 529 Eleanor Parkway, 43055 (614-345-0119); **Ottawa,** Winkle Radio & TV, Route 4, 17 Mi. N. Lima, 1½ Mi. N. Kalida, Route 115, 45875, (419-532-3957); **Pierpont,** G & D Detector Sales, 6500 North Richmond Road, Star Route 6, 44082, (216-577-1496, 576-5967); **Reynoldsburg,** Kirby's Detector Sales, 7336 E. Main St., 43068, (614-868-5754); **Shelby,** Struble Drug Inc. of Shelby, 31 West Main Street. 44875 (419-342-2136 347-2802) **Toledo,** National Camper Sales, 7417 West Central, 43617, (419-841-2444); The Treasure House, 5734 Elmer, 43615, (419-531-7787); **Youngstown,** Ernie's Sales & Service, Inc., 1087 Shady Run Rd., 44502, (216-792-3356).

OKLAHOMA: Ada, Eddie S. Fausett Sales, 2729 Kirby Drive, 74820, (405-332-3156); **Enid,** Cherokee Strip Treasure Shack, Metal Detector Sales, 917 East Locust, 73701, (405-237-3087); **Jenks,** Woodrow J. Russey, 904 N. Juniper, 74037, (918-299-3551); **Maud,** Dewey's Station, 301 West King Street, 74854, (405-374-2786); **Muskogee,** Jack's Lean-To, 1300 Illinois, 74401, (918-687-5198 after 5 P.M.); **Okeene,** Jim N. Pavlu, Rt. 2 Box 118A, 73673, (405-822-4810); **Okemah,** Territory. Town USA, Rt. 2, Box 297A, 74859, (918-623-9933); **Oklahoma City,** Hobby World, 2623 Villa Prom, 73107 (405-942-4556); **Seminole,** Frost Enterprises, Route 4, Box 89, 74868, (405-382-4659); **Tulsa,** Ace's Detector Service, 5622 S. Pittsburg, 74135, (918-742-2214); **Turpin,** Joe Lawder, RR #1, Box 22, 73950, (405-854-6429).

OREGON: Coos Bay, Carla Kay Salvage Co., 471 Bruel Street, 97420, (503-888-4015); **Eugene,** Northwest Mining Supply, Inc., 509 Chambers Street, 97402, (503-343-6502); **Grant's Pass,** Kelly Metalcraft, 5057 Redwood Avenue, 97526, (503-479-1767); **Hillsboro,** D & K Detector Sales, 540 S.E. 10th, 97123, (503-640-9288); **Medford,** Medford Coin & Prospectors Supply, 411 East Main Street, 97501, (502-772-1477, 773-4471); **Oregon City,** Pan Pacific Rare Coins Inc., 1656 So. Beavercreek Road, Suite E, 97045, (503-657-0130); **Portland,** D & K Detector Sales, 13809 SE Division, 97236, (503-761-1521).

PENNSYLVANIA: Carbondale, Elsuroba City, 33 Maple Av., P.O. Box 342, 18407, (717-282-6870); **Gettysburg,** Gettysburg Electronics, 24 Chambersburg Street, 17325, (717-334-8634); **Greensburg,** Sealand's Metal

Detectors, 422 Sells Lane, 15601, (412-834-3429); **Johnstown,** J & D Metal Locating Equip., RD Conemaugh-Johnstown, 15909 (814-749-9411; 814-322-4984); **Meadville,** Miller's Treasure & Metal Detectors, RD #1, Pettis Rd., 16335, (814-336-5453); **Milford,** Warren Pedersen, RR 2, Box 381, 18337, (717-296-7285); **New Castle,** Barker Advertising & Detector Sales, RD #5 Mitchell Road, 16105, (412-652-7596); **State College,** Mid-State Sales, 3410 W. College Avenue, 16801, (814-238-5666); **Williamsport,** K. A. Detectors, RD 4, Box 323, 17701, (717-326-0867), **Zelienople,** Morgan's Furniture, 106 N. Main St., 16063, (412-452-7510).

RHODE ISLAND: Warwick, House of Bargains, 345 Warwick Avenue, 02888, (401-781-8580).

SOUTH CAROLINA: Cayce, Redmond Signs (Leo Redmond), 2021 State Street (Box 945), 29033, (803-796-6862); **Greenville,** Copy Products & Supplies, Inc., 2701 Poinsett Hwy., 29609 (803-232-0794); **Sumter,** Ken Lyles Detectors, 122 Lazy Lane, 29150, (803-775-8840 or 773-9577).

SOUTH DAKOTA: Big Stone City, Big Stone Coinfinders, Rt. 1, Box 323, 57216 (612-826-2286); **Faulkton,** Kenneth Wherry, Box 433, 57438, (605-598-6226); **Rapid City,** Donco Metal Detectors, 2424 Canyon Lake Drive, 57701, (605-343-3103); **Sioux Falls,** Sioux Detector Sales, 6509 Westview Rd., 57107, (605-332-3591).

TENNESSEE: Chattanooga, Chattanooga Detector Sales, 3110 3rd Avenue, 37407, (615-622-8882); Hickory Valley Electric Co. and Metal Detector Sales, 6916 Lee Hwy., 37421, (615-892-0525, 892-3581); **Jackson,** Carmark's Unlimited, 11 Wallace Cove, 38301 (901-668-1167); **Johnson City,** Applachian Detectors, Rt. 8, Box 94, 37601 (615-926-5577); **Memphis,** Memphis Numismatics, Inc., 11 S. Orleans At Madison, 38103, (901-526-5054); Mid South Metal Detector Sales, 3190 Summer Avenue, 38112, (901-452-8860); **Nashville,** Music City Detector Sales, 3716 B Nolensville Rd., 37211 (615-834-2320); **Selmer,** Selmer Service Station & Sporting Goods, 100 West Court Avenue, 38375, (901-645-5431).

TEXAS: Amarillo, Golden Spread Metal Detectors, (Dunkin' Donuts), 2807 Western St., 79109 (806-352-1281); **Aransas Pass,** Aransas Metal Detectors, Hwy. 35 S., 78336, (512-758-8005); **Arlington,** Bill Allmon's Comanche Land Detectors, 1404 Carla Ave., 76014, (817-261-6385); **Austin,** Niles Carter, 2103 Whitestone Drive, 78745, (512-444-0106); **Bastrop,** Ed's Metal Detectors, P.O. Box 637, 78602, (512-321-2444); **Beaumont,** Sanders Sports Shop, Route 8, Box G-36, 77705, (713-794-2560); **Brackettville,** Ft. Clark Metal Detectors, Box 986, 78832, (512-563-2904); **Breckenridge,** Bill's Locksmith Shop, 122 W. Williams Street, 76024, (817-559-8411); **Brownwood,** Morgan's Guns & Ammo., 100 Mayes St., 76801, (915-646-3872); **Bryan,** Treasure Hound Detector Sales, 400 Mitchell, 77801, (713-779-6423); **Conroe,** Bob's Gun Shop, Rt. 9—27425 Robinson Rd., 77302 (713-367-0548); **Corpus Christi,** Bayside Metal Detectors, 9245 So. Padre Island Drive, 78418, (512-937-1682, 937-5334); **Dallas,** United Treasure Hunters, 11602 Garland Road, 75218, (214-328-4327 or 328-1223); **Denton,** Software & Peripherals, 420 D S. Carroll Blvd., 76201 (817-566-3888); **El Paso,** American Camping & Outing, 520 W. San Antonio, 79912, (915-542-1721); **Ennis,** Joe Krajca & Son Supply, Rte. 3. Interstate 45 N., 75119, (214-875-6358); **Ft. Worth,** Gray's Antiques, 1601 West Berry Street, 76110, (817-921-2431); Rex Grove Auto Supply Co. Inc., 4527 E. Belknap, 76117, (817-838-3066); Texas Treasure Hunting Headquarters, 5159 River Oaks Blvd., 76114, (817-626-9162); **Houston,** Alexander Enterprises, 1312 College Avenue, 77587 (713-946-6399); Research & Recovery, 2803 Old Spanish Trail, 77025, (713-747-4647/48); **Kerrville,** Hill Country Detectors, 12 Donna Drive, 78028 (512-257-4760); **Killeen,** CNI/Treasure Trove, P.O. Box 169, 76541 (817-526-5007); **Kountze,** Peterson's Trash & Treasure, P.O. Box 288, 77625, (713-246-2591); **Longview,** Jerry Evans, 1003 Donald Drive, 75604 (214-759-4593); **Manvel,** The Treasure Hunter, Box 558, 77578, (713-489-9156); **Mission,** Mission Rexall Drug, 1030 Conway, 78572, (512-585-1211); **Mt. Pleasant,** Glenn's Pawn & Gun Shop, 1506 W. 1st St., 75455 (214-572-4131); **Orange,** Berry's Detector Sales, 406 S. 43rd Street, 77630, (713-886-7343); **San Antonio,** Owens Detector Sales, 5814 Kepler Drive, 78228, (512-434-1605); **Texas City,** Treasure Hunters Supply, 1819 6th Street North (Loop 197), 77590, (713-948-8312); **Tyler,** Treasure Shop (Wayne Boshears), 620 Clyde, 75701, (214-597-1603); **Uvalde,** Spurgeon Artifacts & Detectors, 205 W. Nueces Street, 78801, (512-278-2164); **Waco,** D&L Detector Sales, 913 W. Denison, 76706 (817-662-1331); **Wichita Falls,** Southwestern Treasure Outfitters, 216 Glasgow, 76301 (817-322-8413).

UTAH: Holladay, Hardrock Rick's, 4000 Highland Dr., 84117 (801-277-8523); **Price,** Don's Detector Den, 810 No., 900 E., 84501 (801-637-5612); **Roosevelt,** Uintah Mountain Cache, P.O. Box 451—155 E. Lagoon, 84066 (801-722-3488); **Roy,** Bryant T. Cash, 2457 West 4975 South, 84067, (801-825-7858); **Salt Lake City,** Gallenson's, 220 S. State Street, 84111, (801-328-2016); **West Valley City,** Valy's Detector Sales, 3874 S. 2570 W., 84119, (801-968-6883).

VIRGINIA: Fairfax, Suburban Detectors, 3169 Spring Street, 22031, (703-273-2542); **Richmond,** Essential Electronics, 10453 Medina Rd., 23235, (804-272-5558); **Virginia Beach,** H & S Detector Center, 2108 Thoroughgood Rd., 23455, (804-464-6072).

WASHINGTON: Bremerton, Alpha Faceting Supply Inc., 1225 Hollis Street, Box 2133, 98310, (206-373-3302); **Coulee Dam,** Earl's Inc., Kit Road, P.O. Box 5, 99116, (509-633-2625); **Kennewick,** The Coin Cradle Inc., 2810 W. Kennewick Avenue, Suite "E", 99336, (509-735-1507); **Kent,** Cache Inn Detectors, 23615, 104th S.E., 98031, (206-852-8258); **Lake Stevens,** Treasure Chest, 8216 158th Drive NE, Everett Area, 98258, (206-691-7683); **Port Angeles,** BC Treasures, 1117 Grant Ave., 98362, (206-457-1497); **Seattle,** Pearl Electronics Inc., 312 Dexter Avenue North, 98109 (206-622-6200); Prospector Ed's Gold Supplies, 5263 Rainier Avenue So., 98118, (206-723-8200); **Spokane,** Bowen's Hideout, S. 1823 Mt. Vernon, 99203, (509-534-4004) **West Richland,** Gold Rush Mining Supplies, 4242 Van Giesen, 99352 (509-967-3307).

WEST VIRGINIA: Paden City, Murdocks Hobby Shop, 137 Work Street, 26159, (304-337-9278); **Shady Spring,** Ray's Leisure-Time Shop, U.S. Highway 19, P.O. Drawer E, 25918, (304-763-3110).

WISCONSIN: Janesville, Cue & Cushion, 1337 Creston Park Dr., 53545, (608-755-0908); **Madison,** Pete's Rock Shop, 1917-19 Winnebago Street, 53704, (608-249-2648); **Menomonee Falls,** Dons Treasure Hunting Supply, N88 W16747 Appleton Avenue, 53051 (414-251-5350); **Sheboygan,** Jetzer's Locksmith Service, 3212 N. 21

Street, 53081 (414-457-9231); **Waukesha,** Outdoor Outfitters, 705 Elm Ct., 53186, (414-542-7772); **Wausau,** Discovery Electronics, 319 So. 10th Avenue, 54401, (715-848-6141).

WYOMING: Casper, Caspar Metal Detectors Sales & Rentals, 1281 Payne and 1017 Cardiff, 82601, (307-235-6323, 234-5205).

INTERNATIONAL

AUSTRALIA: Victoria, Park, P. J. Bridge Hesperian Detectors, P.O. Box 317, 6100, Western Australia, (09-32-57422, 32-58575).

CANADA

ALBERTA: Calgary, Linnwest Prospecting, #12 700 33rd St. NE, T2A 5N9 (403-249-2851, 403-248-7870); **Edmonton,** Bedrock Detectors, 10250-82 Street, T6A 3M3, (403-469-3050); **Milk River,** Jerry's Detectors, P.O. Box 536, 508-4th Avenue N.E., T0K 1T0, (403-647-3851); **Rocky Mountain House,** Discovery Detectors, Box 1284, T0M 1T0, (403-845-3718).

BRITISH COLUMBIA, Surrey, Canada West Gold Bank, 5696-176 Street, V3S 2B3, (604-576-9511); **Vancouver,** Diversified Electronics Limited, 1104 Franklin Street, V6A 1J6, (604-254-0761).

MANITOBA: Winnipeg, O. K. John, Stn. F. Box 54, R2L 2A5, (204-667-6556).

NEW BRUNSWICK: Stanley, York Carleton, Treasure Supplies, P.O. Box 147, E0H 1T0, (506-367-2955).

NOVA SCOTIA: Halifax, Mr. Jim Redden of Hydrostone Surplus Store Ltd., 5535 Young Street, B3K 1Z7, (902-454-5718); **Wentworth Valley,** Four Seasons Recreation, Bob & Carol Hyslop, Station Road, B0M 1Z0 (902-548-2381).

ONTARIO: *Canadian Treasure Trail Ltd., P.O. Box 22, Camden East, K0K 1J0, (613-378-6421) *Distributor and Service Center for Canada; **Ayr,** Treasure Unlimited, Box 257, N0B 1E0, (519-632-7955); **Downsview,** Sub-Mariners Diving Equipment, 954 Wilson Avenue, M3K 1E7, (416-630-2590; **Niagara Falls,** Sandy Cline, 1422 Teal Road, Ridgeway Los Ino, (416-894-4520); **Peterborough,** Leisure Detector Sales, Box 44, K9J 6Y5,

(705-745-7655); **Scarborough,** Buried Treasure Metal Detectors, 3274 Danforth Ave. M1L 1C3 (416-691-5560); Buried Treasure Metal Detectors, #55 John Stoner Ave., M1B 3A2 (416-281-8900); **Stirling,** Tall Pines Treasure Trail, Box 186, K0K 3E0, (613-395-2406); **Strathroy,** L. W. Electronics, Box 42, N7G 3J1, (519-245-1994); **Waterford,** D. Keith Edwards, RR #5, N0E 1Y0, (519-443-5193).

QUEBEC: LaSalle, Detecteur de Tresor Treasure Detectors, P.O. Box 634, Champlain, LaSalle, H8P 3J2 (514-769-9873).

SASKATCHEWAN: Yorkton, John Menken, 67 Darlington Street E., S3N 0C4, (306-783-8336).

CARIBBEAN AREA
DOMINICAN REPUBLIC: Santo Domingo. Detectotesoros, C. X. A. Bloque 24, Numero 5, Costa Brava (809-566-7858, 809-533-1262).

PUERTO RICO: Santurce* Detectometales, Calle Las Marias 1513, Terraza del Parque, 00911, E.U.A. (809-725-7936) *Distributor & Service Center for Caribbean Area.

AFRICA
SOUTH AFRICA: Overport Durban, DECO, P.O. Box 37606, 4067, (031-259008).

GREAT BRITAIN & IRELAND
ENGLAND: London, *Pieces of Eight, 259 Eversholt Street, N.W.1, (01-388-3686) *Distributor and Service Center for UK, **London,** Treasure World, 155 Robert Street, N.W.1, (01-387-3142).

FRANCE
ST. CLOUD: David R. Moore, 17 Parc de Bearn, 92211 (602-8996).

MEXICO
CALIFORNIA: San Diego, Gem & Treasure Hunting Association, 2493 San Diego Avenue, 92110, (714-297-2672.)

PHILIPPINES
MANILA: Makati Metro, Anvil Commercial, 8435 Imela Ave. (89-99-71).

VENEZUELA
CARACAS: Victor Alvares, Box 60705, 1060 (058-272-8320).

RECOMMENDED SUPPLEMENTARY BOOKS

The books described below are among the most popular books in print related to treasure hunting. If you desire to increase your skills in various aspects of treasure hunting, consider adding these volumes to your library.

DETECTOR OWNER'S FIELD MANUAL. Roy Lagal. Ram Publishing Company. Nowhere else will you find the detector operating instructions that Mr. Lagal has put into this book. He shows in detail how to treasure hunt, cache hunt, prospect, search for nuggets, black sand deposits ... in short, how to use your detector exactly as it should be used. Covers completely BFO-TR-VLF/TR types, P.I.'s, P.R.G.'s, P.I.P.'s, etc. Explains precious metals, minerals, ground conditions, and gives proof that treasure exists because it has been found and that more exists that you can find! Fully illustrated. 236 pages. $6.95.

ELECTRONIC PROSPECTING. Charles Garrett, Bob Grant, Roy Lagal. Ram Publishing Company. A tremendous upswing in electronic prospecting for gold and other precious metals has recently occurred. High gold prices and unlimited capabilities of VLF/TR metal detectors have led to many fantastic discoveries. Gold is there to be found. If you have the desire to search for it and want to be successful, then this book will show you how to select (and use) from the many brands of VLF/TR's those that are correctly calibrated to produce accurate metal vs. mineral identification which is so vitally necessary in prospecting. Illustrated. 96 pages. $3.95

GOLD PANNING IS EASY. Roy Lagal. Ram Publishing Company. Roy Lagal proves it! He doesn't introduce a new method; he removes confusion surrounding old established methods. A refreshing NEW LOOK guaranteed to produce results with the "Gravity Trap" or any other pan. Special metal detector instructions that show you how to nugget shoot, find gold and silver veins, and check ore samples for precious metal. This HOW, WHERE and WHEN gold panning book is a must for everyone, beginner or professional! Fully illustrated. 96 pages. $3.95.

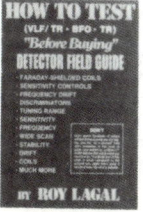

HOW TO TEST "BEFORE BUYING" DETECTOR FIELD GUIDE. Roy Lagal. Ram Publishing Company. Completely explains the inner workings of the BFO, TR, and discriminator types of detectors. You will learn how to test for sensitivity. stability, total response, wide scan, soil conditions, coils, Faraday shields, and frequency drift, and you will be able to expose incompetent detector engineering and overly enthusiastic, misleading advertising. If you own or are thinking of buying a detector, this book is an ABSOLUTE MUST. Fully illustrated. 64 pages. $3.95.

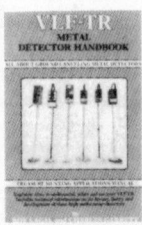

THE COMPLETE VLF-TR METAL DETECTOR HANDBOOK (All About Grand Canceling Metal Detectors). Roy Lagal, Charles Garrett. Ram Publishing Company. The unparalled capabilities of VLF/TR Ground Canceling metal detectors have made them the number one choice of treasure hunters and prospectors. From History, Theory, and Development to Coin, Cache, and Relic Hunting, as well as Prospecting, the authors have explained in detail the capabilities of VLF/TR detectors and how they are used. Learn the new ground canceling detectors for the greatest possible success. Illustrated. 200 pages. $7.95.

ROBERT MARX: QUEST FOR TREASURE. R. F. Marx. Ram Publishing Company. The true story of the discovery and salvage of the Spanish treasure galleon, *Nuestra Señora de la Maravilla*, lost at sea, January 1656. She went to the bottom bearing millions in gold, silver and precious gems. Be there with the divers as they find coins and priceless artifacts over three centuries old. Join Marx's exciting adventure of underwater treasures found. The story of the *flotas*, dangers of life at sea, incredible finds ... all are there. Over 50 photos. 286 pages $9.95.

TREASURE HUNTER'S MANUAL #6. Karl von Mueller. Ram Publishing Company. The original material in this book was written for the professional treasure hunter. Hundreds of copies were paid for in advance by professionals who knew the value of Karl's writing and wanted no delays in receiving their copies. The THM #6 completely describes full-time treasure hunting and explains the mysteries surrounding this intriguing and rewarding field of endeavor. You'll read this fascinating book several times. Each time you will discover you have gained greater in-depth knowledge. Thousands of ideas, tips, and other valuable information. Illustrated. 318 pages. $7.95.

TREASURE HUNTER'S MANUAL #7. Karl von Mueller. Ram Publishing Company. The classic! The most complete, up-to-date guide to America's fastest growing activity, written by the old master of treasure hunting. This is *the* book that fully describes professional methods of RESEARCH, RECOVERY, and TREASURE DISPOSITION. Includes a full range of treasure hunting methods from research techniques to detector operation, from legality to gold dredging. Don't worry that this material overlaps THM #6 ... both of Karl's MANUALS are 100% different from each other but yet are crammed with information you should know about treasure hunting. Illustrated. 334 pages. $7.95.

SUCCESSFUL COIN HUNTING. Charles Garrett. Ram Publishing Company. The best and most complete guide to successful coin hunting, this book explains fully the how's, where's, and when's of searching for coins and related objects. It also includes a complete explanation of how to select and use the various types of coin hunting metal detectors. Based on more than twenty years of actual in-the-field experience by the author, this volume contains a great amount of practical coin hunting information that will not be found elsewhere. Profusely illustrated with over 100 photographs. 248 pages. $6.95.

TREASURE HUNTING PAYS OFF! Charles Garrett. Ram Publishing Company. This book will give you an excellent introduction to all facets of treasure hunting. It tells you how to begin and be successful in general treasure hunting; coin hunting; relic, cache, and bottle seeking; and prospecting. It describes the various kinds of metal/mineral detectors and tells you how to go about selecting the correct type for all kinds of searching. This is an excellent guidebook for the beginner, but yet contains tips and ideas for the experienced TH'er. Illustrated. 92 pages. $3.95.

THE COMPLETE BOOK OF COMPETITION TREASURE HUNTING. Ernie "Carolina" Curlee. Ram Publishing Company. This book gives the details you need to know to sponsor or compete successfully in an organized treasure hunt. All about everything from choosing a name for a hunt and promoting it to receiving the prize you may have won. Whole sections on "How To Sponsor" and "How To Win." Every metal detector owner/treasure hunter can benefit from Ernie's down-to-earth, plainly written information and instructions. A book that will pay for itself many times over! Fully illustrated. 88 pages. $5.95.

PROFESSIONAL TREASURE HUNTER. George Mroczkowski. Ram Publishing Company. Research is 90 percent of the success of any treasure hunting endeavor. You will become a better treasure hunter by learning how, through proper treasure hunting techniques and methods, George was able to find treasure sites, obtain permission to search (even from the U.S. Government), select and use the proper equipment, and then recover treasure in many instances. If treasure was not found, valuable clues and historical artifacts were located that made it worthwhile or kept the search alive. Profusely illustrated. 154 pages. $6.95.

SPECIAL PUBLICATION OF

Search International

Search publishes a journal, THE SEARCHER. Each issue contains carefully selected "how to" information regarding treasure hunting, metal detecting, prospecting, relic hunting, and other projects, as well as the latest successful treasure hunting stories of treasure found world-wide. Information about treasure hunting clubs and competition treasure hunts is also included. Copies are distributed free to Search members.

All treasure hunters, prospectors, recreational miners, rockhounds, and others who search for lost and hidden wealth and nature's precious metals are encouraged to join Search International by sending $3 for the first year's dues to Search International, P.O. Box 3007, Garland, Texas 75041.

BOOK ORDER BLANK

See your detector dealer or bookstore or send check or money order directly to Ram for prompt, postage paid shipping. If not completely satisfied return book(s) within 10 days for a full refund.

- ___ DETECTOR OWNER'S FIELD MANUAL **$6.95**
- ✓ ELECTRONIC PROSPECTING **$3.95**
- ___ GOLD PANNING IS EASY **$3.95**
- ___ HOW TO TEST BEFORE BUYING DETECTOR FIELD GUIDE **$3.95**
- ___ COMPLETE VLF-TR METAL DETECTOR HANDBOOK (THE) (ALL ABOUT GROUND CANCELING METAL DETECTORS) **7.95**
- ___ ROBERT MARX: QUEST FOR TREASURE **$9.95**
- ✓ TREASURE HUNTER'S MANUAL #6 **$7.95**
- ✓ TREASURE HUNTER'S MANUAL #7 **$7.95**
- ✓ SUCCESSFUL COIN HUNTING **$6.95**
- ___ TREASURE HUNTING PAYS OFF! **$3.95**
- ___ COMPLETE BOOK OF COMPETITION TREASURE HUNTING (THE) **$5.95**
- ___ PROFESSIONAL TREASURE HUNTER **$6.95**

Please add 50¢ for each book ordered (to a maximum of $2.00) for handling charges.

Total for Items $ _____

Texas Residents Add 5% State Tax _____

Handling Charge _____

Total of Above $ _____

ENCLOSED IS MY CHECK OR MONEY ORDER $ _____

NAME _____

ADDRESS _____

CITY _____

STATE _____ ZIP _____

PLACE MY NAME ON YOUR MAILING LIST ☐

Ram Publishing Company
P.O. Drawer 38649, Dallas, Texas 75238
Dept. M6
214-278-8439
DEALER INQUIRIES WELCOME